COLONY AND MOTHER CITY
IN ANCIENT GREECE

COLONY
AND MOTHER CITY
IN ANCIENT GREECE

by

A. J. GRAHAM

MANCHESTER
UNIVERSITY PRESS

Copyright © A. J. Graham

First published by Manchester University Press 1964
Special edition for Sandpiper Books Ltd, 1999

Published by Manchester University Press
Oxford Road, Manchester M13 9NR
http://www.man.ac.uk/mup

British Library Cataloguing-in-Publication Data
A catalogue record for this book is available from the British Library

05 04 03 02 01 00 99   7 6 5 4 3 2

ISBN 0 7190 5739 6

Printed in Great Britain by
Bookcraft (Bath) Ltd, Midsomer Norton

CONTENTS

vii

APPENDICES

PREFACE

SINCE I give an account of previous work on my subject in the Introduction, and an explanation of the way in which the material is set out in Chapter I, I confine myself here to the basic functions of a preface, apology and acknowledgment.

The transliteration of Greek names presents a problem beyond satisfactory solution. Andrewes has discussed it sensibly in the preface to *The Greek Tyrants*. Since complete consistency is unattainable some form of compromise is inevitable, and I have preferred to use the 'traditional Latinized form',[1] though without slavishly latinizing rare or obscure Greek names and words. In this, as also in translating most of the Greek passages cited, I have had in mind those who are interested in Greek history but do not know Greek.

Any student of Greek history must be conscious of a great debt to past workers in the same field, and especially one who attempts a synthesis ranging over the whole Greek world and several centuries of Greek history. His widely dispersed material would hardly be manageable if it had not been evaluated in detail by others before him. But the quantity of modern literature more or less relevant to this material makes it almost impossible to escape the charge of failing to take cognizance of all of it. I can only hope that nothing of crucial importance has been missed and all debts have been acknowledged.

If failings of this and other kinds are less numerous than they might have been that is due to the help that I have received from many quarters. Much of this was given when I was preparing an earlier and different form of this work as a Ph.D. thesis; for that I hope a general acknowledgment will be considered sufficient here. In a form much nearer its present shape this essay was awarded the Hare Prize of the University of Cambridge. To the examiners for that prize, Professor V. L. Ehrenberg and Mr. F. H. Sandbach, as also to Dr. A. H.

[1] Hammond, *History of Greece*, p. vii.

McDonald, I am indebted for many valuable criticisms. I also owe a very special debt of gratitude to my colleagues Mr. V. R. d'A. Desborough and Mr. C. A. Rodewald, to whose care in reading my MS. and thoughtful suggestions almost every page bears witness. Finally, I gladly express my thanks to Sir Frank Adcock, who originally suggested the subject to me, guided my early investigations, and helped and encouraged me throughout. It would be churlish not to add that I alone am responsible for the faults that remain.

A. J. G.

Manchester

ABBREVIATIONS

In citing periodicals I employ the abbreviations commonly found in modern learned literature, or, occasionally, a longer self-explanatory form. The following books are cited by the abbreviation indicated:

ATL: The Athenian Tribute Lists, by B. D. Meritt, H. T. Wade-Gery, M. F. McGregor, Princeton N.J. 1939–50.

Beloch: *Griechische Geschichte*, by Karl Julius Beloch, 2nd edition, Strasburg 1912–17.

Bengtson *GG²: Griechische Geschichte*, by H. Bengtson, 2nd edition, Munich 1960.

Bérard: *La colonisation grecque de l'Italie méridionale et de la Sicile dans l'antiquité*, by J. Bérard, 2nd edition, Paris 1957.

Bilabel: *Die ionische Kolonisation*, by F. Bilabel, *Philologus* Supplementband XIV, Leipzig 1920.

BMC: Catalogue of the Greek Coins in the British Museum, edited by R. S. Poole, B. V. Head, G. Hill and others, London 1873–.

Busolt: *Griechische Geschichte bis zur Schlacht bei Chaeroneia*, by G. Busolt, 2nd edition, Gotha 1893–1904.

Busolt/Swoboda: *Griechische Staatskunde* II, by G. Busolt and H. Swoboda, Munich 1926.

CAH: The Cambridge Ancient History, edited by J. B. Bury, S. A. Cook, F. E. Adcock and others, Cambridge 1929–39.

Ditt.*OGI: Orientis Graeci Inscriptiones Selectae*, edited by W. Dittenberger, Leipzig 1903–05.

Dunbabin: *The Western Greeks*, by T. J. Dunbabin, Oxford 1948.

FGH: Die Fragmente der griechischen Historiker, by F. Jacoby, Berlin 1923–9, Leiden 1940–.

FHG: Fragmenta Historicorum Graecorum, by K. Mueller, Paris 1841–72.

Gomme: *A Historical Commentary on Thucydides*, by A. W. Gomme, Oxford 1945–56.

Head, *HN²: Historia Numorum*, by B. V. Head, 2nd edition, Oxford 1911.

Hicks and Hill: *A Manual of Greek Historical Inscriptions*, by E. L. Hicks and G. F. Hill, new and revised edition, Oxford 1901.

Hill, Sources²: *Sources for Greek History between the Persian and Peloponnesian Wars*, collected and arranged by G. F. Hill, 2nd edition by R. Meiggs and A. Andrewes, Oxford 1951.

IC: Inscriptiones Creticae opera et consilio F. Halbherr collectae . . . curavit M. Guarducci, Rome 1935–50.

IG: Inscriptiones Graecae, Berlin 1873–.

Inschr. von Olympia: Die Inschriften von Olympia, edited by W. Dittenberger and K. Purgold, Berlin 1896.

Liddell and Scott: *A Greek-English Lexicon*, by H. G. Liddell and R. Scott, revised and augmented edition by H. S. Jones, Oxford 1925-40.

Milet I.3: *Das Delphinion in Milet*, by A. Rehm and G. Kawerau, Berlin 1914.

OCD: The Oxford Classical Dictionary, edited by M. Cary and others, Oxford 1949.

PA: Prosopographica Attica, by J. Kirchner, Berlin 1901-2.

Pouilloux: *Recherches sur l'histoire et les cultes de Thasos* I, by J. Pouilloux, Paris 1954.

RE: Paulys Realencyclopädie der classischen Altertumswissenschaft, edited by G. Wissowa and others, Stuttgart 1904-.

SEG: Supplementum Epigraphicum Graecum, Lugduni Batavorum 1923-.

SGDI: Sammlung der griechischen Dialektinschriften, edited by H. Collitz, F. Bechtel and others, Göttingen 1884-1915.

Syll.[3]: *Sylloge Inscriptionum Graecarum*, by W. Dittenberger, 3rd edition, Leipzig 1915-24

Tod: *A Selection of Greek Historical Inscriptions*, by M. N. Tod, two volumes, vol. I, 2nd edition, Oxford 1946, vol. II, Oxford 1948.

SELECT BIBLIOGRAPHY

The aim of this bibliography is no more than to provide full descriptions of works cited in the text, excluding periodicals, *Festschriften*, ancient authors, and the works listed above under Abbreviations.

ANDREWES, A., *The Greek Tyrants*, London 1956.

AURIGEMMA, S., *Il R. Museo di Spina*, Ferrara 1935.

BARRON, W., *A History of the Colonization of the Free States of Antiquity, applied to the present contest between Great Britain and her American Colonies*, London 1777.

BEAN, G. E. AND FRASER, P. M., *The Rhodian Peraea and Islands*, Oxford 1954.

BENGTSON, H., *Grosser Historische Weltatlas I, Vorgeschichte und Altertum*, Bayerische Schulbuch Verlag, Munich 1953.

BÉRARD, J., *L'expansion et la colonisation grecques jusqu'aux guerres médiques*, Paris 1960.

BERVE, H., *Das Alexanderreich auf prosopographischen Grundlage*, Munich 1926.

BÉTANT, E. A., *Lexicon Thucydideum*, Geneva 1843–7.

BLINKENBERG, CHR., *Die Lindische Tempelchronik*, Bonn 1915.

—— *Lindos, Fouilles d'Acropole II, Inscriptions*, Berlin and Copenhagen 1941.

BOUGAINVILLE, J. P. DE, *Dissertation qui a remporté le prix de l'Academie Royale des Inscriptions et Belles Lettres en l'année 1745. Quels étaient les droits des Métropoles grecques sur leurs colonies; les devoirs des colonies envers les métropoles; et les engagemens reciproques des unes et des autres*, Paris 1745.

BUCK, C. D., *The Greek Dialects*, Chicago 1955.

BURY, J. B., *History of Greece*, 3rd edition edited by R. Meiggs, London 1956.

BUSOLT, G., *Griechische Staatskunde I*, Munich 1920.

CASSOLA, F., *La Ionia nel mondo miceneo*, Naples 1957.

CHAMOUX, F., *Cyrène sous la monarchie des Battiades*, Paris 1953.

CLERC, M., *Les Métèques Athéniennes*, Paris 1893.

—— *Massalia, Histoire de Marseilles dans l'antiquité*, Marseilles 1927.

COLLART, P., *Philippes, ville de Macedoine, depuis ses origines jusqu' à la fin de l'époque romaine*, Paris 1937.

COMPERNOLLE, R. VAN, *Etude de Chronologie et d'Historiographie Siciliotes*, Brussels 1960.

DEFRADAS, J., *Thèmes de la propagandie delphique*, Paris 1954.

DESBOROUGH, V. R. D'A., *Protogeometric Pottery*, Oxford, 1952.

DIESTERWEG, G., *De iure coloniarum Graecarum*, Berlin 1865.

DUNBABIN, T. J., *The Greeks and their Eastern Neighbours*, London 1957.

EHRENBERG, V. L., *Aspects of the Ancient World*, Oxford 1946.

—— *Sophocles and Pericles*, Oxford 1954.

—— *Der Staat der Griechen*, Leipzig 1957.

Finley, M. I., *Land and Credit in Ancient Athens*, New Brunswick 1951.
—— *The World of Odysseus*, London 1956.
Fouilles de Delphes publiées sous la direction de T. Homolle etc., Paris 1905–.
Frazer, J. G., *Pausanias' Description of Greece*, London 1898.
Frisch, H., *The Constitution of the Athenians*, Copenhagen 1942.
Fritz, K. von, *Pythagorean Politics in Southern Italy*, New York 1940.
Gardiner, E. N., *History and Remains of Olympia*, Oxford 1925.
Gardner, Percy, *A History of Ancient Coinage*, Oxford 1918.
Gilbert, G., *Handbuch der griechischen Staatsalterthümer*, Leipzig 1881.
Glotz, G., *The Greek City*, London 1929.
Grundy, G. B., *The Great Persian War*, London 1901.
Gschnitzer, F., *Abhängige Orte im griechischen Altertum*, Munich 1958.
Guthrie, W. K. C., *The Greeks and their Gods*, London 1950.
Halliday, W. R., *The Greek Questions of Plutarch*, Oxford 1928.
Hammond, N. G. L., *A History of Greece to 322 B.C.*, Oxford 1959.
Hanell, K., *Megarische Studien*, Lund 1934.
Haussoulier, B., *Milet et le Didymeion*, Paris 1901.
Hermann, K. F., *Lehrbuch der griechischen Staatsalterthümer*, Heidelberg 1855.
Hitzig, F., *Altgriechische Staatsverträge über Rechtshilfe*, Zurich 1907.
Hugill, W. H., *Panhellenism in Aristophanes*, Chicago 1936.
Jeffery, L. H., *Local Scripts of Archaic Greece*, Oxford 1961.
Johansen, K. Friis, *Attic Grave Reliefs of the Classical Period*, Copenhagen 1951.
Jones, A. H. M., *Athenian Democracy*, Oxford 1957.
Kahrstedt, U., *Griechisches Staatsrecht*, Göttingen 1922.
Kirchner, J., *Imagines Inscriptionum Atticarum*, 2nd edition edited by G. Klaffenbach, Berlin 1948.
Kirsten, E., *Die Insel Kreta*, Leipzig 1936.
Lampros, S., *De conditorum coloniarum graecarum indole, praemiisque et honoribus*, Leipzig 1873.
Larfeld, W., *Griechische Epigraphik*, Munich 1914.
Lasserre, F., *Les Epodes d'Archiloque*, Paris 1950.
Lerat, L., *Les Locriens de l'Ouest*, Paris 1952.
Macan, R. W., *Herodotus, the Seventh, Eighth and Ninth Books, with Introduction etc.*, London 1895.
Macdonald, G., *Coin Types*, Glasgow 1905.
Magie, D., *Roman Rule in Asia Minor*, Princeton N.J. 1950.
Malthus, R., *Principle of Population etc.*, 4th edition, London 1807.
Martin, Victor, *La vie internationale en Grèce des cités*, Paris 1940.
May, J. M. F., *The Coinage of Damastion*, London 1939.
Meritt, B. D. and West, A. B., *The Athenian Assessment of 425 B.C.*, Ann Arbor 1934.
Meyer, E., *Forschungen zur alten Geschichte*, Halle 1892.
—— *Theopomps Hellenika*, Halle 1909.
Minns, E. H., *Scythians and Greeks*, Cambridge 1913.
Oikonomidis, I., Ἐποικία Λοκρῶν γράμματα τὸ πρῶτον ὑπὸ I. Οἰκονομίδου ἐκδοθέντα καὶ διαλευκαθέντα, Athens 1869.
Page, D. L., *Sappho and Alcaeus*, Oxford 1955.
Pappritz, R., *Thurii*, Berlin 1891.

PARKE, H. W. AND WORMELL, D. E. W., *A History of the Delphic Oracle*, Oxford 1956.
PAYNE, H. G. G., *Necrocorinthia*, Oxford 1931.
PEEK, W., *Griechische Versinschriften*, Berlin 1955.
PHILLIPSON, COLEMAN, *The International Law and Custom of Ancient Greece and Rome*, London 1911.
PORALLA, P., *Prosopographie der Lakedaimonier bis auf die Zeit Alexanders des Grossen*, Breslau 1913.
RANDALL-McIVER, D., *Greek Cities in Italy and Sicily*, Oxford 1931.
RAOUL-ROCHETTE, *Histoire de l'établissement des colonies grecques*, Paris 1815.
RAVEL, O., *The Colts of Ambracia*, New York 1928, (*Numismatic Notes and Monographs*).
Recueil des inscriptions iuridiques grecques, edited by R. Dareste, B. Haussoulier and Th. Reinach, Paris 1891.
ROBERT, LOUIS, *Villes d'Asie Mineure*, Paris 1935.
—— *Etudes Anatoliennes*, Paris 1937.
—— *Hellenica*, Paris 1940–.
ROEBUCK, C., *Ionian Trade and Colonization*, New York 1959.
RÖHLIG, J., *Der Handel von Milet*, Hamburg 1933.
ROSTOVTZEFF, M. I., *The Social and Economic History of the Hellenistic World*, Oxford 1941.
SAKELLARIOU, M. B., *La Migration grecque en Ionie*, Athens 1958.
SANCTIS, G. DE, *Storia dei Greci*, Florence 1942.
SANDYS, J. E., *Aristotle's Constitution of Athens*, 2nd edition, London 1912.
SCHAEFER, A. D., *Demosthenes und seine Zeit*, 2nd edition, Leipzig 1885–7.
SCHAEFER, HANS, *Staatsform und Politik*, Leipzig 1932.
SCHMID, P. B., *Studien zu griechischen Ktisissagen*, Freiburg in der Schweiz 1947.
SELTMAN, C., *Athens, its History and Coinage*, Cambridge 1924.
—— *Greek Coins*, 2nd edition, London 1955.
SHELOV, D. B., *Antichni Mir v severnom Prichernomorye*, Moscow 1956.
STARR, CHESTER G., *The Origins of Greek Civilization*, London 1962.
SYMONDS, JOHN, *Remarks upon an essay entitled the History of the Colonization of the Free States of Antiquity, applied to the present contest between Great Britain and her American Colonies*, London 1778.
SZANTO, E., *Das griechische Bürgerrecht*, Freiburg i.B. 1892.
TAYLOUR, LORD WILLIAM, *Mycenean Pottery in Italy*, Cambridge 1958.
TOD, M. N., *Greek International Arbitration*, Oxford 1913.
URE, P. N., *The Origin of Tyranny*, Cambridge 1922.
VALESIUS, H., *Polybii etc. Excerpta, Henricus Valesius nunc primum edidit, Latine vertit, notisque illustravit*, Paris 1634.
VALLET, G., *Rhégion et Zancle*, Paris 1958.
VINOGRADOFF, SIR PAUL, *Outlines of Historical Jurisprudence*, Oxford 1920–22.
WALBANK, F. W., *A Historical Commentary on Polybius* I, Oxford 1957.
WALDSTEIN, C., *The Argive Heraeum*, New York 1902.
WENTKER, H., *Sizilien und Athen*, Heidelberg 1956.
WILHELM, A., *Griechische Inschriften rechtlichen Inhalts*, Athens 1951.
WILL, E., *Korinthiaka*, Paris 1955.
WUILLEUMIER, P., *Tarente*, Paris 1939.

INTRODUCTION

'QUAENAM porro fuerint haec iura quae originibus debeban-
tur non alienum fuerit paucis hoc loco perstringere,' wrote
Valesius in 1634[1] and initiated the modern investigation of the
relations between Greek colonies and their mother cities. These
relations attract attention not only from the intrinsic interest of
colonizing activity, but also because of the special nature of
Greek colonies. A North-American colonist from Britain was a
citizen of his mother country and occupied land regarded as
British territory—at least in theory a simple position. The
Greek colony's position *vis-à-vis* its mother city was generally
less simple: they had a closer tie of relationship than existed
between Greek states in general, yet as a rule the colony formed
a separate city-state. Thus there was scope for great variety of
relations, a variety which exemplifies the conflict between
diversity and unity constantly found in Greek interstate politics.

There is no need to tell the history of the investigation of these
relations in detail,[2] but the landmarks may be noted. The collection of the relevant passages in ancient authors may be said
to have been virtually completed by J. P. de Bougainville in
1745 with the first separate book on the subject.[3] Later in the
same century the topic received special attention owing to the
conflict between Britain and her American colonies. Many
pamphlets were written both in French and English with the
aim of finding justification in the practices of the ancients for
whatever view their authors supported.[4] The scholarly search

---

[1] In his edition of Polybius, *Polybii etc. Excerpta, Henricus Valesius nunc
primum edidit, Latine vertit, notisque illustravit* (Parisiis MDCXXXIV), 6–8.
[2] For a good bibliography of the early work on the subject see K. F.
Hermann, *Lehrbuch der griechischen Staatsalterthümer (Lehrbuch der griechischen
Antiquitäten, Theil I)*, 1855 edition, section 73.
[3] *Dissertation qui a remporté le prix de l'Académie Royale des Inscriptions et
Belles Lettres en l'année 1745. Quels étaient les droits des Métropoles greques sur
leurs colonies; les devoirs des colonies envers les métropoles; et les engagemens reciproques
des unes et des autres* (Paris 1745).
[4] Two characteristic examples are *A History of the Colonization of the Free
States of Antiquity, applied to the present contest between Great Britain and her
American colonies*, published anonymously but in fact by William Barron,

for truth was not the guiding principle of these works, and the
bias and irrelevance which they introduced into the investigation found their way into later compilations.[1]

The first considerable work of more than antiquarian interest
today is the thesis of G. Diesterweg.[2] For this is the first full
treatment which can be called modern in precision and logical
approach. If the literary evidence alone were available the only
advance on Diesterweg possible would be by reinterpretation.
This might well represent real advance, but it is the archaeological, and especially the epigraphic, evidence which has most
clearly enlarged the material available for the study of this
question and provides the special justification for a new treatment.

Since Diesterweg's work the subject has been treated in sections of more general studies,[3] and several modern articles and
books are concerned with it more or less directly. These will
naturally be considered in the course of the work that follows.[4] It
was Kirsten who suggested that the question needed new investigation as a whole.[5] It is hoped that the present work will go
some way towards meeting that need.

London 1777, and *Remarks upon an essay entitled the History of the Colonization
of the Free States of Antiquity, applied to the present contest between Great Britain
and her American Colonies,* by John Symonds (London 1778).

[1] As e.g. Raoul-Rochette, *Histoire de l'établissment des colonies grecques*
(Paris 1815), 45 ff.

[2] *De iure coloniarum Graecarum* (Berlin 1865).

[3] As e.g. Coleman Phillipson, *The International Law and Custom of Ancient
Greece and Rome* (London 1911), II ch. 19, 'Colonies and their Relationship
to the Mother Country', in which good sense is marred by the acceptance
of errors taken over from the eighteenth-century writers on the subject;
Busolt/Swoboda 1274-9, *Mutterstadt und Pflanzstadt,* a good brief introduction to Greek colonies, very well documented, in which the colony-
metropolis relationship is also briefly considered. The importance and
significance of the relationship is well expressed by Schaefer in his article
'Eigenart und Wesenzüge der griechischen Kolonisation', *Heidelberger Jahrbücher,* 1960, p. 91.

[4] My manuscript was unfortunately already with the printer when
Dr. Jacob Seibert kindly sent me his doctoral dissertation, *Metropolis und
Apoikie,* Würzburg, 1963.

[5] See *R.E.* 2. Reihe VII, 2, 1726.

CHAPTER I

PROLEGOMENA

Principles of arrangement

As GREEK colonization could be said to have gone on from Mycenean times till the Hellenistic period it is necessary to define and defend the time limits observed in this study.

The essential character of Greek colonization which makes the relations between colony and mother city worth study has been stated in the Introduction. It has this character as a product of the world of the polis, of independent city-states. The indications are that this world did not exist in the Mycenean period,[1] so that Mycenean colonization[2] may be excluded. There is more difficulty with regard to the colonies of the migratory period.[3]

Modern historians tend to see a clear difference between these colonies and those founded during the great colonizing movement from the later eighth century onwards. The date of the Ionian Migration (and the Aeolian and Dorian colonization in the same regions) is a matter of great uncertainty, though

[1] This can be said confidently without going so far as Finley in stressing the oriental organization of society in Mycenean times; see M. I. Finley, *The World of Odysseus* (London 1956), 159 ff.; his 'Homer and Mycenae: Property and Tenure', *Historia* vi 1957, 133 ff, illustrates convincingly the break between Bronze Age and Iron Age Greece. See also Starr, *Origins of Greek Civilization* (London 1962) 42 ff.

[2] On the Mycenean colonization in the Aegean see Sakellariou, *La Migration greque en Ionie* (Athens 1958) 325 ff, and Cassola, *La Ionia nel mondo miceneo* (Naples 1957) especially 302–12. For criticism of some of the theories in this book see Mellink's review, *AJA* lxiii, 1959, 294 f. A justifiably cautious attitude to ideas of widespread Mycenean colonization is maintained by J. M. Cook, *Greek Settlement in the Eastern Aegean and Asia Minor, CAH* I and II, revised edition (Cambridge 1961) 14 f, who refuses to assume that Mycenean pottery 'necessarily betokens a Greek population', and convincingly refutes the hypothesis of a continuous Greek occupation of Ionia from Bronze Age times, in which the Dark Age migrations would be merely a reinforcement of existing Greek settlements.

[3] Though even here it seems doubtful if we should talk of a world of independent city states. J. M. Cook sees in the reconstructed Smyrna of the early seventh century 'the first certain and unambiguous apparition of the recognized Hellenic polis' (32).

it now seems certain that there were Greeks in Asia Minor by *c.*
1000 B.C. at the latest, so that some of the settlements there were
fully two hundred years earlier than the earliest historical
colonies.[1] The origins of these settlements were also often not
clear. However, colonies of this earlier stage are described in the
same terms as the historical colonies by Greek writers. To
Thucydides the origin of the Ionian colonies of Athens, or of
Melos, was a reason for close relations with the metropolis in
exactly the same way as that of historical colonies like Potidaea.
It would seem wrong therefore to exclude these colonies completely from discussion. But if it is, as we shall see, very difficult
to find continuity in the relationship between a historical
colony and its metropolis, it is clearly impossible with colonies
of the Greek dark age. So it is best to assume that evidence for
the relations of such colonies with their mother cities cannot be
used to show anything more than ideas of the classical period.

From the Hellenistic and Roman periods there is quite a
body of evidence, much of it epigraphical, concerning the relations between colonies and mother cities. But many of these ties
had been recently revived or indeed created, and where antiquity is claimed for them the evidence is sometimes fabricated
or at best embellished.[2] In addition, the reason for maintaining
or reviving these relationships was a sentimental attachment to
a great past rather than any important practical effect they
might have in a world of great empires. It seems right, therefore,
to exclude this Hellenistic and Roman evidence; for it adds
nothing to our knowledge of a relationship born of the world of
independent *poleis*.

[1] The discovery of protogeometric pottery at Old Smyrna especially has
invalidated the belief, widely held till recently (see e.g. J. H. Jongkees,
Studia Varia Carolo Gulielmo Vollgraff (Amsterdam 1948) 71–7), that the movement should be dated to the ninth century or later. Cook's *Greek Settlement*,
op. cit., is a very good brief treatment of the subject based on the most
recent archaeological exploration. For chronology see especially 4–8 (Áeolic)
and 13 (Ionic). His sober and approximate dating is preferable to the more
ambitious and precise chronology proposed by Sakellariou, op. cit., in an
exhaustive section on the chronology of the Ionian Migration (305–58,
conclusions 357).

[2] The matter is well expressed by Robert, *Etudes Anatoliennes* (Paris 1937)
248. Examples concerning the help given in embassies between colonies and
mother cities were listed by Robert, *BCH* lxii 1938, 498. To these may be
added the inscriptions *Milet* I.3, nos. 141, 155, which are not concerned with
specifically diplomatic assistance.

The material that has been admitted has been organized in a way that requires some explanation. For a study of this kind there would seem to be a choice between two arrangements. First, one could adopt a descriptive principle and try to state the character and scope of the colony–metropolis relationship topic by topic. The advantage of such an arrangement is that it would reveal how far this relationship was uniform or regular in ancient Greece. But it would also be likely to conceal the disparate nature of the evidence and its chance survival. Worst of all, it would inevitably blur important chronological differences.

The second possibility would be to use a chronological arrangement and treat these relations in the various periods from the eighth century to the fourth. To a historian this is obviously an attractive method. Unfortunately, however, the evidence is so predominantly from the fifth century or later that it is impossible to give a satisfactory and convincing general picture of the state of relations between Greek colonies and mother cities in, say, the seventh century. As will be clear from the subsequent discussion of the nature of the evidence, this principle of arrangement would involve a great deal of repetition and continual discussion of the question whether later evidence or later analogies are applicable to the earlier periods.

So neither principle would provide by itself a satisfactory arrangement. The chance character of the evidence also presents a special difficulty. So much of it consists of odd statements referring to one moment in a colony's history, that it is extremely rare to be able to follow the relationship of a colony and its mother city over the years. Aristotle could ask (*Pol.* III 1276 a 35 ff) whether a city could be called the same city when its citizens are constantly changing through birth and death, and the transformation of a community over the centuries, though it keeps the same name, place, and even constitution, can be demonstrated by many examples. When the evidence is confined to one or two moments in a history of some centuries it is too easy to forget these changes, and to assume that the one moment reveals an unchanging relationship between two unchanging communities over the whole period in question. Fortunately we can go some way towards meeting both this difficulty and those inherent in the two possible principles of arrangement, thanks to a special characteristic of colonial affairs.

The history of colonies in modern times shows the difference between the arrangements and aspirations of the original founders and colonists and the subsequent relations of the two communities. Closely linked though they are, the act of foundation is one thing, the subsequent relations another. They are therefore discussed separately in this study. In this way it should be easier to avoid the danger mentioned in the last paragraph. But such a division also allows the two principles of arrangement to operate in the areas where each is appropriate. Greek ideas and practices with regard to the act of founding a colony varied much less than the subsequent relations between colonies and mother cities. Generalization is therefore easier and more justified in discussing the former, so that in this section (Part I) the descriptive principle dominates. Subsequent relations (Part II) are treated broadly chronologically, though the descriptive principle may also be admitted. For the isolated pieces of evidence may be grouped with the few examples where the relations between a mother city and its colonies are illustrated fairly abundantly by the evidence. In this way a mainly chronological treatment nevertheless allows each main topic to be considered as a whole.

Some generalizations and distinctions

Although it would be quite superfluous to give a general account of the nature of Greek colonization,[1] it is necessary to have clear certain general considerations about the colonies of the period from the eighth century to the fourth in order to understand the nature of the problem before us. The normal Greek word for any colony was ἀποικία, but distinctions of language were possible if it was strongly felt that a distinction of form should be recognized. Thus the term cleruchy (κληρουχία) was used to describe a certain type of Athenian colony which will require consideration later, and trading-posts were distinguished by the special name ἐμπόριον. This latter distinction raises two questions. The first is the place of trade in general in Greek colonization.

[1] The general lines are well understood, as can be seen from two recent brief accounts: the article by Burn, *OCD* s.v. Colonization, Greek, and Bengtson's short statement on page 69 of the Erläuterung volume of the *Grosser Historischer Weltatlas I, Vorgeschichte und Altertum* (Bayr. Schulbuch Verlag 1953).

The sane paper of A. Gwynn[1] marshals most of the evidence and arguments to prove that in the main the great Greek colonizing movement was caused by overpopulation and desire for land. This was a necessary correction of earlier ideas of colonization for trade, which arose largely from misapplying the analogy of modern colonization. But in spite of Gwynn's work scholars have continued to attribute commercial aims to early colonization. A notable example is the hypothesis that Corinth had explicit commercial intentions in her Western colonization at the end of the eighth century. It is therefore still necessary to stress that most Greek colonies were founded to be self-sufficient Greek *poleis*, with enough land to feed their population.[2] Thus the nature of their relations with their mother cities is not normally determined by commercial considerations.

The second question concerns the character of the trading stations (ἐμπόρια),[3] which were occasionally established, from the seventh century certainly, and even from the eighth, if this was the nature of the settlement at Al Mina excavated by Woolley.[4] The most famous of these trading stations, Naucratis, was founded in the Nile delta in the seventh century.[5] Its exceptional character as a privileged settlement in a more developed country is rightly emphasized by Gwynn,[6] but for the present purpose it is enough to note that the settlement was unlike most Greek city-states and had no mother city or cities in the normal sense.[7]

---

[1] *JHS* xxxviii 1918, 88 ff.

[2] It is not, however, necessary for me to present the arguments again, as they are well set out elsewhere. Apart from Gwynn's paper, compare R. M. Cook, *JHS* lxvi 1946, 80 ff, and G. Vallet, *Rhégion et Zancle*, 199 ff, who puts the colonizing movement in the general setting of theories about the ancient Greek economy. It is firmly stated in Busolt/Swoboda (1264): 'die meisten Kolonien waren zunächst Ackerbaukolonien'.

[3] The significance of the word is discussed by C. Roebuck, *CP* xlvi 1951, 219 n. 22. Herodotus seems to use the word for any community living from trade, while Thucydides seems to stress more the meaning 'trading-factory'.

[4] See Woolley, *JHS* lviii 1938, 1 ff and especially p. 12; Dunbabin, *The Greeks and their Eastern Neighbours*, 25 ff.

[5] See Roebuck, 'The Organization of Naukratis', *CP* xlvi 1951, 211–20.

[6] p. 106.

[7] This is clear from Herodotus' description, II.178. Roebuck denied this exceptional character in the article cited (see especially 216 f), but his grounds are slight when compared with Herodotus' statements. The good evidence for his view (e.g. the coinage) is late (ibid.), and the existence of

The same characteristics may perhaps be seen in two less famous settlements in the Adriatic, Adria and Spina. Spina is described as a Greek city by Strabo (V.214) and excavation has supported his description.[1] The pottery finds suggest that it was established towards the end of the sixth century. Spina dedicated certain spoils at Delphi which are set beside the dedications of Gyges, Croesus, and Sybaris by Strabo (IX.421), so that presumably the booty was very valuable.[2] In any case the tombs[3] show the wealth of the city and its size. The history of Adria is much the same as that of Spina,[4] and so is its nature; it was a rich trading city. The population of both cities may be assumed to have been mixed,[5] and Adria in particular had a strong Etruscan element, so that some authorities call it an Etruscan city.[6]

We have here, therefore, two large, rich settlements, both of which are mentioned from time to time in the ancient sources; yet no source names the metropolis of either settlement.[7] In view of the regularity with which this information is given it is reasonable to conclude that it was not known. And as they were founded in a period about which there is a good deal of information it may also be confidently conjectured that these were trading settlements of mixed population with no true metropolis, like Naucratis. Trading stations of this sort clearly stand outside the relationship of colonies and mother cities and have no place in this study.

---

the name Naucratis and the ethnic does not prove that it was 'a normal Greek community'. The existence of an ethnic does not prove any particular political status; it could be required for purely geographical description. Thus Thucydides can call Samian exiles in Anaia Ἀναιτῶν(III.19.2; cf. IV.75.1 and Gomme I.375 n. 3). However, in Roebuck's later book, *Ionian Trade and Colonization* (New York 1959) his very good account of the character of Naucratis on p. 135 includes the statement that its organization 'is neither in the pattern usually given a Greek state nor that of its colony'.

[1] See Beaumont, 'Greek influence in the Adriatic Sea before the fourth century B.C.', *JHS* lvi 1936, 179.

[2] Ibid.

[3] Published by S. Aurigemma, *Il R. Museo di Spina* (Ferrara 1935); cf. Beazley, *JHS* lvi 1936, 88.   [4] See Beaumont 180 f.

[5] As Beaumont 179.   [6] E.g. Livy V.33.8, Plut. *Camillus* 16.2.

[7] Beaumont's article offers many examples of Greek settlements in the Adriatic the origin of which is not recorded, and this may be set beside his judgment (194) that colonization in the Adriatic was directed to 'certain specific ends', all of them commercial. Adria and Spina are only the best examples.

Among normal Greek colonies distinctions can also be drawn which are important for our enquiry, but it would be a mistake to try to force them all into rigid categories. Thus colonies founded by fugitives from the mother city might be expected to have a different relationship from those engendered by a peaceably arranged settlement. So Timaeus argued that Epizephyrian Locri could not have been founded by slaves, criminals and the like, as one account went, because he had seen important evidence to show good relations with the mother city.[1] But Taras appears to provide a warning not to rely on such arguments too confidently. The tradition was that its founders were people of scandalous origins; yet its relations with Sparta seem to have been generally close and friendly.[2]

Another distinction of clear relevance to the relations between colony and mother city is that between state and private enterprises. This is perhaps particularly important in the later period, when definite imperial ambitions can be recognized in some Greek colonization; much of the argument is around this point, for example, in the question of the nature of Miltiades the Elder's colony in the Chersonese.[3] But even in earlier times it is a relevant distinction. Oversimplifications, such as that all early colonies were private,[4] or that colonial enterprises were generally official,[5] should be avoided. For though it is clear that the interest of ancient writers in individuals[6] stresses the private

[1] See Polyb. XII.9.

[2] The fullest and best account and discussion of the foundation of Taras is in Bérard, 162–72. Dunbabin agrees in accepting the main lines of the tradition, 29 ff. The relations with Sparta will be seen later; they are not necessarily particularly close, as Dunbabin affirms (31); Wuilleumier's judgment of the matter is more reasonable: 'Tarente a eu de bons rapports avec Sparte'; see Tarente, by P. Wuilleumier (Paris 1939) 43.

[3] See Hdt. VI.34 ff. The modern discussion will be resumed below.

[4] As e.g. Clerc, Massalia (Marseilles 1927) I.124.

[5] As Bengtson, 'Einzelpersönlichkeit und Athenischer Staat', Sitz. Bayr. Akad, 1939, p. 10, who maintained that even in mid-sixth century Greece a colonizing expedition without a decree of the community is unthinkable. In his Griechische Geschichte[2] (Munich 1960) Bengtson merely says that the community named the oikist (89).

[6] This is to be seen most clearly in the poetical foundation stories which have been studied by P. Benno Schmid, Studien zu griechischen Ktisissagen (Freiburg i.d. Schweiz 1947); see his generalizations, p. 5. But the same tendency affects prose accounts, exaggerating the private initiative of the oikist, as e.g. in the story about Archias, the oikist of Syracuse, related in [Plut.] Am. Narr. 772 f.

nature of colonial undertakings, it seems right to infer from two examples in Herodotus that both state and private enterprises existed throughout the historical colonizing period. The foundation of Cyrene in c. 630 is clearly described by him as a state act,[1] while Dorieus' abortive colonial expedition of c. 514–512 is equally clearly a private enterprise.[2] On the other hand it is probably a vain hope to try to draw a firm line in the early period between colonies founded on individual initiative and approved by the state and those established by a decision of the community. So these distinctions do not provide an easy or unvarying way of assessing the relations of colonies and mother cities.

The character of the evidence

In the past most writers have simply asked: what was the relationship of a Greek colony with its mother city?[3] But this was to ignore the existence of various special problems, which are so important that they determine the way in which the main question should be answered, and perhaps destroy the validity of any single answer. These problems are created by the nature of the sources.

Even if we confine ourselves to the great colonizing movement Greek colonies were being founded from the middle of the eighth century; yet articulate evidence, literary or epigraphic, for their relations with their mother cities hardly begins until the fifth century. Thus even if the source relates earlier events, as for example Thucydides' mention of a sea-battle between Corcyra and Corinth in c. 664 B.C. (I.13.4), the account may clearly be unreliable and will certainly be written from the standpoint of a later age. Even this unsatisfactory evidence is rarely available. It is much more common to know virtually nothing of a colony's relations with its mother city until the

---

[1] See especially IV.153.

[2] V.42.2. For the date see Dunbabin, 349. Dunbabin (ibid.) rightly states that Dorieus must have had permission from the Spartan state, but appears to make too much of this passive approval in calling the enterprise 'Sparta's effort' (348). For, as he admits, it is very doubtful whether the state knew of the direction and intention of the expedition, and the undertaking of the colony at all is very hard to reconcile with Spartan policy of the time.

[3] Compare the form of the question which De Bougainville, op. cit., sets out to answer: 'Quels étaient les droits des Métropoles grecques sur leurs colonies etc.?'

fifth century or later, though this will generally be some two centuries or more since its foundation. Thus the relations of Olbia, one of Miletus' greatest colonies, with her mother city are in almost complete obscurity until the later fourth century, when they are briefly but brightly illumined by an inscription (Tod 195).

To Greeks of the fifth and subsequent centuries colonization and the relations between colonies and mother cities were of vital and immediate interest. Nicias encourages his army before its retreat from Syracuse with the reflection that they can settle down and form a city;[1] Xenophon (*Anab.* V.6.15 ff) entertains seriously the idea of persuading his men to found a city on the coast of the Black Sea; the same author takes great pains to point out the advantages of a site he noted, stating the population it could support,[2] the quality of its harbour, the water-supply and many other details (*Anab.* VI.4.3 ff); Plato's references to colonization in the *Laws* (740 e; 708 b) show the same close familiarity; to him it is 'the ancient remedy' in case of overpopulation, and he is well aware of the difficulties both of foundation and in subsequent relations with the mother city. It is unnecessary to multiply examples, but Thucydides requires more careful consideration. For it is from Thucydides that we have not only some of our best early information about Greek colonies, but also some of the most explicit statements about the relations of colony and mother city to be found in a classical author.

It is his practice to take great care to give the origins of any colony he mentions. This is clearest in the famous account of the settlement of Sicily at the beginning of Book VI, but perhaps more striking when it occurs by the way in normal narrative, as for example at V.6.1.

ὁ δὲ Κλέων . . . ὁρμώμενος ἐκ τῆς Ἡιόνος Σταγίρῳ μὲν προσβάλλει Ἀνδρίων ἀποικίᾳ καὶ οὐχ εἷλε, Γαληψὸν δὲ τὴν Θασίων ἀποικίαν λαμβάνει κατὰ κράτος.[3]

[1] Thuc. VII.77.4.
[2] Ten thousand. This was widely regarded as a good size for a city in the fifth and fourth centuries, as Schaefer has shown in *Historia* x 1961, 292–317. See 309 f for Xenophon's ideas about colonization in the Pontus.
[3] 'Cleon . . . set out from Eion and attacked Stagirus, a colony of the Andrians, but did not take it. However, he forcibly captured Galepsus, the Thasian colony.'

Even more significant for our purposes are his references to the relations between colonies and mother cities. Of the remarks concerning the dispute between Corinth and Corcyra over Epidamnus[1] John Symonds wrote in 1778,[2] 'Thucydides has thrown more light on the Graecian colonization, in the passages that are referred to, than any other ancient writer whatever.' From them we learn of a colony transferring itself to a new metropolis and by implication recognizing the metropolis' supremacy, of the shame attached to a war between colony and mother city, of various religious obligations which a colony was expected to fulfil, and of an undefined hegemony which a metropolis expected to enjoy. According to Thucydides (I.60.1; 66) Corinth also regarded herself as the natural protector of her colony Potidaea, and saw the Athenian attack on Potidaea as a reason for war. But Thucydides stresses this matter so strongly in his enumeration of the opposing forces at Syracuse that we need not list all the other examples.

In this long chapter (VII.57) Thucydides is concerned to show that just causes and the claims of kinship were largely displaced as reasons for going to war by chance, expediency or compulsion. To mention some of his examples: the Rhodians fought against their colonists the Geloans; the people of Cythera fought Spartans, though they were Spartan colonists; the Corcyreans fought against Corinthians and Syracusans; a few Megarian exiles fought against Selinuntians, who were of Megarian origin; and Cretans, who had joined in founding Gela, fought against their colonists. The whole chapter reveals the importance Thucydides set on origins, and his view that these should normally determine alignments in war. He is so meticulous in finding examples that even a few exiles from Megara did not escape him.

As Thucydides provides so much of our evidence, it is important to see if his interest in the relations of colonies and mother cities is peculiar to him. For this would make him less valuable as a witness to common Greek ideas on the subject in his day, and might even cast doubt on his statements of facts, motives or political arguments in this field. For example, he

[1] Thuc. I.24 ff.
[2] Op. cit., 35.

states that Athens was the metropolis of the Ionian cities.[1] But although it seems probable that the Athenian share in the origin of the Ionian cities was exaggerated in the fifth century as a justification for the Athenian empire,[2] both Herodotus and Aristophanes make the same statements, and stress the political significance of the Athenian connection with the Ionian cities.[3] This shows that Thucydides is at least reflecting correctly an opinion commonly held at the time.

Another example is Melos' status as a colony of Sparta, which Thucydides makes an important matter both in debate and behaviour during the Athenian attack on the island.[4] But the connection is also emphasized as a matter of practical importance by Xenophon (*Hell.* II.2.3) when he describes the fears at Athens on the news of Aigospotami. The Athenians expected to suffer the fate they had administered to others; and he names the Melians first, implying that it is their destruction that the Spartans would especially be expected to avenge. Herodotus (VIII.48) also shows interest in this relationship.

---

[1] I.12.4; cf. I.2.6. and the two occasions where he described the Ionians as ἀπ' Ἀθηναίων (II.15.4. and VII.57.4), both of which the scholiast explains as meaning the Ionians were *apoikoi* of Athens (Thuc. Scholia, pp. 121, 394).

[2] Since Wilamowitz' treatment (*Sitz. preuss. Akad.* 1906, 57–79 = *Kleine Schriften*, Berlin 1937, V.1. 156 ff) the view has gained ground that the Athenian connection was a comparatively late invention. Jacoby, following Wilamowitz in the main, affirms that the claim of Athens to be the founder of the Ionian cities was not consolidated or widely acknowledged till the time of the Delian League (see *FGH* IIIB (Supplement) I.32–4). Similar views, though putting the invention further back, are expressed in Nilsson's paper 'Political propaganda in sixth-century Athens', *Studies presented to D. M. Robinson*, II (St. Louis 1953). Sakellariou follows the same line in considering the view that Athens was the metropolis of all Ionia a fifth-century invention (see *La Migration grecque en Ionie*, 21 ff and especially 29 ff). But, as his work shows, the origin of these cities was very mixed. The existence of different traditions does not, therefore, deny the Athenian connection; only the Athenian monopoly of origin. A more respectful and very satisfactory treatment of the tradition is to be found in Roebuck, *Ionian Trade and Colonization* 25 ff and a vigorous defence of it against the modern attacks in Bérard, *L'Expansion et la Colonisation grecques* (Paris 1960), 50 f. J. M. Cook also provides strong reasons for accepting the kernel of truth that 'Athens was the main focus of emigration,' op. cit., 12 f.

[3] Hdt. I.147.2; VII.46.2; IX.106.3. Arist. *Lys.* 582. This line and its context are convincingly elucidated by Hugill (*Panhellenism in Aristophanes*, by W. H. Hugill, Chicago 1936) 67 ff. He shows that 'the cities . . . the colonies of this land' must mean the Ionian cities and Aegean islands.

[4] See V.89; 104; 106.

Probably then Thucydides is not untypical of his age in stressing the importance of the relations between colonies and mother cities. But even if Thucydides himself should not be regarded as isolated, the view has been advanced that the idea of the relationship between colonies and mother cities was especially influential in his time.[1] Now it is true that many of the best examples of the practical effectiveness of the relationship come from this period. In addition to the examples known from Thucydides there is the notable control exercised by Sinope over her colonies, which Xenophon describes (*Anab.* V.5 ff), and the hegemony of Argos over colonies in Crete which seems to be revealed in the inscription Tod 33.

It is not difficult to show that the idea of the relationship was similarly effective in the fourth century, and, if this period be admitted as relevant, in Hellenistic times; for the inscriptions reveal a strong belief in the importance of the relationship.[2] But the important question is whether the interest in colonies and the active relations between colonies and mother cities found in the fifth century arose at that time, or existed in the previous two centuries, only hidden by the lack of source material capable of revealing it.

In a recent article,[3] Will has suggested implicitly that the idea of the relationship became politically effective in the sixth century. He simply assumes that early colonies were independent, and thus quite different from the colonies of Corinth under the tyrants and of Athens in the sixth and fifth centuries, which form the main subject of his study. In his view the dependent colony appears in association with the attempt to build up overseas empires. There is, as we shall see, some truth in this picture,[4] but though the shortage of source material may make it very difficult to investigate the character of the earlier

[1] Notably by Kirsten, *Die Insel Kreta* (Leipzig 1936) 17 f; cf. *R.E.* s.v. Tylissos 1726 ff.

[2] The Hellenistic ones are mentioned above, p. 2. From the fourth century there are the stones concerning Epidaurus and Astypalaea (*I.G.* IV^2.1.47) and Miletus and her colonies (*Milet* I.3 nos. 136, 137).

[3] 'Sur l'évolution des rapports entre colonies et métropoles en Grèce à partir du VIe siècle', *La Nouvelle Clio* vi 1954, 413-60.

[4] Though the attempt to classify colonies into different categories sharply distinguished from each other (on p. 459 we are given a list of five distinct types) seems unhistorical, and leads to inconsistencies and difficulties of interpretation.

colonies, it is unsatisfactory simply to assume their nature without discussion.

In looking back to the sixth century for the appearance of the relationship's effectiveness, Will is implicitly approving the extrapolation to earlier times of the attitude found in the fifth century. But can we accept the fifth-century sources and their attitude as valid even for the sixth century? To argue back from later conditions to earlier times is clearly dangerous; but to assume that there was no effective relationship simply because we hear nothing of relations until, say, the fifth century is, given the state of the sources, too negative. The assumption of continuity and the argument from silence are the Scylla and Charybdis of this investigation. It is therefore extremely important to remember these dangers, and in each case to make the origin and nature of the source material one of the first considerations.

But there are ways of escaping in part from the stranglehold of the fifth-century sources. The most obvious is to use the archaeological evidence from the earlier period. While this has the great advantage that it is primary and unaffected by the ideas of later periods, the information yielded by material objects must remain very limited. Occasionally they show artistic connections between a colony and its mother city. For example, Taras seems to have been influenced by Sparta in sculpture and architecture in late archaic times,[1] and Syracuse and Corcyra were so markedly under Corinth's influence in these fields from an earlier date, that Dunbabin affirmed[2] that there must have been continuous interchange of men and ideas.

Again this evidence sometimes suggests a close commercial link between a mother city and a colony, but this is even harder to prove. While Corinthian pottery is dominating all markets in the West, its appearance at Syracuse does not necessarily signify special commercial relations between colony and mother city. Similarly Miletus' trade with her colonies must be set beside her trade in other directions.[3] Furthermore, if the Attic ware found in Etruria was largely brought in Ionian ships,[4] this

[1] See Wuilleumier, *Tarente*, 260, 314, 334; Ashmole, *Proc. Brit. Acad.* xx 1934, 11.   [2] p. 284.
[3] See Röhlig, *Der Handel von Milet* (Hamburg 1933) especially 26 f and the section 37–52.
[4] As Vallet seems to have shown, *Rhégion et Zancle*, 191.

shows that commercial links suggested by pottery finds may sometimes have been exceedingly tenuous.[1] And it is pottery that forms the dominating part of all finds. Coins are a specially informative category of material objects, but their significance is often very hard to interpret, even when they obviously bear on the colony–metropolis relationship, as do those of the Corinthian colonies, which will be considered below. Thus the directness of the archaeological evidence is often offset by its limited application and by difficulties of interpretation.

A second way is the investigation of what we may, after Thucydides, call *nomima*.[2] As we should expect, it was normal for the colony to continue the cults, calendar, dialect, script, state offices and citizen divisions of its mother city. Two modern studies, Bilabel's of Ionian colonization[3] and Hanell's of the Megarian colonies,[4] have shown this beyond doubt. This material, being embedded in the continuous life of the community, is not subject to the objections which we have seen can be made against much of the literary and epigraphic evidence bearing more directly on the relationship between colony and metropolis. On the other hand it is necessary to discern clearly just how far it reveals these relations. It could be said that the careful maintenance of the mother city's customs in the colony shows at least a living realization of origin. But we have examples where an institution which was later changed in the metropolis was preserved in the colony.[5] This may show that the preservation of the *nomima* of the metropolis could be entirely due to the colony's conservatism and owe nothing to a continued connection with the mother city. It is therefore important to recognize that there may be a distinction between the preservation of the metropolis' *nomima* by a colony and an active relationship between the two cities.[6]

---

[1] Compare also R. M. Cook's very just warnings against drawing conclusions about commercial and political connections from the evidence of painted pottery; *Jahrbuch d. deutsch. arch. Inst.* lxxiv 1959, 114–23.

[2] E.g. VI.5.1.

[3] *Die ionische Kolonisation* by F. Bilabel, *Philologus* Supplementband XIV.1 (Leipzig 1920).

[4] *Megarische Studien* by Krister Hanell (Lund 1934) Part II.

[5] See Bilabel, 126 and 129, on the Milesian official, the ἐπιμήνιος; 174, on the *phylae* of Samos.

[6] This has not always been recognized in modern studies, though it was stressed more than a century ago by K. F. Hermann, op. cit. Thus Bilabel

A more subtle inference from the preservation of some of these institutions has been suggested, which would bring them into direct (if ill-defined) connection with an active relationship between colony and mother city.[1] In the primitive city the family organization was extremely important, and the sub-divisions of the city were based on it, genos, phratry, tribe. But these family groupings were also indissolubly bound up with religion,[2] and it is therefore possible that identity of cult between colony and metropolis implies that connections were maintained between the kinship groups of colony and mother city. Identity of cult between colony and metropolis can very often be found, as the studies mentioned have shown; it may be taken to have been the rule. So that we have here a possible sign of living connection between colonies and mother cities through their family organizations. Unfortunately it is impossible to be more definite than this, and impossible to be at all precise as to the detailed way in which these connections might work. To unearth and list all examples of identity of cult between colonies and mother cities would therefore seem a fruitless labour, and would add nothing to our knowledge of the colony–metropolis relationship.

So in general the *nomima* of a colony are much more important in determining the origins of a colony, where these are disputed.[3] They contribute at best indirectly to our knowledge of the relationship between colonies and mother cities.

If these two ways of reaching back beyond the fifth-century sources only help a little, some of the evidence concerning mixed colonies seems to show that the relationship was important from the beginning. It was very common in Greek colonization for settlers of different origins to join in one colonial

---

lumps together preservation of *nomima* and political relations under the one term 'Beziehungen'. Another bad example is provided by Röhlig, 17 f.

[1] See Bérard, *L'Expansion et la colonisation grecques*, 89.

[2] One very interesting example of this comes from Selinus; we have attested Zeus Meilichios of the Kleulidai, i.e. of a certain genos. But in this instance the mother city, Megara, provides evidence of the same deity connected with another *genos*. On all this see Hanell, 178.

[3] For example, they are most profitably used in this way by Hanell to establish the origins of the population of Byzantium; see 123–8, 142, 169, 183, 201, 211 f.

c

enterprise. In late instances we are sometimes informed that this mixture of origin militated against good relations with the mother city. At Amphipolis the settlers of Argilian origin were under the influence of Argilus and so encouraged to betray their new city to Brasidas.[1] These events followed quite shortly after the colony's foundation, but at Cyrene the groups of different origin at least remained distinct over a long period. When Demonax of Mantinea was called in to settle civil strife, he divided the inhabitants into three tribes: one of Theraeans and perioikoi, one of Peloponnesians and Cretans, and one of all the islanders.[2] This was five generations after the foundation and two after the subsidiary immigration.[3] It may be that the preservation of such distinctions implies a living connection with the place of origin. And the same inference could be drawn from the general statement of Aristotle that difference of origin was very often a cause of civil strife (*Pol.* 1303 a 25). Most of his examples concern colonies that received later immigrants, but at Sybaris and Thurii *stasis* occurred among the original mixed settlers.

The persistence of distinctions of origin may be found in mixed colonies even if they had one titular metropolis. But mixed colonies said to have two or more mother cities seem to reveal further significant information. There are a few passages in ancient authors which throw light on this situation. First, Strabo relates (VI.243) that the leaders of the expedition to found the colony of Cumae, Hippocles from Cyme and Megasthenes from Chalcis, agreed that Chalcis should be the mother city but the name should be taken from Cyme. Then Plutarch (*Q.G.* 30) tells that when Acanthus was founded jointly by Andrians and Chalcidians, the Chalcidian leader ran ahead to claim it for Chalcis, but the Andrian leader anticipated him by throwing his spear into the city. The Andrian claim was later upheld by arbitration. Finally Strabo (VI.264) relates (his source being Antiochus) that Taras and Thurii settled a long struggle over Siris with the agreement that they should make a

---

[1] Thuc. IV.103.3 f.

[2] Hdt. IV.161.2 ff. For these events see Chamoux, *Cyrène sous la monarchie des Battiades* (Paris 1953) 139 ff. He suggests that the reason for the disturbance was that the later immigrants had been kept underprivileged, but this is not stated by Herodotus.

[3] Hdt. IV.159.2.

joint settlement but that it should be adjudged Tarentine. Doubt might be cast on the first two passages, though they seem too circumstantial to dismiss out of hand. If they are accepted they show, together with the third which refers to a much later period, that the attempt was sometimes made in mixed colonies to recognize one city only as metropolis. This must therefore have been thought to be of importance for the future.

Other examples can be found revealing the same tendencies, even when the ancient sources do not say this expressly. The joint foundations of Corinth and Corcyra are particularly good examples of the tendency for one mother city to monopolize a mixed colony, but they are rather late for our present purpose.[1] There are, however, two early examples: one, Rhegium, which seems to show the persistence of distinctions of origin, the other, Gela, revealing the tendency of one mother city to arrogate that title to itself alone.

Rhegium's foundation is variously told in the tradition.[2] Strabo (VI.257) quotes Antiochus as saying that the Zancleans summoned the settlers from Chalcis and provided the oikist, Antimnestus. Strabo himself[3] gives the initiative to Delphi, after the Chalcidians, who had suffered a bad harvest, had dedicated one-tenth of their citizens to the god. He adds that some Messenian exiles were associated in the foundation. Though details may vary, the other sources also clearly state that it was a Chalcidian colony.[4]

Its Chalcidian nature is revealed not only by its close connection with Zancle, at the foundation, if we accept Antiochus'

[1] I treat them fully in Chapter VII.
[2] Vallet gives a full account of the literary tradition, *Rhégion et Zancle*, 66 ff. His conclusion (80) virtually agrees with Dunbabin's (12) and accepts Antiochus' account. His most important remarks concern the question when the Messenians were introduced. After presenting other rather slight arguments he decides (77) that they must have been there from an ancient period for Anaxilas to be able to use their origin for political purposes early in the fifth century. He then goes on to explain the confused and anachronistic account of Pausanias (IV.23.6–10) as reflecting several successive waves of Messenian settlers over the centuries (72 ff). This is conjecture, and it may be safer to ignore Pausanias, whose confusion has been recognized since Bentley; cf. *JHS* lxxiv 1954, 34 n. 2.
[3] Vallet seems right in deciding (71) that we cannot really tell whether all Strabo's account is from Antiochus or not.
[4] As Thucydides also; see III.86.2; cf. VI.44.3.

account, but also in its subsequent history.[1] Like the Chalcidian cities of Sicily it followed the laws of Charondas of Catane.[2] Its coinage too shows that it turned towards the Chalcidian cities of Sicily rather than to Southern Italy. No coins of other Italian cities have been found at Rhegium, though many of Sicily and Athens, while conversely, coins of Rhegium are rare in Southern Italy but have been found on many sites in Sicily.[3] The passage of Androdamas of Rhegium to the Chalcidians of Thrace, presumably via the mother city, is also a slight indication of contacts with Chalcis itself.[4]

But in spite of this we know that in the fifth century and later the dialect was mixed.[5] Moreover, Strabo relates (VI.257) that the rulers of the city were Messenians till the time of Anaxilas,[6] himself, according to Thucydides,[7] a Messenian. If these statements are true, Anaxilas is known as a Messenian some two hundred and forty years after the colony's foundation[8] and the Messenians had kept themselves separate and privileged all

[1] Vallet's work shows in detail how the two cities go together in commerce, coinage and where we know it (e.g. regarding Anaxilas), in political history.

[2] Heraclides Lembus *de. reb. pub.* 25 (*FHG* II p. 219).

[3] Milne, *Num. Chron.* 1938, 36 ff.

[4] See Arist. *Pol.* 1274 b 23, and Dunbabin 75. The origin of Chalcidian Ware seems too uncertain to add to these indications of Chalcidian connections. It is discussed at length by Vallet 211-28.

[5] See *R.E.* s.v. Rhegion 493, where the relevant inscriptions are listed. They show a mixed Doric-Chalcidic dialect. They are all later than Anaxilas, however, and Dunbabin infers that he introduced more Messenian settlers, so that it might be urged that these were responsible for the mixed dialect. Dunbabin's argument is from the analogy of Zancle (pp. 12, 396), but it remains uncertain that the new inhabitants of Zancle/Messene were Messenians. Though Strabo says so plainly (VI.268), Thucydides only mentions people of mixed origin (VI.4.6). Vallet discusses this conflict (344 ff) and follows Wallace (*JHS* lxxiv 1954, 32 ff) in arguing that Messenians were introduced into Zancle in the early years of the fifth century. The arguments for this are good if not compelling, and it is also reasonable to assume that some Messenians would have settled in Rhegium. In any case, if one accepts Vallet's hypothesis of several waves of Messenian immigrants into Rhegium, the dialect could owe its Doric element to these later arrivals of undetermined date.

[6] The exact words are:
οἱ τῶν Ῥηγίνων ἡγεμόνες μέχρι Ἀναξίλα τοῦ Μεσσηνίων γένους ἀεὶ καθίσταντο.

[7] VI.4.6.

[8] The exact date of Rhegium's foundation is not given in the tradition, but the modern calculation *c.* 730-20 seems reasonable: see Vallet 56, Dunbabin 13, Bérard 104 f.

those years in a Chalcidian colony. However, Vallet (77) has
argued recently that Strabo's statement cannot be accepted,
because 'comme l'indique formellement un passage d'Aristote'
Anaxilas overcame an oligarchy to install his tyranny, an oligarchy which had held power until that date and consisted of
descendants of the old Chalcidian colonists. But this is to go
beyond the sources. Aristotle merely states (*Pol.* V.1316 a) that
the tyranny succeeded an oligarchy, and the description of that
oligarchy by Heraclides Lembus[1] does not include information
about the origin of the oligarchs.[2] Vallet's view (336) that
Anaxilas replaced Chalcidian rulers and based his power on the
popular element in which the Messenians were important is
therefore a conjecture. If we accept it and combine it with his
other conjecture that there had been several waves of Messenian
settlers,[3] we need not conclude that the Messenian element had
kept itself separate and privileged over a very long period. But
it would still be legitimate to ask why Messenians were allowed
regularly to settle in the colony over these years; and the obvious answer would be that the Messenian element already in
the colony was important. Vallet's conjectures do not seem
preferable to Strabo's clear statement, but even if one accepts
them the distinctions of origin among the settlers of Rhegium
remain.

Gela was founded, according to Thucydides (VI.4.3) by
Antiphemus of Rhodes and Entimus of Crete, and evidence for
the influence of both these islands[4] can be seen in archaeological finds and cults. Imports of certain Cretan pottery, found
nowhere but at Gela, preceded the foundation, and continued
for a short time in the seventh century.[5] The pithoi used for
infant burials in the seventh [century were Cretan in type and
some, at least, were Cretan in manufacture.[6] The story that
Antiphemus carried off a statue made by Daedalus from

[1] *De reb. pub.* 25.3; *FHG* II p. 219.
[2] It is not necessarily right to identify Strabo's leaders (ἡγεμόνες) with the
1000 oligarchs of Heraclides (as Dunbabin 75 n. 1); but they were chosen
by wealth.
[3] See above p. 17 n. 2.
[4] Neither island was a political unity at this date, and the sources do not
reveal which cities the oikists came from.
[5] For this pottery see Blakeway, *BSA* xxxiii, 1933, 183, and Orsi, *MA
Linc.* xxxi.337 f; cf. Dunbabin 4.
[6] Payne, *Necrocorinthia*, 5 n. 1.

Omphace[1] seems to show Cretan influence.[2] The Rhodian connection is shown by Gela's original name, Lindioi,[3] by offerings to Athena Lindia as early as the seventh century,[4] and by the importance of the cult of Apollo, who may be assumed to be Apollo Lindios.[5]

But later evidence gives the impression that the Rhodian connection became predominant. The plain or simply decorated Rhodian ware found in Sicily almost solely at Gela, the local imitation of Rhodian forms, the very close agreement in burial methods between Rhodes and Gela at the turn of the seventh and sixth centuries, seem, taken together, to justify Dunbabin's suggestion that there was a fresh Rhodian immigration into Gela at the time of the foundation of Acragas in c. 580 B.C.[6]

In addition Dunbabin suggests that the immigration was part of Rhodian policy in connection with the foundation of Acragas and the contemporary attempt of Pentathlus to settle Lilybaeum with Rhodian and Cnidian forces. Although Strabo and Ps-Scymnus, hardly independent witnesses, agree with Thucydides that the Geloans founded Acragas,[7] Polybius says plainly that the colony was founded by Rhodians,[8] and Rhodian participation is indicated by a fragment of Pindar and Pindaric scholia.[9] The cults earliest attested at Acragas are Rhodian, as Dunbabin notes (311). Further, if the founding of Acragas is regarded as part of a Rhodian policy, its great size, which was

[1] Paus, VIII.46.2.
[2] Dunbabin suggests (112) that this might be a 'plant' to establish a Cretan claim.
[3] Thuc. VI.4.3.
[4] *Lindian Chronicle* XXV, in *Lindos, Fouilles d'Acropole II, Inscriptions*, by Ch. Blinkenberg (Berlin and Copenhagen 1941); cf. Dunbabin 112. The source of information is the historian Xenagoras, whom Jacoby considers (*FGH* IID. *Commentary* 702 f.) to be of early Hellenistic date. He also regards Wilamowitz's very low opinion of Xenagoras' reliability as too hasty, and I do not see any general *a priori* reasons for doubting records of dedications of the seventh century.
[5] Diod. XIII.108; cf. Dunbabin 236.
[6] See Dunbabin 138 ff and for the pottery Appendix IIc.
[7] Thuc. VI.4.4; Strabo VI.272; Ps-Scymnus 292 f.
[8] IX.27.7 f; Bérard's view (236) that they need not have come direct from Rhodes seems to be an attempt to get round the disagreement among the sources.
[9] Frg. 105 (OCT), and schol. to *Ol.* II.15 (c). On these see Dunbabin 310 f.

planned from the beginning,[1] is more easily intelligible. It was to eclipse Gela, and it would be strange for Gela to found a colony comparatively nearby greater than itself.

This combination of evidence and argument by Dunbabin hangs together well. The great stumbling-block remains Thucydides' statement that Acragas was a Geloan foundation.[2] There are, however, two points to note in Thucydides' sentence: that there were two oikists and that he thought it necessary to say that a Geloan colony received Geloan customs. It is possible to explain the two oikists as being one from Rhodes and one from Crete,[3] but the lack of firm evidence for a Cretan connection with Acragas seems against this interpretation.[4] Dunbabin's view (310) that one was Geloan and one Rhodian[5] fits the other evidence better, and would explain Thucydides' slightly unexpected information about Geloan *nomima*. For if Thucydides' source contained the information (which he has not passed on)[6] that one of the oikists was Rhodian, his remark about the *nomima* becomes meaningful.

If this view of the relations between Rhodes, Gela and Acragas is right, then Rhodes was dominating Gela's policy in a way that a truly joint metropolis could hardly hope to. It would be more natural to suppose that she had effectively ousted Crete from the position. This would explain why many sources refer to the Rhodian origin of Gela to the exclusion of Crete. Antiphemus is far more often mentioned as sole oikist than as sharing the honour with Entimus,[7] and Herodotus can

[1] See Dunbabin 312 f.
[2] VI.4.4:
ἔτεσι δὲ ἐγγύτατα ὀκτὼ καὶ ἑκατὸν μετὰ τὴν σφετέραν οἴκισιν Γελῷοι Ἀκράγαντα ᾤκισαν, τὴν μὲν πόλιν ἀπὸ τοῦ Ἀκράγαντος ποταμοῦ ὀνομάσαντες, οἰκιστὰς δὲ ποιήσαντες Ἀριστόνουν καὶ Πυστίλον, νόμιμα δὲ τὰ Γελῴων δόντες.
[3] As Bérard suggests (236), though tentatively.
[4] Theron is said to have sent Minos' bones to Crete (Diod. IV.79.4), and Phalaris' krater dedicated to Athena Lindia bore the inscription Δαίδαλος ἔδωκε ξεινιόν με Κωκάλωι (*Lindian Chronicle* XXIV), in which the name Daedalus suggests a Cretan connection. But these need show no more than a consciousness of the partially Cretan origin of Gela.
[5] As he notes, Zancle provides an analogy for such a procedure (Thuc. VI.4.5). If Vallet's conjecture is accepted, Rhegium is also an example. But it rests merely on the two oikists recorded separately in different sources (see Vallet 68 nn. 1 and 2).
[6] Unless, as Professor Gomme suggested to me, the words <μετὰ Ῥοδίων> should be read before or after ᾤκισαν.
[7] See Bérard 228 f. The inscribed base of an Attic kylix of the fifth century

think of Gela as a purely Rhodian foundation (VII.153.1). It therefore seems that in this mixed colony one metropolis came to monopolize that position.

If we may conclude that distinctions of origin remained important in mixed colonies and that an attempt was sometimes made to monopolize the position of mother city, it is reasonable to proceed to the further conclusion that the relations between colonies and mother cities were considered important from the beginning of the great colonizing movement.

It is clear that the ways of reaching back beyond the fifth-century sources only provide very general or very occasional help. But their existence allows some confidence in accepting statements about earlier times in fifth-century sources, and slightly weakens the argument from silence implicit in the view that the idea of the relationship between colony and metropolis was especially effective in the fifth century. Hence an attempt to investigate the relations between colonies and mother cities in Greece is not made hopeless by the great chronological gulf between the foundation of most colonies and the articulate source material. But such an attempt is only justified if the problems arising from the nature of the evidence are constantly borne in mind.

---

dedicated to Antiphemus (first published and recognized as a dedication to the oikist by Orsi, *Not. Scav.* 1900, 273 ff; photograph *Annuario d. Scuola arch. d. Atene* n.s. xi–xiii 1949–51, 108) may suggest the same thing. For he is mentioned alone with no distinguishing epithet (*Μνασιθάλες ἀνέθεκε 'Αντιφάμōι*) as if he were well known as sole oikist, or had a separate cult. The authenticity of the inscription is convincingly defended by Guarducci, *Annuario d. scuola arch. d. Atene* n.s. xxi–xxii 1959–60, 264 ff.

PART I

THE ACT OF FOUNDATION

CHAPTER II

TRADITIONAL PRACTICES

COLONIZATION was a regular activity in classical and pre-classical Greece; as we have seen, interest in it was also great from the time of the first sources likely to reveal this; it is not therefore surprising that the ideas and practices regarding the procedure of establishing a colony were also fixed and well-known. Thus Herodotus refers to the omission of these actions in terms which show their traditional character;[1] and Thucy-dides can say that the oikist for Epidamnus was summoned from Corcyra's mother city, Corinth, 'according to the ancient custom' (I.24.2).

The antiquity of these actions and beliefs is also suggested by their religious character. It was the rule for the colonists to take with them fire from the sacred hearth (Hestia) of the mother city, in order to kindle with it the sacred hearth of the colony.[2] The intention of this ritual act was clearly to make the new community in the deepest possible way continuous with the old.

According to Herodotus (V.42.2) it was also obligatory to consult the oracle at Delphi before undertaking a colonial expedition.[3] If this was so from the earliest times it is unlikely

---

[1] Herodotus (V.42.2) only specifies Dorieus' failure to consult Delphi. It is a pity that he did not give details of the other traditional practices which he says Dorieus omitted.

[2] Though the precise statement of this is in a late compilation (*Etym. Magn.* s.v. πρυτανεία), Herodotus seems to refer to the practice (I.146.2).

[3] It has been maintained that Delphi did not become an international centre until some date after the beginning of the colonizing movement, and only influenced colonization 'à partir du VIᵉ siècle'; see J. Defradas, *Thèmes de la propagandie delphique* (Paris 1954) 233 f. This would require the rejection of all the traditions of Delphi's part in the colonization of the eighth and seventh centuries, especially that of Sicily and Magna Graecia. Desborough, *Protogeometric Pottery* 304, believes that the pottery finds at Delphi show that it was an international sanctuary in the ninth century. This is not the view of W. G. Forrest, 'Colonization and the Rise of Delphi', *Historia* vi 1957, 160 ff; he does not think it attained this character before the later eighth century. Though his arguments rest too much on fargoing reconstructions

that it was originally an application for practical advice.[1] It is true that the oracle may have built up a useful store of geographical knowledge and may thus have led colonists to areas not yet occupied by Greeks, or advised against ill-chosen sites. Good examples of this would be Cyrene and Taras.[2] But, as most of the oracles we possess are probably forgeries,[3] we can hardly be certain that the oracle gave such practical advice in the early period. It was probably rather a matter of obtaining the god's sanction. The foundation of a city was a sacred act, sacred enough to be performed by a god. Apart from the cities of Greece proper, like Athens, many colonies claimed Apollo as their oikist,[4] and mortals who performed this act were worshipped as heroes after their death. As a home of gods as well as men, a Greek city could not be founded without the sanction of the gods.[5] The recourse to Delphi seems also to show that the colonists realized that they were extending the human and divine community not only of their own city, but of the Greeks in general. This is the way to understand Thucydides' information (VI.3.1) that the altar of Apollo Archegetes at Naxos was especially sacred, so that all Sicilian Greeks going to the great Panhellenic festivals sacrificed on it first before their departure. This was the first place where the worship of the Greek gods had been established in the new country.

It seems probable that through this constant connection with colonial expeditions Delphi acquired the position of arbiter in colonial matters. Various examples, inevitably comparatively late in date, suggest that specifically colonial matters were referred to the oracle for judgment. When the people of Thurii were divided as to who was their oikist, they sent to Delphi for the answer, and the god himself assumed the role.[6] Epidamnus,

---

concerning the Lelantine War and too easy acceptance of early oracles, Forrest is surely right to see that the participation of Delphi in the early colonization attested by the tradition should not be denied.

[1] As it is in Hdt. V.42.2.

[2] See Hdt. IV.150–8, and Parke and Wormell, *A History of the Delphic Oracle* I.71 ff. This work contains a good survey of the oracle's part in colonization, I.49–81.

[3] This was convincingly shown by A. S. Pease, *CP* v 1917, 1–20.

[4] The instances were collected by S. Lampros, *De conditorum coloniarum graecarum indole, praemiisque et honoribus*, diss. Leipzig 1873, 8–20.

[5] As stressed by Parke and Wormell, 49 f.

[6] Diod. XII.35.2.

desiring to transfer itself from its metropolis, Corcyra, to Corinth, also asked Delphi for advice.[1] Thasos' relations with her colonies seem to have been adjusted under the guidance of Delphi.[2] If the oracle did discharge this function, it may have been partly responsible for any regularity that can be found in Greek ideas on these subjects.

As we have seen, Thucydides states (I.24.2) that it was the ancient custom when a colony itself founded a colony to summon the oikist from its mother city. It is characteristic of our scanty knowledge of these practices that we only hear of this from Thucydides, and that he provides our only definite examples, Epidamnus and Selinus.[3] But there is no reason to doubt his statement. The practice is a further indication of the desire in early times to represent even colonies at one remove as continuations of the original community.

Other more narrowly political practices are mentioned or implied by decrees arranging colonial enterprises, which must be examined separately. But it is worth noting that there is a little evidence to suggest that the colonists made an agreement on oath with the community they were leaving. The decree of Thera arranging for the foundation of Cyrene, which is preserved in a fourth-century Cyrenean inscription,[4] is followed by the information that those leaving and those staying behind swore to keep the agreement they had made, and a picturesque and primitive ceremonial of curses against transgressors is also described.[5] With this may be compared Herodotus' information regarding the Phoenicians (III.19.2) that they refused to sail against their colonists the Carthaginians on the grounds that they were bound by great oaths. This is not a Greek colony but as it is a Greek historian his testimony may perhaps be set beside

[1] Thuc. I.25.1.

[2] See Pouilloux, *Recherches sur l'histoire et les cultes de Thasos I* (Paris 1954) 181 ff, especially 183.

[3] Thuc. VI.4.2.

[4] *SEG* IX.3. The question whether this document represents the original seventh-century Theraean decree is very complicated. I have treated it elsewhere (*JHS* lxxx 1960, 94 ff) and tried to show that what we probably have is the seventh-century document edited for re-publication in the fourth. The matter in it may be taken as authentic, if some of the wording may not.

[5] 40 ff. Dr. Kathleen Forbes, who has written a thesis on the dialect of Cyrene, has informed me (by letter) that she considers these curses to be the latter part of the original oath sworn by the colonists.

the evidence from Thera. Such agreements on oath may well
have preceded the more formal decrees arranging foundations,
and show the aspirations of founders and colonists to keep some
permanent relationship between the new and old communities.

CHAPTER III

THE ROLE OF THE OIKIST

ἔνθεν ἀναστήσας ἄγε Ναυσίθοος θεοειδής,
εἷσεν δὲ Σχερίῃ, ἑκὰς ἀνδρῶν ἀλφηστάων,
ἀμφὶ δὲ τεῖχος ἔλασσε πόλει, καὶ ἐδείματο οἴκους,
καὶ νηοὺς ποίησε θεῶν, καὶ ἐδάσσατ᾽ ἀρούρας.[1]

Homer, *Od.* vi. 7–11.

EVIDENCE for the oikist's activities in the early period is unfortunately very meagre, and even in later times we know less of his duties than of the honours paid him.[2] The most important of these was his worship as a hero after his death,[3] which shows that the foundation of a colony was thought of in terms which we should call religious. However, practical duties may easily be inferred. Homer provides a minimum list in the lines quoted above[4] and the account of the foundation of Cyrene in Herodotus offers further evidence.

The oikist Battus was pointed out to Delphic Apollo by the king of Thera (IV.150.3) and he was chosen by the state (153), as is also stated in the Theraean foundation decree.[5] He then led the expedition (156.2), ruled as king for about forty years (159.1), and established his family as a dynasty (163.2 e.g.). In ruling as king Battus may have been exceptional, but the early oikists certainly went as participants in the new community; for the sacrifices and rites paid to them clearly grew up round their tombs, which were situated in distinguished places in the colony.[6] Herodotus' remarks on Dorieus (V.42.2)

[1] 'Godlike Nausithous made them arise from there and led them away and settled them in Scheria, far from mortal men who live by gain. He surrounded the city with a wall, built houses, made temples of the gods and divided the land.'

[2] They are listed in detail by Lampros, op. cit.

[3] A pleasing memorial of such cults is the fragment of a fifth-century Attic kylix dedicated to Antiphemus, oikist of Gela; see above p. 21 n. 7.

[4] The close connection between the Odyssey and colonization is stressed by Schaefer in his article 'Eigenart und Wesenzüge der griechischen Kolonisation', *Heidelberger Jahrbücher* 1960, p. 77.

[5] See above p. 27 n. 4.

[6] E.g. those of Battus, Pind, *Pyth.* V.124 f and schol., and of Brasidas, Thuc. V.11.1. For the rites attached to them see Thuc. ibid; Hdt. VI.38.1

29

suggest that the oikist was expected to manage everything from consulting the Delphic oracle onwards. We need not doubt that in such early colonies the oikist was generally an independent leader, and would satisfy both colony and metropolis by carrying out the general conditions laid down for the settlement[1] and especially by performing the right ritual acts in establishing the new polis.

From the early period there is no sure example of an oikist who was intended by the metropolis to further its imperial or commercial policies.[2] The first oikists who may be confidently regarded as chosen in order to maintain a political link with the metropolis were the sons of tyrants. In Corinth's striking colonial activity under Cypselus and Periander the rule seems to have been for the sons of tyrants to serve as oikists of the new settlements. We are told that the oikists of Ambracia, Leucas and Anactorium were sons of Cypselus,[3] and the oikist of Potidaea was Euagoras, son of Periander.[4] The effect of this family relationship was presumably never legally defined, but the leaders of the colonies were members of the ruling house in the mother city.[5] That this created a political link is suggested by the events on Corcyra in Periander's reign.

It is clear from the foundation of Epidamnus in 627 (Euse-

(of Miltiades, oikist of the Chersonese). For the importance of the tombs of heroes in general see, e.g. W. K. C. Guthrie, *The Greeks and their Gods* (London 1950) 232–5.

[1] As in the foundation decree for Cyrene, to be discussed in the following chapter.

[2] Such a role has been attributed to Archias and Chersicrates, oikists of Syracuse and Corcyra, in the eighth century, but, as I try to show in Appendix I below, this hypothesis is not convincing.

[3] Ambracia: Ps-Scymnus 435 f, Strabo X.452; Leucas: Strabo loc. cit., who attributes its foundation to the same expedition, led by Gorgos, son of Cypselus, which was responsible for Ambracia; but Nic. Dam. frg. 57.7, *FGH* IIA p. 357, names Echiades, son of Cypselus, as oikist; Anactorium: Strabo loc. cit., though the oikist given by Nic. Dam., loc. cit., is Pylades, son of Cypselus.

[4] Nic. Dam. frg. 59, *FGH* IIA p. 358.

[5] To make the tyrant something almost separate from the city he ruled seems a mistake. This is done by Berve in his *Miltiades, Hermes*, Einzelschriften II, 1937; cf. the criticisms of his thesis by Bengtson, 'Einzelpersönlichkeit und athenischer Staat', *Sitz. Bayr. Akad.* 1939, 7–67, and by Ehrenberg, 'Early Athenian Colonies', in *Aspects of the Ancient World* (Oxford 1946) 116–43. Will seems to make the same mistake, when he asks if the family connection could turn into a civic connection after the fall of the tyranny; see *La Nouvelle Clio* vi, 1954, 418.

bius) that Corcyra was then independent of Corinth. For though
she behaved correctly in inviting a Corinthian oikist and even
invited Corinthian settlers,[1] the colony was always recognized
as Corcyrean. The other colonies in which both Corinth and
Corcyra were involved were never known as purely Corcyrean.[2]
If, however, Corcyra was then independent but on friendly
terms with her mother city,[3] under Periander she was hostile
and became dependent. The story as told in Herodotus and
Nicolaus Damascenus is not entirely clear in detail.[4] According
to Nicolaus Damascenus Periander's son was merely living on
Corcyra[5] when he was killed by the Corcyreans, though the
description may conceal his real power. However this may be,
in revenge for his death Periander conquered the island, and
made his nephew its ruler.[6] Thus conquered territory was put
under the rule of a member of the tyrant's family. This suggests
that it is right to infer some measure of control by the metropolis over colonies founded under the leadership of tyrants' sons.

Although the choice of oikists suggests that this colonization
was of an imperial nature, it has sometimes been thought to
represent only family aggrandizement.[7] That this is to draw too
definite a line between the tyrant and the community he ruled
is, however, proved by the subsequent relations between these
colonies and the mother city, which will be treated later. For
these too were close and show some dependence. If the colonies
were merely private possessions of the tyrant house the connection should have died with the last tyrant.

[1] Thuc. I.24.2.
[2] They were Leucas, Anactorium and Apollonia in Illyria. Leucas may
be inferred to have been a joint foundation from Plut. *Them.* XXIV. For
Anactorium see Thuc. I.55.1; for Apollonia in Illyria Ps-Scymnus 439,
Strabo VII.316. As the sources concentrate on the Corinthian connection
in these colonies, Beaumont's suggestion (*JHS* lvi, 1936, 166) that the Corinthians were strong enough to force the Corcyreans to let them participate
in the colonization of Epidamnus seems unlikely. If this had been so it seems
difficult to believe that Epidamnus would have been a Corcyrean colony;
at best it would have been a joint foundation of Corinth and Corcyra.
[3] Wade-Gery's conjecture (*CAH* III.550 ff) that Corinth and Corcyra
may have clashed in two contemporary battles in the North West seems
improbable in view of the behaviour of Corcyra at the foundation of
Epidamnus and of Cypselus' pacific nature, which Wade-Gery notes.
[4] Hdt. III.52 f; Nic. Dam. frg. 59, *FGH* IIA p. 358. They differ on the
son's name.
[5] διαιτώμενον παρὰ σφίσιν.
[6] Hdt. III.49 ff; Nic. Dam. loc. cit.   [7] See above p. 30 n. 5.

D

The Athenian colony of Sigeum[1] was likewise placed by Peisistratus under the control of his son Hegesistratus in about 530 B.C.[2] From that time until the expulsion of Hippias we may assume that it was in a dependent position similar to that of the Corinthian colonies. Sigeum lies near the south side of the Hellespont. On the north is the Thracian Chersonese. To this Miltiades the Elder had brought an Athenian colony at an earlier date, probably between 561 and 556 B.C.,[3] and between 524 and 513 B.C. the younger Miltiades was sent out to rule it by the Peisistratids.[4]

It seems entirely reasonable to see the recolonization of Sigeum, the sending of Miltiades the Younger to the Chersonese and his later colonization of Lemnos[5] as parts of a single

---

[1] Herodotus' account (V.94f) seems to mean that there was an Athenian colony planted at Sigeum at the end of the seventh century, which was recolonized by Peisistratus. This is the interpretation of Berve, op. cit. (26–8), accepted by Bengtson, op. cit. (20) and Ehrenberg, op. cit. (117). Will interprets Herodotus' account as telling of only one war, under Peisistratus; see *La Nouvelle Clio* vi 1954, 422, *Rev. de Phil.* xxv, 1951, 178–81, and *Korinthiaka*, 381–91. But this interpretation of Herodotus and what follows from it seem very doubtful. For a convincing defence of the view that Herodotus is telling of a series of wars see Page, *Sappho and Alcaeus* (Oxford 1955) 152–8. Beattie misunderstands Page in his review (*JHS* lxxvii (pt. II) 1957, 322). The Herodotean ending 'and thus Sigeum came under Athenian control' does not imply that there were two accounts of the way in which this had happened; it is merely the conclusion of the whole story. Will's interpretation is part of his view of Cypselid chronology, in which he follows Beloch (I.2.274 ff) in drastically lowering the traditional dates. See below, p. 118 n. 4.

[2] Hdt. V.94.1. For the date Berve's calculation (28) from the probable age of Hegesistratus seems acceptable.

[3] See Hdt. VI.34 ff; Marcellinus, *Vita Thuc.* 5 ff. See Berve, 8. The *terminus ante quem* is 546 when Croesus lost his empire, for Croesus saved Miltiades when he was captured in his war against Lampsacus. Wade-Gery (*JHS* lxxi 1951, 219 n. 38) would accept a lower date for the fall of Sardis, namely 544, based on interpretations of Herodotus. In this case the definite *terminus ante quem* is lowered by two years, and Miltiades could just have left Athens after the battle of Pallene in 546. But the events have to be crowded to fit this time-scale, and the arguments for the lower date are a little tenuous, even if the date in the Babylonian Chronicle (546) is also uncertain, as Wade-Gery (loc. cit.) maintains. Lydian chronology is treated in full by H. Kaletsch, *Historia* vii 1958, 1 ff, who arrives at the date 547/6 for the fall of Sardis after an exhaustive study of Greek chronographers and the Babylonian Chronicle; see 39–44.

[4] Hdt. VI.39.1. For the date see Berve 40 n. 1; Bengtson 28 n. 1.

[5] See Hdt. VI.140; Diod. X.19.6; Zenobius, *Prov.* III.85, *Paroem. Graeci* ed. Gaisford (Oxford 1836), p. 288.

Athenian policy aimed at controlling the straits.[1] But it is unlikely that the first colonization of Sigeum by Phrynon at the
end of the seventh century[2] was already directed to this end, as
has been argued,[3] for at that time Athens was unable to hold
Salamis.[4] Thus Phrynon's settlement at Sigeum is best seen as
an independent colony.[5] Miltiades' expedition to the Chersonese is more difficult to judge, but it certainly left Athens at
some date before Peisistratus was firmly in power,[6] and it therefore seems more likely that the great noble Miltiades was acting
independently,[7] than that Peisistratus was already directing
ambitious foreign policies.

Thus both at Corinth and at Athens tyrants used colonies
for imperial ends, choosing for the purpose oikists closely

[1] This is the view of Bengtson and Ehrenberg, op. cit. They oppose
Berve's view (op. cit.) that this colonization represents the quest for power
by private individuals.

[2] The date is established by the Eusebian dates for the oikist, Phrynon;
see R.E. s.v.

[3] As by Bengtson, 21; but the arguments are slight. They rest on Strabo's
wording (XIII.599), 'Αθηναῖοι Φρύνωνα τὸν 'Ολυμπιονίκην πέμψαντες, and the
description of Phrynon in the Suda (s.v. Πιττακός) as the strategos of the
Athenians. The wording of these late sources should not be pressed to show
the nature of the undertaking. An example of the dangers of such a procedure is provided by Will, La Nouvelle Clio vi 1954, 453 f, who uses the words
of the Suda to show that the colonists remained citizens of the metropolis:
'that is why the Sigeans are called Athenians'. But what else would the
Athenian settlers led by Phrynon be called?

[4] Cf. Solon frg. 2 and Berve, 28.

[5] In ATL III it is suggested (289 n. 75) that Elaious in the Chersonese
was colonized by Phrynon in the late seventh century. This is arrived at by
emending Φορβοων (sic) of the MSS. of Ps-Scymnus (708) to Φρύνων. In that
case Phrynon's colonization of Sigeum would look like part of an attempt to
control both sides of the straits. But until we have something which can be
truly called evidence it seems safer to argue from the circumstances of the
time.

[6] Even if one accepts Wade-Gery's rather unlikely suggestion that Miltiades could have left after Pallene, Peisistratus was hardly firmly in control
so soon.

[7] The ancient evidence could perhaps be interpreted either way. Both
Herodotus' and Marcellinus' words (see above p. 32 n. 3) point strongly to
a private act. But those who argue that it was a 'political not a private enterprise' (Ehrenberg, 120) concentrate attention on Herodotus' remark that
Peisistratus had τὸ πᾶν κράτος, which is interpreted as implying that it was a
state enterprise, finally emanating from Peisistratus. Berve's arguments for
the view that the enterprise was private from the suggested enmity between
Philaids and Peisistratids are rightly shown by Bengtson (8 ff) to be of small
importance. But Bengtson's own arguments for the opposite conclusion
(10 ff) are all open to objection.

connected with themselves. Sigeum's connection with the mother
city depended more on the tyrant, it seems, than that of the
Corinthian colonies. For Hippias was able to retire to Sigeum
on his ejection from Athens,[1] and we shall see that subse-
quently Sigeum does not appear to have been a dependent
colony.

In four colonies of the fifth century, three Athenian, Brea,
Thurii and Amphipolis, and one Spartan, Heraclea in Trachis,
the role of the oikist is even more clearly dictated by the policy
of the metropolis.

The decree concerning the foundation of Brea[2] shows how the
Athenians arranged for the settlement of a colony at the height
of their power. We have no other knowledge of the colony,[3] but
the nature of the foundation is clear from the decree. Founded
within the context of the Athenian empire, it was intended to be
a bulwark in the important Thraceward region, as we may see
from the arrangements for the colony's defence (13–16). It is
provided that, if the land of the colonists is attacked, the cities
(τὰς πόλεις) must come to its aid as quickly as possible, according to the treaty made at an earlier date concerning the cities of
the Thraceward region. The term τὰς πόλεις seems likely to
refer to those of the Thraceward region mentioned immediately
afterwards, and Aristophanes' usage shows that 'the cities' could
mean the allies,[4] so that this provision seems to show that the
Athenians had agreed with the allies in the Thraceward region

[1] Hdt. V.94.1.
[2] Tod 44; the decree is discussed further in the next chapter, and translated in Appendix II.
[3] A recent discussion is that of Woodhead, *CQ* n.s. ii 1952, 57–62. The
choice of date is restricted to 445/4 or 440/38 by the character of the writing
and the information that an Athenian army is in the field (26–9); but the
arguments in favour of either are not sufficient to exclude the possibility of
the other (see Busolt III.417, who favours the earlier date, and Woodhead,
60 ff, who prefers the later). As for the site, Woodhead's suggestion (57–9)
that *Βρέαν* be read instead of *Βέροιαν* in Thuc. I.61.4 would put it in N.W.
Chalcidice, but Edson convincingly defends the correctness of the reading
Βέροιαν (*CP* l 1955, 169–90, especially 176 f). However, the general conclusion that it lay in the Thraceward region follows from ll.13 ff. The lack
of any subsequent history is possibly to be explained by its absorption in
other Athenian settlements in the area (see Nesselhauf, *Klio*, Beiheft xxx
1933, 130 ff, who suggests Amphipolis, and Woodhead, 62, who argues for
Potidaea); or by its forcible inclusion in Olynthus after the Athenian defeat
at Spartolus (as Woodhead, ibid.).
[4] See Hugill, *Panhellenism in Aristophanes*, 67.

to found a colony, and bound these allies to support it in case of need.

The position of the oikist Democlides should therefore be considered in the light of the colony's clearly imperial character. Though it is expressly decreed (8 f) that he shall have full powers (αὐτο]κράτορα) to establish the colony, there are various indications in the decree of limitations on his authority. For one thing the state decides details beforehand, who shall be eligible to sail (40 f), and when the expedition shall depart (29 f), and it chooses the officials (γεώνομοι) to divide the land (6 f). But the greatest encroachment is the presence of ten ἀπ[οικισταί (5).[1] Tod (p. 89) describes these as 'apparently the adjutants of the οἰκιστής', and compares the ten men sent to Thurii to found it (Schol. Arist. *Clouds* 332). If they have this character, as seems likely, Democlides was not an independent autocrat.

Furthermore, if he is identified with the Democlides who proposed a later Athenian decree,[2] then he returned to Athens and did not live with the community he had founded. This is uncertain; the colony may have failed and this have been the reason for his return; or the identification may be wrong. But as he is clearly an Athenian state official carrying out fairly detailed instructions of the Athenian demos, it would not be surprising if he returned on the completion of his temporary task, as did the oikists of Thurii, Amphipolis and, probably, Heraclea in Trachis.

The Athenian aims in the foundation of Thurii are perhaps not so clear-cut. For Thurii was a refoundation of an ancient Greek city, and also it was not a purely Athenian colony.[3] However, one can recognize the Panhellenic nature of the

[1] This restoration appears to be generally accepted, though Tod himself (p. 89) states that the word does not occur elsewhere. Liddell and Scott, however, refer to Menander Rhetor, p. 356 in Spengel's edition *Rhet. Graec.* (Teubner) III, where the word has a quite general sense of 'founders'.

[2] *I.G.* I².152. Ever since Pittakis first published this inscription ('Εφ. 1860, no. 3806) editors have suggested that he might be the same man as the oikist of Brea, though Kirchner does not follow them (*PA* 3474f). Tod (p. 88) goes so far as to say the identification is probable. Meanwhile Wade-Gery conjectures (*CP* xxvi 1931, 313) Δεμ[οκλείδες on the fragment he publishes there belonging to *I.G.* I².50. But his argument 'not many names fit' is admittedly very slight. This inscription refers to the peace with Samos of 440/39.

[3] The main account of the foundation is Diod. XII.10 f.

foundation without denying that the colony was also designed
to further Athens' own aims.[1] Athens' interests in the West at
this period are revealed by her treaties with Leontini and
Rhegium[2] and the important Athenian participation in the
foundation of Neapolis (Naples).[3] The Athenians also tried to
provide for these interests in the act of founding Thurii, within
the limits prescribed by the special circumstances of the
settlement.

The oikist(s) and leading men in the expedition were
Athenians,[4] and the Athenians sent the largest group of settlers.[5]
The constitution was a democracy[6] and there were ten tribes.[7]
It seems overcautious not to conclude from this that the con-
stitutional arrangements had Athenian models, even though the
Solonian code was not adopted.[8] In the arrangement of the
tribes[9] the only tribe deriving from a single city was the
Athenais from Athens. Thus in the establishment of this ostensibly Panhellenic colony the Athenians established a constitution likely to be pro-Athenian[10] and an Athenian tribe likely to
provide an organized pro-Athenian core.

As at Brea, the oikist Lampon[11] seems to have been a state
official performing a temporary task. The unimportance of his
role is shown by the fact that he is only mentioned as sole oikist
in one source;[12] Diodorus (XII.10.4) associates him in the task
with Xenocritus, and Photius mentions,[13] besides these two,
three others to whom the foundation had been attributed. In
434/3, a bare ten years after the foundation,[14] an argument arose

[1] This has been convincingly stated by Ehrenberg, *AJP* lxix 1948,
149 ff, so the arguments need not be repeated. He refutes Wade-Gery's far-
going thesis that the colony was established by Thucydides, son of Melesias,
as a sincerely Panhellenic venture (*JHS* lii 1932, 217–19).

[2] Tod 57; 58.   [3] See Bérard, 58 ff.
[4] See Ehrenberg, 164 ff, for details.   [5] Diod. XII.35.1 f.
[6] Diod. XII.11.2 f; Arist. *Pol.* 1307a.   [7] Diod. loc. cit.
[8] Diod. XII.11.4 ff.   [9] Diod. XII.11.3.
[10] See Thuc. III.47.2; cf. A. H. M. Jones, *Athenian Democracy* (Oxford
1957) 67 ff, and Sainte-Croix, *Historia* iii 1954, 1–41.
[11] We may accept Lampon as the oikist, however small his powers and
shortlived his honour, as he appears more consistently than anyone else in
the sources; cf. Ehrenberg, 164.
[12] Plut. *Praec. reip. ger.* 823 D.   [13] s.v. Θουριομάντεις.
[14] Ehrenberg, 157, explains the two traditions about the date of Thurii's
foundation in a way that seems acceptable: 446/5 foundation of the third
Sybaris, 444/3 foundation of Thurii. This is neatly confirmed by the coins;
see Ehrenberg, 152.

as to who should count as oikist.[1] This was caused by political
motives, but if the matter was arguable, the oikist cannot have
been a monarchic leader and a hero. The ten men sent to found
the colony,[2] whom, as we have seen, Tod regards as corresponding to the ἀποικισταί of the Brea decree,[3] represent a sharing
and thus a lessening of the oikist's powers.

Furthermore, Lampon did not live and exercise citizenship in
the community he had helped to establish, but kept his Athenian
citizenship, returned to Athens, and played an important role in
public life there. He is the first Athenian signatory at the Peace
of Nicias and at the Spartan/Athenian alliance of the same
year,[4] and Aristophanes makes fun of him in the Birds (521,
988). Though we cannot say when he returned to Athens, it
seems unlikely that he was still in the colony when the dispute
about the oikist arose in 434/3.

Hagnon's role in the foundation of Amphipolis seems to have
been closely alike. The Athenian aims in this foundation were to
establish a strong point of Athenian power in the Thraceward
region, able to exploit the natural resources of the immediate
area, and to protect the Athenian allies of the district.[5] Hence
the expedition's size,[6] hence Thucydides' exile for allowing
Brasidas to capture the city,[7] and hence its special position in the
Peace of Nicias,[8] not to mention later attempts to regain the city.[9]

Of the act of foundation we know only that it was an official
venture[10] under the leadership of Hagnon and that a democratic
constitution was established.[11] The choice of Hagnon shows the
importance of the undertaking to Athens. He was a leading

[1] Diod. XII.35.2.   [2] Schol. Arist. Clouds 332.
[3] This seems preferable to identifying them with the γεώνομοι of the same
decree, as Pappritz, Thurii (Diss. Berlin 1891) 20, as these would be less
likely to be mentioned virtually as founders.
[4] Thuc. V.19.2; 24.1.   [5] Thuc. IV.108.1.
[6] The abortive expedition of 465/4 (for date see Thuc. IV.102.2 with
Diod. XII.32.3; cf. Gomme I.390 f) had 10,000 settlers (Thuc. I.100.3;
IV.102.2). Since the aims and requirements were similar in the successful
expedition it can hardly have been smaller.
[7] Thuc. V.26.3; Marcellinus Vita Thuc. 23.   [8] Thuc. V.18.5.
[9] Thuc. V.83 f; VII.9, not to go beyond the fifth century.
[10] The wording of Thucydides in describing the foundation (IV.102.2), in
which the subject of the sentence is οἱ Ἀθηναῖοι, puts this beyond doubt.
[11] This seems a reasonable conclusion from the passages IV.104.4; 105.1.
In the first the pro-Athenian party convince τῷ πλήθει,, in the second
Brasidas is worried because the πλῆθος τῶν' Ἀμφιπολίτων is not coming over to
him. Both suggest that the people had political power.

figure at Athens, especially in the military field,[1] both before and after the foundation of Amphipolis. At Amphipolis he named the city[2] and was honoured as founder until the title of oikist was transferred to Brasidas.[3] On the other hand his early return to Athens, at the latest in time to be *strategos* in 430/29,[4] shows that his task was probably confined to the preliminaries of the settlement; again it was temporary state employment for an Athenian citizen. This explains too how the colonists could deprive him of the position of oikist. These examples show the status of the oikist in Athenian imperial foundations of the fifth century.[5]

The Spartan colony of Heraclea in Trachis, settled in 426,[6] was closely connected with their war aims. Thucydides tells us (III.92.4) that it was considered a suitable place for preparing a naval descent on Euboea and the journey to Thrace. It was a large,[7] mixed settlement, and was established by three Spartan oikists: Leon, Alcidas and Damagon.[8] Of the last-named we know nothing further. Alcidas played a considerable if ignoble role in the earlier part of the war; he was admiral of the Spartan fleet that failed to help Mytilene, and commander of unsuccessful expeditions in the north-western theatre.[9] Leon was one of the Spartan ambassadors sent to Athens about the Athenian/Argive alliance, and held the office of eponymous ephor at Sparta in 419/18; in 411 he took over command at Chios.[10] So

---

[1] Cf. Thuc. I.117.2, Hagnon's part in the reduction of Samos; II.58.1, his generalship at Potidaea.

[2] Thuc. IV.102.3.   [3] Thuc. V.11.1.   [4] Thuc. II.58.1.

[5] A similar status, of temporary state servants, should probably be attributed to the Athenian oikists sent to settle Notion, especially as it was not a settlement of Athenians at all; see Thuc. III.34.4.

[6] The settlement is related by Thucydides, III.92 f; cf. Diod. XII.59.5.

[7] Diodorus' figure (loc. cit.) of 10,000 may be too round, and Schaefer shows why it is unlikely to be correct (*Historia* x 1961, 292), but the passage Thuc. III.93.2 shows the size of the settlement.

[8] Thuc. III.92.5.   [9] See Thuc. III.16.3; 26.1; 69.1 f; 76.

[10] See Thuc. V.44.3; Xen. *Hell.* II.iii.10; Thuc. VIII.61.2. This depends on accepting Poralla's suggestion (*Prosopographie der Lakedaimonier bis auf die Zeit Alexanders des Grossen* (Breslau 1913) 83 f) that the various Leons we meet at this time were one and the same man. Thucydides' four references to the Spartan Leon contain on only one occasion any delimiting word (Σπαρτιάτης, VIII.61.2; the others are III.92.5; V.44.3; VIII.28.5), which seems to mean that there was only one Leon to whom he could be referring. Poralla has shown that chronological considerations fit this thesis perfectly well.

Leon at least returned to public life at Sparta after founding Heraclea. That none of the oikists stayed to govern the colony seems probable from the fact that the Spartan Xenares is described as the Heracleot governor, ἄρχων αὐτῶν, in 420,[1] and when the Boeotians took control of the place immediately afterwards, the Spartan expelled for misgovernment was Hagesippidas.[2] So it seems that in this foundation clearly designed to further the strategic aims of the mother city the oikists were carrying out a temporary state task as Spartan citizens.

The evidence on the oikist's role discussed here is admittedly limited; we know of few in any detail even in the later period and in the earlier only general inferences are possible. For all that, the marked change or development in the role which has been illustrated has probably general validity and mirrors a general development in Greek ideas about colonies over this long period. In the earlier colonies the oikists seem to have been all-responsible, even monarchical; in the dependent colonies of the tyrants the oikists chosen are closely attached to the ruler of the metropolis; in the imperial colonies of the fifth century the oikist is no longer even a participant in the new community. Other factors no doubt played a part in changing the role of the oikist. In Athenian colonies with democratic constitutions, for instance, a monarchical oikist would be an impossible anachronism. But in general the changing role of the oikist reflects the increasing dependence of the colony, or the increasing interference of the mother city.

[1] Thuc. V.51.2.   [2] Thuc. V.52.1.

CHAPTER IV

FOUNDATION DECREES

THE arrangements made by a mother city for the foundation of a Greek colony were, sometimes at least, set down in writing. Timaeus claimed to have seen such a decree in Locris, referring to Epizephyrian Locri, which began 'as parents to children' (ὡς γονεῦσι πρὸς τέκνα),[1] and the Theban claim to rule Plataea seems to have been based on a decree of this sort, whether or not it had, in fact, existed.[2] Moreover, Hyperides even used the word *apoikia* for such provisions (τὰ γράμματα καθ᾽ ἃ ἀποικοῦσί τινες).[3]

Some of these documents have, at least in part, come down to us. Three are particularly important: the foundation decrees for Cyrene,[4] for a settlement of Hypocnemidian Locrians at Naupactus,[5] and for Brea.[6] There is also an inscription arranging a colonial settlement on Black Corcyra,[7] but this evidently contains only part of the arrangements for the colony.[8] Another inscription (*IG* I² 46) is concerned with the foundation of a colony, but is unfortunately too fragmentary to yield any information of value. A foundation decree is also presupposed by an inscription concerning the despatch of an Athenian colony to the Adriatic (Tod 200), but the inscription itself is only a record of equipment taken over by the oikist.

These decrees, the first three of which will provide most of the material for this chapter, sometimes arrange directly for the relations that the colony and mother city intended to maintain, and thus provide primary evidence for Greek ideas and practices in this field. Even when they do not, they can throw light

---

[1] See Polyb. XII.9. Polybius' disbelief does not seem very well founded.
[2] See Thuc. III.61.2. [3] See Harpocration s.v. ἀποικία.
[4] *SEG* IX.3; see above p. 27 n. 4. For translations of these foundation decrees see Appendix II below.
[5] Tod 24. [6] Tod 44. [7] *Syll.*³ 141.
[8] As was recognized long since; see Wilhelm, *Neue Beiträge zur griech. Inschriftenkunde III* (*Sitz. Wien. Akad.*, Phil. Hist. Klasse, 175, 1913–14) 16, and Brunsmid, *Die Inschriften und Münzen der griechischen Städte Dalmatiens* (*Ab.d. Arch. Epig. Seminares d. Univ. Wien* 1894) 14.

on such relations indirectly. The information from them must, however, be considered in relation to their date and historical circumstances. Brea and Naupactus are settlements of the fifth century,[1] and the actual inscription regarding Cyrene is of the fourth. However, the matter of the decree preserved in this inscription is probably authentic[2] even if the wording is not, so that in this one instance we have the substance of a foundation decree from the seventh century.

The circumstances of Cyrene's foundation are well known. Herodotus' account shows that the colony was a simple colony of need.[3] It was sent out in time of famine at Thera (IV.151.1) to reduce the population. In all its provisions the decree suits these circumstances. It has compulsory enlistment (28 f), severe limitations on the right to return (32 ff), and fierce threats against defaulters (37 ff). It is fortunate that one of the three decrees refers to a colony of the most usual Greek type, a new place to live for people grown too many for the land of the mother city to support.

There is no direct literary reference to the settlement at Naupactus. Its historical setting must therefore be conjectured, and the starting-point for such conjecture is the fact that 'the character of the writing forbids our assigning the law . . . to a date later than the close of the Peloponnesian War'.[4] Tod therefore dates the inscription to about 460,[5] since Naupactus was held by Messenians under the protection of Athens from about that time till 404. The second important factor to be remembered is that Naupactus was a considerable city of

[1] On the date of Brea see above p. 43 n. 3. On that of the colony at Naupactus see the discussion below.

[2] As I have tried to show elsewhere; see above p. 27 n. 4.

[3] The scholiast to Pindar *Pyth*. IV.100 relates that Menecles (*FGH*. IIIA p. 83) gives a stasis at Thera as the reason for Battus' resort to Delphi and the colonizing expedition, Battus being the leader of the losing side. This is incompatible with the general conscription of the colonists found in both Herodotus (IV.153) and the decree. Menecles' account is preferred by the scholiast because it is less mythical than the story of Battus' vocal impediment. This may be true, but that is not the true choice, which lies between famine and stasis. The account of Menecles might be an attempted rationalization of a later age, conjectured from the passage Hdt. IV.156.3 (the refusal to allow the colonists to land when they attempted to return).

[4] Tod I p. 33.

[5] An earlier date, the first quarter of the fifth century, is tentatively proposed on the grounds of the letter forms by Jeffery, *Local Scripts of Archaic Greece*, 106.

ancient standing,[1] so that the settlement is a re-colonization, or, more probably, reinforcement, of an existing city.

Any reconstruction must be based mainly on the internal evidence of the decree itself. Some have been overimpressed by provisions which seem to emphasize the military nature of the settlement, as, for example, those which aimed at keeping the number of male heads of houses constant and allowed for un-conditional return if the colonists were driven out (6 ff, 9 ff). So Curtius[2] proposed an ingenious theory that Corinth was responsible for the re-colonization, which was intended to pre-vent Athenian encroachment, and used these provisions to show that the settlement had the nature of a garrison. Oldfather, for similar reasons, made a more convincing suggestion that it was a move in the Locrian struggle with the Aetolians of the hinter-land, who may have been so successful against Naupactus that large losses in population had to be made good.[3] But there is no need to refer these provisions to a definite warlike threat. A Greek city always felt its existence to be precarious, and the campaigns in the Archidamian War show the troubled charac-ter of this area.

It is unnecessary to go into detailed conjectures here. The general character of the undertaking is clear from the decree. That it was not economically necessary for the metropolis, as Cyrene was, is shown by the easy terms of return, provided the claims of Naupactus were satisfied. But that it served political ends seems clear from the whole tone of the decree, and es-pecially, for instance, from the oath of loyalty (11–14). This decree, therefore, arranged for the reinforcement of an existing community in connection with certain political aims of the metropolis.

The historical circumstance of the Athenian colony at Brea have been described in Chapter III. This was a colony sent out by an imperial state to strengthen its empire in an important region.

As the inscription concerning Black Corcyra is occasionally useful for purposes of comparison, an account of the circum-stances of this expedition is also required. Once again there is only the internal evidence from the document itself. The ex-

---

[1] For its history see *RE* s.v. Naupaktos 1983 f.
[2] *Hermes* x 1876, 237 ff.   [3] See *RE* s.v. Lokris 1194–6.

pedition was probably small. This is a reasonable inference from the fact that over 150 names of settlers are inscribed below the decree on the extant fragments of the stone. Only if the stele were abnormally large could more than 300 names have been inscribed. The inscription may be roughly dated to the fourth century on epigraphical grounds; a more precise date is given in *Syll.*[3], c. 385, because the colonization has been connected with the activity of Dionysius I in the Adriatic.[1] But though it is possible that the mother city, Issa, was a foundation of Dionysius,[2] there is nothing in the inscription to indicate that the colony was the result of Syracusan imperial ambitions. The tone of the inscription rather suggests that it was a regular agricultural settlement.

A slight difficulty is presented by the information from ancient authors[3] that the island was settled by Cnidians. Beaumont made out a plausible case for setting this event in the sixth century after the Cnidians had helped the Corcyreans against Periander,[4] so that it seems he must be right in thinking that the Cnidian settlement had died out in some way before the new Issaean foundation.[5] It might explain how the compilers of the decree had such a clear idea of the available land, its quality and the difference between 'the city' and the outer country, if they were resettling and refortifying a place already occupied in the past by Greeks.[6]

[1] See *Syll.*[3] notes to 141.

[2] The only precise testimony is the passage Ps-Scymnus 413 f, where it is said to have been founded by Syracusans. Its proximity to Pharos, however, where Dionysius helped the Parians to settle a colony (Diod. XV.13.4), combined with Ps-Scymnus' statement, has led to the assumption that it was founded by Dionysius. Cf. Gitti, *La Parola del Passato* vii 1952, 179.

[3] Ps-Scymnus 428, Pliny *N.H.* III.152, Strabo VI.315.

[4] *JHS* lvi 1936, 173 ff.

[5] This seems more likely than that there were two Greek cities existing on this remote island at the same time, as Brunsmid suggested; see Klaffenbach, 'Zur Siedlungsinschrift von Korkyra Melaina', *Studid in Honorem Acad. D. Decev* (Sofia 1958) 220.

[6] The reading of this inscription demands a word. Wilhelm's restorations οἰκιστ]ᾶν and οἰκισταί (1–2) are merely suggestions (see above p. 40 n. 8), so cannot be used as evidence about oikists. Brunsmid's earlier λογιστ]ᾶν (see *Syll.*[3] notes ad. loc.) seems just as good, and the office is known to have existed at Issa (ibid.). The disharmony between the restored συνθήκα etc. of 1–2 (i.e. the record of the agreement between certain officials and the lords of Black Corcyra) and the later part of the inscription, which is patently a decree, makes the restorations of the opening lines suspect. A new restoration of these should perhaps be made, taking account of the two facts that

Of the three decrees concerning Brea, Cyrene and Naupactus the last stands apart in that it contains no practical provisions for settling the colony. No oikist is appointed and there are no arrangements for division of land, much less any of the smaller administrative details found in the Brea decree, like travelling expenses (30 f) or a time limit for the colonists' departure (29 f). Athens may have been more paternal about such administrative details, as the careful provision of equipment for the colony to the Adriatic[1] over a hundred years later might be held to show, but even the Cyrene decree begins with the provision that the colony be sent and Battus be its oikist (24–27).

The absence of such practical matters convinced Oldfather[2] that we have only part of the foundation decree for Naupactus. He noted in support of this view that there is also no mention of the body which passed the decree. But this omission has been adequately explained by Meyer,[3] who pointed out, with examples, that it was not normal in archaic documents to express everything which a member of the community would automatically understand or which necessarily followed from the context. It was unnecessary to say that the assembly of Opus, or whatever body it was, had passed the decree. Furthermore the beginning of the inscription is recognizably a beginning: ἐν Ναύπακτον κα τῶνδε ⱶαπιϝοικία. There may have been another decree arranging the practical matters, but our decree is complete. The fact that it is 'the colony' shows either that there was another decree, arranging for the colony to be sent and other practical matters, or that these things were known and agreed beforehand, and a decree was unnecessary. Whichever was so, for our purposes it is fortunate that the decree has as its main subject the colonist's position, especially with regard to the mother city, for the practical arrangements in the other decrees are inevitably less informative about the relationship between colony and mother city.[4]

---

it is a decree and that Pyllos and his son are natives not Greeks. Klaffenbach has improved the reading of line 5 in the work cited in the preceding note, but the larger problem remains.

[1] Tod 200. [2] *RE* s.v. Lokris 1240.

[3] *Forschungen zur alten Geschichte* I.295.

[4] As, for instance, the inscription about Black Corcyra, which arranges one practical matter, land division.

It is because it is so much fuller on these topics than the other decrees that the Naupactus decree will be investigated first, and the others compared with it where possible. Then provisions in the other decrees which have no counterpart in that about Naupactus will be considered.[1]

One of the most striking aspects of the Naupactus decree is its form. After the first paragraph (1–11), which covers several topics, the remaining paragraphs are numbered,[2] and each contains strictly one provision only. The significance of this distinction is disputed, but there are good reasons to believe that the first, unnumbered section contains the general matters regarded as most important by colonists and metropolis.[3]

A second general question is the exact scope of the decree. It has often been erroneously stated that the purpose of the decree was to regulate relations between colony and metropolis.[4] In fact there are provisions regulating not only these relations, but also the affairs of Naupactus,[5] and there are also two passages in which affairs of all the West Locrians appear to be the decree's concern (10 f; 14–16). The fact that the decree contains all these matters raises the question of the relations of Opus, or more generally, the Hypocnemidian Locrians, with Naupactus (that is, the inhabitants already there), and with West Locris as a whole.

The relationship of Opus with Naupactus is brought into prominence by paragraph 1 (A.11–14). The colonists are to swear not to secede from the Opuntians and the oath may be renewed in thirty years time by a hundred Opuntians and a hundred Naupactians. This provision for renewal shows clearly that the state of Naupactus was to be dependent on Opus.[6]

---

[1] Of the many works on the Naupactus inscription (for a good bibliography see Hicks and Hill p. 7, to be supplemented by Tod I p. 31), the fullest and most fundamental discussion remains that of R. Meister, 'Das Colonialrecht von Naupaktos' (*Ber. d. sächs. Gesell. d. Wiss. zu Leipzig*, Phil. Hist. Klasse, 1895, 272–334).

[2] This is the first example in Greek epigraphy of such numbering by letters of the alphabet; see Tod *BSA* xlix 1954, 1 ff.

[3] For the detailed arguments for this conclusion see Appendix III.

[4] By Meyer, *Forschungen zur alten Geschichte* I.291; Hicks and Hill, p. 33; the editors of the *Recueil des inscriptions iuridiques grecques*, 184; and Jeffery, *Local Scripts of Archaic Greece*, 106. Meister rightly objected to this, 287 n. 2.

[5] As Meister 287 f.

[6] This is not accepted by Meister (302), who assumes that Naupactus was an independent state, and that the oath of loyalty could only be laid on

As it is reasonable to assume that there was a considerable population already at Naupactus,[1] their relationship with Opus must have been of the same sort as the colonists achieved by taking the oath not to secede. How had this relationship arisen?

Thucydides' account of the relations between Corinth and Epidamnus may provide an analogy. After previous negotiations the Epidamnians handed over the colony to Corinth (παρέδοσαν τὴν ἀποικίαν, I.25.2), and as a consequence the Corinthians were able to announce a colonial expedition to Epidamnus on terms of equality for the colonists (I.27.1).[2] Presumably the Naupactians could have converted themselves into colonists of Opus in the same way, and, if it were thought necessary, taken a similar oath of loyalty to that of the colonists.

---

individual colonists, not the state of Naupactus. This leads him to the unlikely position that the oath bound the individual colonist to resist if the majority at Naupactus voted for secession and that the provision for return (8–10) was designed to offer them a retreat if this very situation arose. But if Naupactus were independent it would be most unsatisfactory for them to have a body of citizens bound in allegiance to another state. Nor would Opus be likely to bind in allegiance colonists likely to be outvoted in an assembly. Further, as the oath thirty years later was clearly to be sworn on behalf of Naupactus, Meister is forced to maintain that this would not be a renewal, and support this by the arguments that the original oath was not sworn for a definite time, and many of the original colonists would have returned or be dead in thirty years. His view is that this provision allows for the possibility that the whole city will swear loyalty next time. But the fact that the original oath was not sworn for a definite time does not mean that it could not be renewed; cf. Athens' treaties with Leontini and Rhegium, which were renewed in 433/2 (Tod 57, 58), although they were made, according to Meritt (CQ xl, 1946, 91), in c. 448, and, if his ingenious arguments (85–91) are accepted, for ever (ἐς ἀίδιον). Furthermore, since from paragraph 1(A) onwards, one paragraph contains strictly one subject, it would be strange to provide within the paragraph, without warning, for two oaths with very different validity. The simple explanation is better: the colonists are to become Naupactians (2); their oath can be renewed by Naupactus in the next generation.

[1] This follows from the knowledge of its previous existence; see above p. 42 n.1. But Meyer also argues (op. cit. 292) that the frequent use of the word ἐπιϝοίϙοι to describe the colonists shows that it was a reinforcement; the word may well have this technical sense here. Meister's view about the religious provision (to be considered fully below), which seems right, demands that some of the earlier citizens of Naupactus remained.

[2] Meister rightly brings forward the example of Epidamnus (288), but uses it to support his idea that there was a treaty between Opus and Naupactus. Thucydides' simple phrase hardly suggests such a treaty, and Corinth's subsequent actions seem to be made on her own initiative entirely, based on Epidamnus' single act of handing itself over to Corinth.

However, it may not have been necessary for the Naupactians to convert themselves into colonists of the Hypocnemidian Locrians. An inscription is recorded in Strabo (IX.425) which states that Opus was metropolis of all the Locrians:

> Τούσδε ποθεῖ φθιμένους ὑπὲρ Ἑλλάδος ἀντία Μήδων
> μητρόπολις Λοκρῶν εὐθυνόμων Ὀπόεις.[1]

As this was set up at Thermopylae to commemorate those who fell in the battle of 480 it is of the right date to illustrate a belief current at the time of our decree. It may be that this fact or belief was the justification for the colony's despatch, and for the oath not to secede, and that it determines the relationship between Opus and the inhabitants of Naupactus.[2]

The same fact or belief may explain the two provisions which seem to imply that Opus exercised some control over the affairs of the West Locrians. The second (2(B), 14 f) decrees that a tax-defaulter from Naupactus be excluded from the Locrians until he has paid his lawful debts to the Naupactians. This shows that Opus could apparently legislate for all the Locrians to this extent.

In the first (10 f) the colonists are to pay no tax except in common with the West Locrians. It has been suggested[3] that the tax referred to is a tribute paid by the West Locrians to Opus. This point cannot be definitely decided, because the very brief words of the inscription, Τέλος μὴ φάρειν μηδὲν Ϝό,τι μὴ μετὰ Λοκρῶν τῶν Ϝεσπαρίων, are open to various interpretations. The tax or tribute is probably not to be identified with taxes paid in Naupactus, the existence of which is shown by paragraph 2(B), nor with those of the Hypocnemidian Locrians, for that subject is settled in lines 4–6, where it is stated that the colonists are to pay no taxes among the Hypocnemidian Locrians unless they return. It would be wrong to conclude that this provision precludes the possibility of a tribute paid to

---

[1] 'These men, who died defending Hellas against the Medes, are mourned by the metropolis of the Locrians of righteous laws, Opus'.

[2] For a similar view see Lerat, *Les Locriens de l'Ouest* II.14, who decides that the best explanation for the geographical division of the Locrians is that Western Locris was colonized by Eastern, as the ancient sources say; cf. the epitaph quoted in Strabo and Ps-Scymnus 480–2.

[3] By Oikonomides, Ἐποικία Λοκρῶν γράμματα τὸ πρῶτον ὑπὸ Ἰ. Οἰκονομίδου ἐκδοθέντα καὶ διαλευκαθέντα (Athens 1869) 125.

Opus, for Opus was not a tightly-knit, single-city state; the diversity and number of communities in Hypocnemidian Locris are attested by lines 22 and 30. The provision of lines 4–6 presumably refers to the taxes to be paid by the colonists in their several local communities if they return, and that in line 10 could still refer to a tribute paid to Opus. There seem, therefore, to be two possibilities: either a tribute paid by the West Locrians to Opus, or taxes paid by them to a common state of West Locris to which Naupactus belonged. Such taxes may well have existed, for the league (*koinon*) of the West Locrians is attested as early as the fourth century.[1] In that case Opus is merely assuming the right to guarantee her colonists equal rights in West Locris.

These provisions were said by Meyer[2] to show that the *Stammverwandschaft* of the Locrians had political expression, though since Opus is at least legislating for all the Locrians it is also her supremacy that is revealed. Oldfather in a full discussion of the *Stammverfassung* of the Locrians,[3] considers the implications of this inscription, but takes the view that the 'legend' according to which West Locris was colonized from East Locris was an attempt by the Hypocnemidian Locrians to bring the West Locrians into dependence as colonists. So he would rather explain these provisions by assuming a former agreement between East and West Locris. While this may be so, his main argument for it, from the final provision of the document (45 f), does not seem compelling. This provision states that 'the statute for the Hypocnemidian Locrians is to be valid in the same way for the settlers from Chaleum with Antiphatas'. Oldfather considered that the action of the Chalean settlers in adopting the same status as the colonists from Hypocnemidian Locris was so important a matter that it must have been of interest to all West Locrians. But this is hardly necessary; it was a common practice in colonial expeditions to invite

---

[1] See Lerat, op. cit. 55 ff, for a decree found at Malandrino in West Locris (see map in Lerat I) which begins ἔδοξε τῶι κοινῶι τῶν Λοκρῶν τῶν Ἐσ[περίων. Lerat himself will not accept (31) the idea of a common tax paid to the *koinon* of the West Locrians, because he imagines that the provision about tax-defaulters in Naupactus (14 f) refers to the same tax as that of the passage under discussion. But there seems no reason for this connection.

[2] *Forschungen* 293.

[3] *RE* s.v. Locris 1239 ff.

settlers from other cities, and the Chalean settlers would have naturally adopted the arrangements made for the other colonists, without necessarily considering that their action affected their fellow West Locrians. There are difficulties in the detailed interpretation of this provision,[1] but one point relevant here seems clear. These settlers were ready to take the oath not to secede from Opus. They would have undertaken this obligation more easily if Opus were regarded as the metropolis of all the Locrians, and this is perhaps a further indication that this belief or fact was the basis for the supremacy of Opus attested by the two provisions under discussion.

The first provision of the decree (1–4) concerns the religious position of the colonists. Editors differ on its interpretation. There is no dispute about the letters on the bronze but the 'o' of Ναυπακτιον(ων) could represent either omikron or omega, and the accent on ὅσια must be placed according to interpretation. Meister (274) read in line 2 Ναυπακτίων ἐόντα Ϝόπω ξένον ὁσία λαγχάνειν καὶ θύειν ἐξεῖμεν κτλ.; Tod[2] Ναυπάκτιον ἐόντα Ϝόπω ξένον ὅσια λαγχάνειν καὶ θύειν ἐξεῖμεν κτλ. There is a third difference: Tod takes Ϝόπω as representing ὅπως, though he recognizes that it could be a local adverb (ὁπόθεν), which is how Meister takes it; this can be paralleled from some Doric inscriptions.[3]

Tod's translation reads '(The Hypocnemidian Locrian, after becoming a Naupactian) may, being a Naupactian, participate in social life and offer sacrifice as a ξένος etc.' Meister translates, '(Dem Burger des hypocnemidischen Lokris soll, nachdem er Naupaktier geworden ist,) wenn er in Naupaktos da sich befindet, von wo ein Fremder nach heiligem Recht Antheil erhalten und opfern darf, dies gestattet sein usw.' This he explains grammatically (287): Ϝόπω steht in prägnanter Weise

---

[1] As Meister points out (328) the provision cannot mean that the Chalean settlers would be subject to the same provisions in respect of Hypocnemidian Locris. He lists various unacceptable suggestions and adds that it cannot be taken quite literally. Neither the provisions for return to Opus, for example, nor those about inheritance there, seem likely to have applied to these Chalean settlers. My translation above therefore follows that of Tod (I p. 36), who rightly recognizes that the provision should be interpreted in a general rather than a literal way.

[2] I take Tod as a representative of the editors who have not followed Meister's (to my mind) convincing interpretation (278 ff).

[3] See Liddell and Scott s.v. ὅπω.

für ἐνταῦθα ὁπω und Ναυπακτίων ist der partitive Genitiv, der von dieser Lokaladverbe abhängt.'[1]

In choosing between these interpretations the first step is to decide the force of ὅσια. Meister's reading of ὁσία has a grammatical advantage, which he himself does not point out, in that it leaves λαγχάνειν καὶ θύειν absolute, a formula, just as they are a line later. But he is also able to give many examples (283) of ὁσία (ὁσίη) in this sense, used without ἐστι. But it is its advantage in meaning that makes this reading clearly superior. Meister (282) rightly objects that if the colonists were merely to have the rights of a ξένος in their mother city, not only did they receive no privilege over other foreigners, but it would have been unnecessary to mention it. Further, if they were only to receive the rights of a ξένος in their new city, to take the other possibility, in a vital aspect of citizenship they were to be no better than foreigners, which is at variance with the whole tone of the decree; for throughout every encouragement is given to attract settlers. Thus 'as a stranger ὅσια λαγχάνειν'[2] seems very unsatisfactory, whatever view is taken of the locality of the cults mentioned. Meister, on the other hand, is able to point to an excellent example for the sort of action that his interpretation proposes. In the inscription IG II[2] 1214, 14–17, one Callidamas, an Athenian, is given the same rights as the Piraeans in sacrifices, with a limitation of exactly the same sort as that seen by Meister in the lines under discussion:

συνεστιᾶσθαι Καλλιδάμαντα μετὰ Πειραιέων ἐν ἅπασι τοῖς ἱεροῖς, πλὴν εἴ που αὐτοῖς Πειραιεῦσιν νόμιμόν ἐστιν εἰσιέναι, ἄλλωι δὲ μή.[3]

The early editors[4] all took this provision to refer to cults in

[1] Tod does not represent Meister correctly, I p. 33. Meister's interpretation, just quoted, is not 'so far as religion allows a stranger (to do so)', but refers simply to place. Lerat, op. cit. 30 n. 1, misrepresents Meister in the same way, but rightly, in my opinion, will not take ὅσια as the object of λαγχάνειν καὶ θύειν.

[2] Tod's translation 'participate in social life' seems to derive from a suggestion of Meyer, Forschungen 297, but for λαγχάνειν in close connection with θύειν not to mean 'to receive one's share (in a sacrifice)' is very hard to accept. This translation, and the many others quoted by Meister (278 ff), show the difficulties in the reading ὅσια.

[3] 'Let Callidamas participate with the Piraeans in all the religious festivals except if there is any place where the Piraeans themselves are permitted by law to go, but no one else.'

[4] See Meister 287.

Naupactus, but later it was referred to cults in the mother country.[1] To obtain this meaning one must translate ἐπιτυχόντα as 'when the colonist happened to be in the mother country', which seems more than it can bear,[2] especially as there is no indication in the Greek that any other cults are in question than those of Naupactus, the only name mentioned. It is therefore easier to suppose that the cults are those of Naupactus,[3] especially if one accepts Meister's interpretation of ὁσία and Ⱶόπω, for it seems unlikely that colonists for whom return was envisaged as a clear possibility should be excluded as strangers from any cults in the mother country. If we take this view we have an interesting example of the way subsidiary immigrants were treated regarding their religious status, but no information about their relations with the mother city.

Taxes or tribute are dealt with in three provisions of the decree (4–6, 10 f and (2.B) 14–16), of which the last merely protects Naupactus against absconding tax-defaulters and the second is too brief to admit of certain interpretation. The first, however, throws interesting light on the colonists' relations with their mother city. It runs thus:

Τέλος τοὺς ἐπιϝοίκους Λοκρῶν τῶν Ⱶὑποκναμιδίων μὴ φάρειν ἐν Λοκροῖς τοῖς Ⱶὑποκναμιδίοις φρίν κ'αὖ τις Λοφρὸς γένηται τῶν Ⱶὑποκναμιδίων.

It has been seen[4] that this presumably refers to the normal taxes paid by citizens of the Hypocnemidian Locrians in their local communities. If the colonist returns he is once more liable to these.

Now the decree makes quite plain that the colonist is to become a Naupactian and cease to be a citizen of Hypocnemidian Locris.[5] Yet it is thought necessary to state that the

[1] See Meyer op. cit. 291, Hicks and Hill p. 33, *Recueil des inscriptions iuridiques grecques* p. 181. Tod's translation does not show his opinion, but his immediately subsequent explanation of the words κὴ δάμω (4) by a description of the division of *Eastern* Locris into demes shows that he takes the provision as referring to cults of the mother city.
[2] Vischer's interpretation 'when he is present' (*Rh. Mus.* xxvi 1871, 38 ff) is accepted by Tod and Meister. This must mean, as the Greek stands, 'present at the sacrifices'.
[3] It does not alter this conclusion whether one reads Ναυπακτίων with Meister or Ναυπάκτιον with Tod, and both are possible, but the order of the words seems to make Tod's the more natural reading.
[4] Above pp. 47 f.   [5] See e.g. 1 f, 6, 22 f.

colonists will not be liable to taxes paid by Hypocnemidian Locrians. It would be strictly logical to infer that but for this provision they could still be required to pay taxes in Hypocnemidian Locris although they had ceased to be citizens of it. But the wording of the provision reveals an immediate connection between citizenship and the payment of these taxes, so that it seems better to assume that the decree here expresses something inherent in the loss of citizenship.

This strictly unnecessary expression may be explained by the circumstances of the expedition. It can be seen throughout the decree that the colonists are encouraged to go; every discouraging fear is removed. Furthermore the possibility of easy return and the provision for inheritance by citizens of one state from those of the other, which will be considered below, must have had the effect that the colonists felt far less cut off from their old home than those of a colony like Cyrene. For these reasons it was found necessary to express the automatic effect of the change of citizenship on the colonists' tax liability.

The provisions for return in the Naupactus decree are most revealing. This is not only because they are full and informative, but also because their significance is precisely established by the decree's insistence that the colonist is to become a Naupactian. By joining the colony he loses his original citizenship; the provisions for return give the legal conditions for its recovery.

Paragraph 4 (Δ 19–22) states the procedure which the returning colonist must follow: he must make a public announcement in Naupactus and among the Hypocnemidian Locrians. The conditions for return are given in lines 6–10. A colonist may return voluntarily without penalty,[1] if he leaves a grown son or brother in Naupactus (i.e. if the number of male heads of families in Naupactus is not reduced), or if he is compelled 'by necessity'. This implies that he might also return, with a penalty, if neither of these conditions was fulfilled. These are very easy terms. It seems clear from them that the colony did not arise from need at home; the colonists are discouraged from

---

[1] ἐνετήρια probably means entry fees or the like. So Tod translates (p. 34), but Meister (295–8), who argues the point very closely with full discussion of earlier commentators' views, decides that they represent a sacrifice that a new citizen had to offer (298). This does not alter the general significance, however.

returning only in order to protect the colony. This would be necessary to ensure the success of any colony; it is therefore a minimum limitation of the right to return.

The provision for return in the Cyrene decree (33–7) makes a profitable comparison. There a return to full citizen rights was only allowed if the Theraeans had not been able to help the colonists, if they were under pressure of necessity, and if they returned within five years.[1] This very grudging right of return fits the circumstances of the foundation of Cyrene, a colony founded to relieve the pressure of population at home. In the event, when the colonists tried to return, they were not allowed to do so.[2] However, if in this forced colonization a right of return was still conceded to the colonists, it may be assumed that it was normal to provide in the act of foundation for return if the expedition failed.

If the right of return in the Cyrene decree may be regarded as the minimum, that at Naupactus must be near the maximum. Yet even here it was necessary expressly to provide for unconditional return under pressure of necessity. It is interesting and possibly significant that both decrees use the word $\dot{a}v\dot{a}\gamma\varkappa\eta$ in this context. This was perhaps a matter regularly arranged at the despatch of colonies. If so, it is not surprising that it comes in the first paragraph of the Naupactus decree, as a matter of general and fundamental importance to colonists and metropolis.[3]

The first numbered provision is the oath of the colonists not to revolt from the Opuntians (11–14). The significance of this regarding Naupactus' relations to Opus has been discussed above, where it was seen to be probable that the oath meant the allegiance of Naupactus to Opus. The degree of allegiance is not clear. Meyer[4] thought that it meant only that the colonists should remain true to the mother city and not fight against it. Hicks and Hill (34) took it as merely showing an alliance. But

---

[1] The phrase $\dot{a}\lambda\lambda\dot{a}$ $\dot{a}v\dot{a}\gamma\varkappa a\iota$ $\dot{a}\chi\theta\tilde{\omega}v\tau\iota$ $\ddot{\varepsilon}\tau\eta$ $\dot{\varepsilon}\pi\dot{\iota}$ $\pi\dot{\varepsilon}v\tau\varepsilon$ $\dot{\varepsilon}\varkappa$ $\tau\tilde{a}\varsigma$ $\gamma\tilde{a}\varsigma$ $\varkappa\tau\lambda$. might mean that they could not return until they had suffered under necessity for five years, but this seems less likely. It is most inhumane and seems less suitable for Thera's needs. If any colonists remained after enduring five years it might be thought that the colony was established and should continue. In either case the right of return is strictly limited.

[2] See Hdt. IV.156.3.

[3] For further discussion of the right to return see Chapter VI.

[4] *Forschungen* I.299.

the words μὴ 'ποστᾱμεν imply at least some measure of dependence, not an alliance of equals. Herodotus and Thucydides frequently use the same word in the sense 'to revolt from'[1] and Tod's translation accepts this meaning. An admissible parallel may be seen in the oath sworn by the Chalcidians in the inscription Tod 42, 21 f: οὐκ ἀπο[σ]τήσομαι ἀπὸ τοῦ δήμου τῶν 'Αθηναίων κτλ. It is true that the provision for renewal implies mutual benefits, as Meyer rightly pointed out.[2] These obviously include the privileges about return, inheritance, etc., which the mother city could withdraw if the colonists broke their oath. But it is also to be assumed that Opus' reinforcement of Naupactus was part of her policy of protecting the city, and that this was the main benefit for Naupactus and the new colonists. In this again Epidamnus in her relationship to Corinth may be cited as a parallel. Thus mutual benefits are not inconsistent with dependence and we may conclude from paragraph 1(A) that the colony was to be established as a dependent of the mother city.

This provision is clearly determined by the circumstances of the expedition. Opus is interested in the strength of Naupactus, and this only has meaning for her if Naupactus remains loyal. An oath of political allegiance in the Cyrene decree would be surprising in view of the different circumstances of the colony. In the Brea inscription it would be in place; its absence may be due to the fact that the text is incomplete. But while the circumstances of the Naupactian colony should be remembered, the extreme brevity and simplicity of the provision suggest that it was not arranging anything exceptional. For the Locrians at this period the establishment of a politically dependent colony was nothing unusual.

There are three provisions about inheritance in the decree about Naupactus. The first (paragraph 3 (Γ), 16–19) refers to the inheritance of property in Naupactus. There are difficulties in the details of interpretation,[3] but it seems that there is pro-

[1] Liddell and Scott s.v. ἀφίστημι B.2. The use of the word for the secession of allies from Sparta (e.g. Thuc. V.30.1) is also, if not quite so strong as 'to revolt from', at least the description of an inferior deserting a superior, who will try to prevent or punish the desertion.
[2] Loc. cit.
[3] It is unlikely that the punctuation of the sentence will ever be definitely settled. Meister (304–6) treats these problems in detail, but Tod has not

vision for inheritance in the following order:[1] first, descendants in the family, next, rightful heirs[2] among the colonists in Naupactus, and finally, next of kin in Hypocnemidian Locris. Only then, if all heirs fail, shall the laws of Naupactus (laws, no doubt, regulating inheritance from people without heir) be observed.

The provision allows for inheritance by people from the mother community, but the colony is protected from the possible ill effects of such an arrangement. For though the next of kin among the Hypocnemidian Locrians are admitted, the words αὐτὸν ἰόντα (18) imply that they had to take up residence in the colony in order to inherit. This protected the colony against a reduction of population by absentee ownership. It is worth noting how easily the decree assumes that citizens of one community could transfer themselves to the other.

Paragraphs 6 and 8 (F.29–31; H.35–37) arrange for the colonists to inherit property in Hypocnemidian Locris. In contrast to the provision about inheritance in Naupactus, no general order of precedence or principles governing all inheritance are given; instead two specific possibilities are provided for. The first of these concerns inheritance from a brother: 'If the settler in Naupactus shall have brothers, as the law stands in each city of the Hypocnemidian Locrians, if the brother die, the colonist shall take possession of the property, that is shall possess his due share.'[3] The second reads 'whoever

---

followed him in some points. The differences are: in line 17 Tod puts the comma after ⊦Ὑποκναμιδίων, Meister after Ναυπάκτωι; in line 18 Tod puts the comma after Λοϙϙῶν, Meister after κϙατεῖν. Thus Meister makes τὸν ἐπάνχιστον dependent on Λοϙϙῶν τῶν ⊦Ὑποκναμιδίων and joins the later Λοϙϙῶν to ⊦όπω κ̓ ῆι, translating (276) 'von wo in Lokris er immer her sei'. Tod's punctuation leads to the translation (p. 34) 'the next of kin among the Locrians, whencesoever he be'. So Meister keeps the provision confined to the Naupactians and Hypocnemidian Locrians, while Tod (as also Meyer op. cit. 300) refers it also to all the Locrians. There seems to be no good grammatical criterion to determine which is right, but Meister's interpretation seems slightly preferable because of the probability that the Hypocnemidian Locrian colonist's kin would be Hypocnemidian Locrians. Oldfather, however, accepts Meyer's interpretation (RE s.v. Lokris 1241), which demands Tod's punctuation.   [1] As Meister 304–6.

[2] The exact meaning of the word ἐχεπάμων is obscure, but the general translation 'heir' (as Tod p. 34) probably embraces whatever precise meaning it may have had.

[3] My translation follows the general lines of those of Tod (p. 35) and Meister (277).

of the colonists to Naupactus leaves behind a father, and leaves his property with his father, shall be allowed, when the father dies, to recover his share'.

The position regarding inheritance in Hypocnemidian Locris, in so far as it can be learnt from these provisions, does not seem to have been entirely simple. The arrangements cover the case of the death of a brother and of the death of the father, but in the latter instance the inheritance is only of the share that the colonist has left with the father. One notes that what might be called normal inheritance, of the father's goods by the sons on the father's death,[1] is not provided for. It is noteworthy too that the brother's goods are to be inherited by brothers. One must assume that he died without issue, though this is not said, in contrast to paragraph 3 (Γ) where the conditions are clearly stated (αἴ κα μὴ γένος κτλ.). A possible explanation for this would be that the father and grown-up sons shared the family property and if one died the shares of the others were equally increased.[2] To keep his share intact the colonist left it with his father. In relation to such circumstances the two provisions become intelligible. If they do imply this position, they may be said to provide for the colonist's regular inheritance within the family. In the ordinary way he would have his share, and it is the difference made to this by his becoming a colonist of Naupactus that gave rise to the need for these two provisions.

These were, however, by no means the only rights of inheritance known among the Locrians, who were particularly interested in these rights.[3] As has been seen, paragraph 3 recognized the inheritance rights of people outside the family, and it is not the only example. In a decree of about the same date concerning a small settlement in West Locris,[4] the in-

---

[1] Normally in Greece the first heirs were the legitimate sons; cf. *RE* s.v. Erbrecht 391.

[2] Sharing of property among adult sons during the father's lifetime is attested in Attic literature; see [Dem.] XLVII.34, (cf. XLIII.19) and Lysias XIX.37. It would not be surprising, when one considers the very ancient Greek practice of brothers' equal shares in inheritance (cf. *Od.* XIV.208 f and K. F. Hermann, *Lehrbuch d. griech. Antiquitäten II.1, die griech. Rechtsalterthümer*, 3rd edition, 54 f), and the circumstances of an agricultural community.   [3] See Oldfather, *RE* s.v. Lokris 1257.

[4] Buck, *The Greek Dialects*, no. 59; see lines 3–6. First published by N. G. Pappadakis in 'Αρχ.' Εφ. 1924, 119–41; edited with commentary by Wilamowitz, *Sitz. Berl. Akad.* 1927 no. 1, 7–17. Illustrated in Jeffery, *Local Scripts of Archaic Greece*, plate 14. Tentatively dated by her to the last quarter of the

heritance of grazing rights is provided for in the following order of precedence: son, daughter, brother, next of kin, neighbour(?).[1] The conclusion follows: if the position of the colonist as regards all rights of inheritance was not settled by the Naupactus decree, it was not because such rights did not exist. The two possibilities covered must, therefore, have been chosen because these were the matters in which the colonist's new status might have made a difference. It is presumably right to assume the corollary, that there was no difficulty about the remainder of the colonist's rights to inherit in his old community. The same conclusion is made probable by the content of these provisions. If there was such care to protect his part of a deceased brother's share, the colonist's right to inherit as, for instance, sole legal heir, must surely have been maintained. The rights of inheritance in Naupactus were handled more fully, it is true; but that would be natural for a new community, where new rules needed to be established. It is not unreasonable to assume, therefore, that the colonist had full rights of inheritance in his old community. This not only suits well the general nature of the colonial expedition, but also the fact that the *kleros* in Locris was only allowed to be sold in cases of undoubted need.[2] The desire to keep the *kleros* in the family, implied by this law, is reflected in these inheritance provisions, and may in part explain them.

The question arises whether the colonist could own property in the mother country without returning and recovering his previous citizenship. It is clear from the provision about the Percothariae and Mysacheis (paragraph 5(E), 22–8) that the

---

sixth century, and considered near in time to the Naupactus foundation decree (106). She makes the interesting suggestion that it is tempting to connect the two, and regard the second as fulfilling the provision for reinforcement in the first (see below p. 65). One wonders, however, whether the many and detailed provisions of the Naupactian decree are appropriate to a small subsequent reinforcement.

[1] The last is doubtful. I follow Wilamowitz. Buck (pp. 255 f) assumes an engraver's error and reads τōι ἐπινόμοι (ὁμ) οἱιον (translated 'to the assignee from those of like family'). Jeffery (105 n. 1) regards the last five letters as cancelled and would insert at this point the detached line from the back of the plaque (see below p. 65 n. 4). Georgacas' suggestion (*CP* li 1956, 249 ff) that ouov = oἱιων meaning 'whomsoever' relies on doubtfully apposite parallels from much later Greek and yields a poor sense—'to the heir from among whomsoever'.

[2] See Arist. *Pol.* 1266 b 18; cf. too the inscription *Syll.*[3] 141, in which part of the settler's land is made inalienable (8 f).

colonists from these two clans[1] kept property in Hypocnemidian Locris. For it is said (23 f) that their property in Naupactus shall be subject to the laws of Naupactus, while that among the Hypocnemidian Locrians to the laws of the Hypocnemidian Locrians. Meister (311) takes χρήματα for property in land, which seems probable in view of the primitive character of the Locrian community even in the fifth century.[2] It was possible, then, for at least some of the colonists to own property in the mother country, although they were citizens of Naupactus.

Unfortunately it cannot be decided whether the ordinary colonist had the same right. The two inheritance provisions under discussion do not answer this question. They may merely have preserved his rights to property and inheritance against his possible return, for which such generous provisions had been made. The second provision, referring to the colonist who leaves his share to his father, might be interpreted as showing that a colonist could not continue to own property in the mother community. For if he could, why should he leave it with his father? But the position about property implied by this provision cannot be reconstructed with sufficient certainty to allow a definite conclusion.

The long provision about the Percothariae and Mysacheis (5(E), 22–8)[3] seems to imply that these were specially privileged groups.[4] If the etymological explanation of the names is correct,[5] they had a special religious status, and it is presumably a mark of wealth that they were expected to own property in both Naupactus and Hypocnemidian Locris.[6] The natural assumption from the wording of the provision is that their special status gave them privileges about property.[7]

For the purposes of this enquiry the important point is that their special position at home was not to be maintained in the

[1] Tod (p. 34) follows the generally accepted belief (see Meister 306 f) that these were 'two clans or castes, possibly sacerdotal'.

[2] Cf. Thuc. I.5.3, though this, it is true, refers to West Locris.

[3] This receives convincing grammatical treatment from Meister (306–10), whom Tod follows in his translation (I pp. 34 f).

[4] The general opinion; see Meyer, *Forschungen* I 301.

[5] See among others Meister 307.

[6] Tod (ibid.) therefore seems wrong to allow for the possibility that they were people with lesser rights, a suggestion made in *Recueil des inscriptions iuridiques grecques* (p. 191).

[7] Meister simply assumes this.

colony. Here we have an example of the principle that the colonist should go on equal terms. When the Corinthians advertised for colonists to go to Epidamnus, they assured them equality of status (ἐπὶ τῇ ἴσῃ καὶ ὁμοίᾳ; Thuc. I.27.1). The same words are used in the foundation decree for Cyrene (27 f) and the same principle explains the appointment of special commissioners to allot the land (γεώνομοι) by the Brea decree (6–8), whose duty it would be to ensure this equality in the vital matter of land division. This division of land is the subject treated by the decree about Black Corcyra. There the first settlers each received an equal allotment of land, though their share was a privileged one compared with that of later settlers; this was because they had fortified the city (3 ff). It may be that this fact—that the colonists started equal and this equal start was a historical and perhaps recent event—explains the provision in the mountain settlement of West Locris.[1] In this one of the criminals for whom dire penalties are prescribed is ⱶόστις . . . στάσιν ποιέοι περὶ γαδαισίας (11).[2] Similarly the rulers of Black Corcyra are to swear never to redistribute the land.[3]

So it can be seen that the principle that the colonists should participate on equal terms had definite practical force even among oligarchic peoples like the Locrians and the Corinthians. It therefore seems reasonable to assume that it was a regular feature of Greek colonial enterprises.

Paragraph 7 (I.32–5) concerns legal procedure. It runs: 'the colonists to Naupactus shall have precedence in bringing suits before the judges; the Hypocnemidian Locrian shall bring suits and answer suits against himself in Opus on the same day etc.'.[4] A legal provision of this sort was clearly necessary when, as is suggested here by the inheritance provisions, frequent intercourse between the colonists and citizens of the mother community was envisaged. The precedence given to the colonists

[1] See above p. 56 n. 4.
[2] 'Whoever . . . causes civil strife over division of land.'
[3] *Syll.*[3] 141, 10 f.
[4] For uncertainties and difficulties of detailed interpretation see below pp. 227 n. 2, 228 n. 1, and Meister's discussion, 313–23. The special difficulty of the meaning of the word προστάταν (34) is perhaps removed by Hitzig's suggestion (see *Altgriechische Staatsverträge über Rechtshilfe* 50 f) that the word means 'surety'.

is a good example of the favourable terms offered to those who took part in this expedition. No doubt an arrangement about legal procedure would be required whenever the colonists were expected to maintain close relations with the mother city, and it may be that the first incomplete sentence of the surviving part of the Brea decree formed part of a similar provision.[1]

The protection of the laws against changes and transgressors is the one provision common to all three decrees (Cyrene 40 ff; Naupactus paragraph 9 (Θ), 38–45; Brea 20–6). Similar provisions are very common in all decrees, but they show the importance placed on the foundation decree and this in turn shows that both colony and metropolis expected the connection between them to persist and have value.

There are differences between the provisions of the three decrees not only in administrative details but also more generally. In the Cyrene decree there is no thought of any possible change, and this suits well the finality of the break between the colonists and the citizens of the metropolis which the decree assumes, and the distance which was to separate them. On the other hand the severity of the penalties against anyone who violated the decisions of the decree in the Naupactus text (38) does not preclude the possibility of changes agreed by the assemblies of Opus and Naupactus.[2] This shows that the decisions of the decree were thought of as valuable to both parties, as one would expect, since so many aspects of the relationship between them are arranged.

In the Brea decree, however, the severe penalties for anyone who even proposes any change are simply modified by the phrase (25 f) ἐὰμ μή τι αὐτοὶ ⊦οι ἄποικ[οι περὶ (?) σφῶν δέ]ωνται.[3] The value of the decree seems thus to belong chiefly to the colonists, whereas in the other two both mother city and colony were equally interested in its preservation. This difference may, however, be illusory, for the control of the Athenian demos over any alteration in the provisions remains. If the colonists request

[1] See Tod 1 p. 89. The new restorations due to Wilhelm and Meritt (see *SEG* X 34) which would remove this possibility, are no longer supported, as was first thought, by the new fragment of this inscription. For it does not join the fragments possessed before and so cannot be definitely assigned to the beginning of the decree; see *SEG* XII 15.

[2] See Tod p. 36.

[3] 'Unless the colonists themselves make some request . . . (?) . . .'

a change, the demos will discuss the matter; any change will therefore be, like those concerning Naupactus, agreed by the two communities; the Athenian demos controls such changes but denies itself the right to initiate them. It was evidently confident that it would remain satisfied by the position established by the decree; the colonists might naturally want changes after testing the arrangements in practice.

If it was necessary to provide for future changes, it is clear that both colony and metropolis regarded their relationship as likely to persist in the future and be important. On the other hand the political purposes in the colonization of Brea and Naupactus should not be forgotten. It may have been more normal not to provide for changes in foundation decrees. The decree for Cyrene, a colony of necessity, may be more typical.

When one turns to consider the provisions in the other decrees which have no counterpart in the Naupactus decree one notes first that they include practical arrangements. As has been seen, these are strikingly absent from the Naupactus decree, while the Brea decree consists largely of such provisions. The appointment of the oikist and of commissioners to distribute the land has already been discussed. Both the Brea decree and that for Cyrene make arrangements about the personnel of the expedition. The Brea decree limits volunteers to those from the Thetes and Zeugitae (39–42), that for Cyrene prescribes methods of conscription (28–30).[1] Other purely practical matters in the Brea decree which need only be mentioned are the provisions for sacrifices preceding the colony (3–6), for men absent on campaign to participate (26–9), for the time limit for the expedition's departure and for expenses (29–31). As was noted in the discussion of the oikist's role,[2] these show the detailed way in which Athens organized a colonial foundation to serve imperial ends. But that is all they contribute to our understanding of the colony–metropolis relationship. Nor does the arrangement that the sacred domains in the colony should not

[1] This is clear too from Herodotus (IV.153). The reading and interpretation of the inscription is difficult in detail; I discuss it in my article, *JHS* lxxx 1960, 94 ff. Interesting new suggestions about the personnel of the expedition are made by Jeffery, *Historia* x 1961, 139 ff; but they are inevitably conjectural. Robert rejects her restorations on grounds of syntax (*Bull.* 1962, 364; *REG* lxxv 1962, 218).

[2] See Chapter III.

be increased (9–11)[1] imply anything more than the determination to maintain the amount of land available for ordinary settlement. It is not comparable to the first provision of the Naupactus decree, which arranged for the colonist's religious activity in his new home.

On the other hand there are provisions which concern more closely Brea's relations to Athens. The provision for the colony's defence (13–17), while it is clearly a protection of Athens' imperial interests,[2] is also an example of the mother city's assumption of responsibility for the colony's safety. As such it may be compared with the implications of the provision for return in the Cyrene decree. The colonists were allowed to return if, among other conditions, the Theraeans could not help them. Here too the mother city assumed some responsibility for the colony's protection. It was seen that the forced nature of the Theraean expedition to Cyrene makes it probable that a minimum right of return was granted. This suggests that in all regular Greek colonies the mother city was responsible for the colony's protection at least in its early years. Hence it had to concede the colonists a right of return if it failed in this duty.

It is provided in the Brea decree (11–13) that the colonists should contribute a cow[3] and a panoply for the Great Panathenaea and a phallus for the Dionysia. These offerings by the colonists at the festivals, or to the gods, of the mother city can be paralleled by several other examples, which suggest that it was a widespread practice. These other examples, however, are all instances of subsequent relations, so they will be considered below (pp. 159 ff). The Brea decree is the only example we have where the practice was provided for in the act of foundation.

The same duty was, however, imposed on allies in the Athenian Empire, and in the Great Reassessment of Tribute of 425 it was applied universally to all the allies who paid tribute.[4]

[1] See Tod I p. 89 for the uncertainties in precise interpretation.

[2] See Chapter III.

[3] Or ox, but the sex seems to be established by the words τῆς βοὸς in a provision about similar offerings in Kleinias' decree (*ATL* II.D7.42).

[4] See *ATL* II.A9.55 ff. Mattingly has suggested that this was the first time that the allies were obliged to make these offerings (*Historia* x 1961, 153), but Meritt and Wade-Gery show that this is not a necessary assumption (*JHS* lxxxii 1962, 69 ff). Offerings, but not the same offerings, were imposed as a duty on Erythrae (*ATL* II.D10.2–8; cf. Meritt and Wade-

It is therefore necessary to consider whether the Athenians were imposing on Brea a duty taken from the practices of their empire, or applying a colonial practice to their allies. The question seems to be settled by an Athenian inscription, probably to be dated 372/1, which shows that the Parians made offerings at Athenian festivals according to traditional custom ([κ]ατὰ τὰ πάτρια) because they were colonists of Athens (ἐπειδὴ [τ]υγχά νουσ[ι] ἄποικοι ὄ[ντες τ]οῦ δήμου τῶ ᾿Αθηναίων).[1] This supports the restoration of Meritt and West in the Great Reassessment of Tribute of 425 by which the colonies are expressly named as the models for the behaviour of the allies.[2] We may thus assume that a practice originally colonial was applied to the allies in general,[3] which recalls the tendency of Athens to exaggerate her share in the colonization of Ionia as a way of justifying her empire.[4] These religious offerings may be seen as an expression of the tie between a colony and its mother city, which made them a suitable means for Athens to make a closer link between herself and her allies.

Finally, the provision for the public record of the decree (17–20) may be set beside the provisions about changes and transgressors. For it shows that the exhibition of the mother city's decree regulating their foundation was an important matter for the colonists. It is significant that they are to meet this expense. For the sake of our evidence about Greek colonization it is fortunate that they did.

Gery op. cit. 71). The date of the Erythrae decree is uncertain, but Meiggs has convincingly shown that it probably belongs to the years 452–449 (his arguments are preferable to those used by Accame in support of the date *c.* 460, *Riv. Fil.* xxx 1952, 119–23); see *JHS* lxiii 1943, 23–5. A provision in Kleinias' decree (*ATL* II.D7.41–3) suggests that allies were offering the cow and panoply by the time of that document (see Meritt and Wade-Gery op. cit. 69). That was in 447, according to the authors of *ATL* and Meiggs, but this inscription is dated by some scholars as late as the 420s; see Meiggs, 'The Crisis in Athenian Imperialism', *Harvard Studies in Classical Philology* lxvii, 1963, 29. For further suggestions on the date of the introduction of these practices in the Athenian Empire, see Meritt and Wade-Gery op. cit. 71.

[1] See Meritt and Wade-Gery op. cit. 70.

[2] πεμπόντων δ[ὲ ἐν] τῆι πομπῆι [καθάπερ ἄποι]κ[οι.See Meritt and West, *The Athenian Assessment of 425 B.C.*, 63, and Meritt and Wade-Gery, *JHS* lxxxii 1962, 70.

[3] This is the conclusion of Meritt and Wade-Gery, who argue the matter more fully, op. cit. 69–71.

[4] See Chapter I.

F

There remains one provision in the Cyrene decree, which has no counterpart in those for Naupactus and Brea but contributes important information about the relationship between colony and metropolis. If the colony succeeds in establishing itself, anyone who later sails from Thera[1] shall have a share in citizenship and rights and receive an allotment from the unowned land (30–3). It is this fargoing right of the metropolis which the people of Cyrene recognized in the fourth century, when they decided to give the Theraeans citizenship according to the traditional arrangements made by their ancestors (4–6). Their recognition of the validity of this provision[2] may suggest that this was not an abnormal right for mother cities. It should be noted that this principle, if principle it was, that the citizens of the mother city could settle in the colony, is different from isopolity.[3] There are examples of isopolity between colony and mother city, but this right is one-sided. However, it too is not without parallel.

The decree arranging for the settlement on Black Corcyra provides for later settlers (9 f), but it is not clear whether they are simply settlers enrolled beforehand who were not wanted

[1] This may seem a very free rendering of τῶν οἰκείων τὸγ καταπλέον[τα] ὕστερον, for it might be thought that οἰκείων means kinsmen in a narrower sense. It is thus translated by Meiggs (Bury, *History of Greece*[3], 862). However Oliverio translates it 'concittadini' (*Riv. Fil.* lvi 1928, 227) and Chamoux 'compatriotes' (*Cyrène sous la monarchie des Battiades*, 107). I discuss the meaning of οἰκεῖος in this context in detail in my article Οἰκήιοι Περίνθιοι (to appear in *JHS* lxxxiv 1964) where I have tried to show that the word could express the kinship in a wide sense that existed between a colony and its mother city. Apart from verbal parallels (which I assemble ibid.), the chief argument for such an interpretation here is that the only part of the foundation decree which directly justifies the Cyrenean action in giving the Theraeans citizenship (cf. 4–11) is this passage. οἰκείων was therefore understood by the people of Cyrene in the fourth century to mean all the Theraeans.

[2] Attempts to find other reasons for the Cyrenean action have been unconvincing. Thus Ferrabino (*Riv. Fil.* lvi 1928, 253 f) suggested that it might be an attempt to gain good relations with the Second Athenian League, to which Thera belonged. But it seems a most roundabout way of doing this. Nor does there seem good reason to connect it with Alexander's agreement with Cyrene (Diod. XVII.49.3; Curt. Ruf. IV.7.9) as Zhebeliov (*CR Acad. Sc. USSR.* 1929, 429 n. 2). Such attempts all fail in face of the objection that a great city like Cyrene could hope for no political advantage from pleasing little Thera.

[3] Chamoux describes the decree as arranging isopolity; see *Cyrène sous la monarchie des Battiades*, 108, 241. Nowhere is it stated or implied that the Cyreneans had citizenship in Thera.

for the advance party, or any later colonist from the metropolis, for the key phrase, τοὺς ἐφέρποντας, could be translated in either sense. In the decree arranging for the settlement in West Locris mentioned above[1] provision is made for new settlers to be introduced in case of war. The translation by Wilamowitz[2] is '(the law stands) unless under the necessity of war 101 men (chosen) according to worth decide by majority to bring in at least 200 warlike men as inhabitants'. It is not certain what body passed this law, but the indications of the text[3] are that a Locrian community is arranging to settle some land, and it may be inferred from the provision under discussion that this settlement would itself form a community. The mother community makes provision for reinforcement in case of need, but allows the new community to make the actual decision if the reinforcement should take place. Both the form and the size of the reinforcement and the way in which the new community should make the decision are fixed in advance by the mother community. In this instance the right of the mother community to send in new settlers is limited. The limitations may have been accepted because the land available was strictly confined, as may be inferred from the later provision[4] that the land be halved between the first settlers and the newcomers.

If, as was seen to be probable,[5] Rhodes poured new settlers into Gela at the time of the foundation of Acragas, this may be another example of a mother city exercising its right to reinforce its colony. It has already been suggested that Corinth could send settlers to Epidamnus simply on being named Epidamnus' mother city, so that Corinth's action may also perhaps be seen as the exercise of this particular right. And if, as was suggested, Epidamnus' relations with Corinth provide a good analogy for Naupactus' relations with Opus, Opus may have exercised the same right in sending a reinforcing colony to Naupactus. But there is also clearer evidence from the Naupactus inscription. When it was arranged for the next of kin among the Hypocnemidian Locrians to inherit property in Naupactus, it was laid down that they should go to Naupactus

[1] See p. 56 n.4 .   [2] Ibid.
[3] See Wilamowitz, 9.
[4] Lines 16–18; see Wilamowitz, 11, on the intrusive line 17. For another view see Jeffery, *Local Scripts of Archaic Greece*, 105 n. 1.
[5] See Chapter I.

to take up the inheritance.[1] This suggests again that citizens of the mother city could take up residence in the colony.

The man who practised the trade of a sophist under the cover of gymnastics, Herodicus, may possibly have exercised the right to take up citizenship in a colony of his original city. Protagoras is made to describe him[2] as ʽΗρόδικος ὁ Σηλυμβριανός, τὸ δὲ ἀρχαῖον Μεγαρεύς. He is generally described as a Selymbrian elsewhere, as for instance in the Suda.[3] However, as a clearly notable figure, to whom a special grant of citizenship could well have been made, Herodicus may not be a typical example.

While these instances are of varying certainty and worth it seems reasonable to conclude from them that the provision in the Cyrene decree is not isolated, but an example of a right regularly enjoyed by Greek mother cities.[4]

It would be wrong to hope to obtain a complete picture of Greek ideas and practices in the field of colonial foundations and colonial relationships from these foundation decrees. The examples preserved are too few to allow many certain conclusions of general validity to be drawn from them. Furthermore the special circumstances of the several expeditions can be seen to have influenced the character of the detailed provisions. Every colonial expedition will have had circumstances peculiar to itself, but the colonies at Brea and Naupactus were certainly far from typical of Greek colonization in general.

It is also likely that some aspects of the colony-metropolis relationship were of such a traditional nature that they did not need legal provision. For example, the remarks of the Corinthians and Corcyreans in the dispute about Epidamnus seem to be made in reference to generally accepted beliefs rather than to legal arrangements.[5] It would be wrong, therefore, to make much of matters absent from these decrees. They show us rather what the Greeks felt it necessary to lay down.

It is important to remember these provisos, but the three main decrees are still of great value in showing the arrangements made by Greeks for expeditions varying in date and

[1] See p. 55.
[2] Plato, *Prot.* 316 d.
[3] S.v. ʽΙπποκράτης.
[4] Schaefer notes the frequent reinforcement of colonies by mother cities (*Heidelberger Jahrbücher* 1960 p. 87), though both here and elsewhere in his article he does not use the evidence from inscriptions.
[5] Thuc. I.34.1; 38.

ranging in character from the remote colony of need to the reinforcement of an existing, closely-related city.

The special circumstances of the colony at Naupactus caused its foundation decree to look forward to certain relations with the mother community which may be regarded as special and unusually close. Provision for inheritance between colony and mother city, for example, would have been unrealistic at Cyrene. It presupposes frequent and easy relations between the citizens of the two communities. The same is true of the provision about legal procedure, and the very easy conditions for return. The practical arrangements for the foundation of Brea must also be seen as special and determined by Brea's character as an imperial foundation; though the choice of the oikist, which is also found in the Cyrene decree, was probably a regular provision in foundation decrees. The same may be true of arrangements about the personnel of the expedition, which are also found in both decrees. An important practical arrangement stated in the Cyrene decree, implied in that for Naupactus, and to be assumed at Brea, is that the colonists should start on equal terms. This is an instance where we seem to have a provision of general application.

The forced nature of the colonization of Cyrene gives a special value to the provisions looking to future relations between colony and metropolis. Where the minimum of such relations might be expected, the metropolis undertook to help the colony, or (under certain conditions) to allow the colonist to return to full citizen rights at home, and citizens of the mother city had the right to go and settle in the colony.

In the Brea decree the most important provision about future relations is that arranging for the colonists to make religious offerings in the metropolis. As other examples (not to mention the implications of the passage Thuc. I.25.3 f) show that this was a widespread practice, it is perhaps legitimate to ask why there is no such provision in the Naupactus decree. The answer seems to lie in the possibility mentioned earlier, that certain fundamental and generally agreed matters would not need legal provision.

In the Naupactus decree there are provisions of fundamental importance in revealing Greek ideas on the subject of the relations between colony and mother city. The oath not to secede has been seen to show the easy acceptance of the idea of a politically dependent colony, but more interesting perhaps is the evidence about the colonist's citizenship. It is clearly stated that by becoming a colonist he loses his old citizenship and takes up that of Naupactus. On the other hand it is necessary expressly to free him from the tax obligations of a citizen of Hypocnemidian Locris, and family ties are allowed to have continuing practical effect, as the inheritance provisions show. So while the legal position is clearly stated, ties of blood and origin are recognized and keep their practical force in spite of the change of citizenship. These indications may imply that the Greeks were less clear and definite that the colonist ceased completely to be a citizen of his mother city than some modern scholars have been.[1]

Finally, the provisions for changes, for public record and for penalties against transgressors all show in a general way that colonies placed a high value on the mother city's decree regulating their foundation. This was not only the legal basis for their very existence, but also a sign that the community was seen as born of the mother city, as a continuation of it. It was shown that the same conclusion is to be drawn from the character of the traditional arrangements in the act of foundation and from the position and honours of the oikist. However great the differences in detail, it was this fundamental basis for the relations between the two communities which was regularly expressed in the act of foundation.

[1] E.g. Busolt/Swoboda 1265.

PART II

SUBSEQUENT RELATIONS

CHAPTER V

THASOS AND THE EFFECT OF DISTANCE

THASOS had the dual rule of colony and metropolis. In both, owing to unusually rich documentation, the city provides illuminating evidence on the relations of Greek colonies with their mother cities. The evidence for Thasos' relations with her mother city Paros is unusually good not merely in quantity but also because it stretches from the seventh to the fourth centuries. This exceptional position is partly due to the rich finds of epigraphical material on the island; but the existence of evidence for the seventh century is largely explained by the poetic genius of Archilochus of Paros. Thasos' role as metropolis of several colonies on the mainland is largely known from evidence of the fifth century and later, but it also is exceptional in quality and fullness. Thasos' own colonies were all at a comparatively short distance, and it will be seen that the closeness of her relations with them probably required such geographical proximity. It is therefore convenient to consider with Thasos other examples where it seems that the relationship of colony and mother city was affected by the same factor.

Anyone who writes about the history of Thasos must lean heavily on J. Pouilloux' book *Recherches sur l'histoire et les cultes de Thasos*, I. This contains a considerable amount of important new epigraphical material, as well as careful reconsideration of both literary and epigraphic evidence previously known. It is therefore possible on many difficult or controversial matters to avoid repetition by referring to Pouilloux' treatment. It is, for example, unnecessary to reconsider here the question of Thasos' foundation and its date. For it seems reasonably certain that Thasos was founded from Paros in the first quarter of the seventh century, and that its oikist was Archilochus' father, Telesikles.[1]

---

[1] See Pouilloux 22 f. Conjectures of the exact year of foundation remain unproved; for these see Pouilloux ibid.

The first evidence for Thasos' relations with Paros comes from Archilochus, through the surviving remains of his poetry[1] and through the *Monumentum Archilochi* of Paros,[2] which expressly depends on the poems for its statements. The interpretation of this evidence is so difficult that many of the historical details remain quite uncertain. But it must be used as far as possible, for it represents a great rarity, direct evidence for the seventh century itself, originally written within a generation of the colony's foundation. Its fragmentary character makes detailed reconstructions from this evidence quite unjustified, but the general historical worth of the poems of Archilochus has been demonstrated recently by the discovery at Thasos of a monument to the Glaukos[3] who appears several times in the poems.[4] Conclusions must be very general not to risk forcing the evidence, but they are not for that reason unimportant.

In the first place it seems clear that in the first generation after the colony was founded relations with Paros remained very close. So Archilochus talks of the affairs of both communities with equal familiarity; to him the life of the two peoples was intermingled.[5] It also appears from the *Monumentum Archilochi* that Parians helped the Thasians in their struggles with the Thracians of the mainland.[6] The only reason to doubt this (though the details are frustratingly obscure) is that the settlers on Thasos could perhaps still be called Parians in contrast to the Thracians and other mainland tribes. Another fairly definite feature of the relations in these early days were the reinforcements from Paros. Archilochus himself was presum-

---

[1] Diehl *Anth. Lyr. Graeca*[3] Fasc. 3. The fragments from Oxyrhynchus (Peek *Philologus* xcix 1955, 193 ff.; c 1956,l ff) add nothing for the present purpose.

[2] For the text see Diehl[3] 51. This is based on the text of Hiller; see *Nach.gött.Akad.* Neue Folge 1, 1934, 41–58. A new text of I.1–20 is offered by Peek, *Philologus* xcix 1955, 41. For further fragments of the monument discovered since Hiller's work, see *SEG* XV.517.

[3] *SEG* XIV.565. A full study of the inscription is provided by Pouilloux in *BCH* lxxix 1955.75 ff, with interesting, if necessarily hypothetical, suggestions about Glaukos.

[4] Diehl[3] 13, 56, 59, 68; see also *Mon. Arch.* IVA.6.

[5] Examples may be seen in Diehl[3] 19, 53, 54. But the *Mon. Arch* provides the best evidence; e.g. IA.40–55.

[6] *Mon. Arch* IA.40–52. Cf. Pouilloux 30, 33. Some of Archilochus' famous lines about fighting are also to be referred to this campaigning, as the names show; see ibid.

ably one,[1] and it is probably right to conclude, with Pouilloux, that there were other, perhaps considerable, groups of further settlers from Paros.[2]

It was seen in the previous chapter that there may well have been a widespread right for the mother city to send further settlers to its colonies. Perhaps Paros' action is a very early example of this. On the other hand it is taken by Pouilloux (26) to show that the establishment of the colony was not a single act but required several efforts over a long period. If this is the correct interpretation it may exemplify the kind of practice that gave rise to the mother city's right to send in further settlers. This could well have grown out of the reinforcements necessary to establish a colony in its early years.

Similarly the help given to Thasos in wars against the mainland tribes could be regarded rather as the mother city's help in establishing the colony[3] than as an example of a general principle that a metropolis should help its colony in war. There are later examples, to be considered below, which show that colonies and mother cities sometimes gave each other help in war on the grounds of their relationship. But the early examples of such activity which may be compared with the Parian act are not surprisingly rather shadowy. Firstly there is the help given to Chalcis by at least one of the Chalcidians in Thrace in what appears to be the Lelantine War.[4] The information is given by Plutarch (*Amat.* 761A) alone, and nothing further is known of the circumstances, but his authority is Aristotle,[5] so that it is at least worth a mention beside the rather better evidence from Thasos.

[1] This seems the right way to interpret the oracles and information preserved by Oenomaus of Gadara (Eusebius, *Praep. Evangel.* V.33.1; VI.7.8.); see Lasserre, *Les Épodes d'Archiloque*, 211–13, and Pouilloux 26 (especially n. 3).

[2] See Pouilloux 26 f, where the mutilated lines of *Mon. Arch.* IVA.15ff are referred, with much probability, to such an expedition. And there 1000 men are mentioned (23).

[3] As Thera undertook responsibility for Cyrene's protection in its first years; see Chapter IV.

[4] It appears to be the Lelantine War because it is against Eretria and because the Thessalians were also fighting on Chalcis' side. On this war see below p. 222 n.3.

[5] The whole passage Plut. *Amat* 760E ff. is thought to derive from Aristotle's dialogue *Erotikos* and is given as fragment 3 of this dialogue by Ross in his edition (Aristotle, *Fragmenta Selecta, OCT* 1955).

The second example concerns Samos and Perinthus. Perinthus was a Samian colony (Strabo VII.331, Ps-Scymn. 714 f) founded, according to the chronographers, c. 600. Plutarch records (*Q.G.* 57) that the Megarians attacked the Perinthians and were defeated by an expedition sent from Samos. The expedition was sent by the Geomoroi who ruled at Samos after the end of Demoteles' tyranny. It is unfortunate that this information still leaves the chronology very uncertain, but the latest possible date cannot be long after the colony's foundation.[1] This is also the most probable time for a Megarian expedition against Perinthus, since Megara was no doubt trying to exclude the Samians at the outset from an area where the only competition she was prepared to admit was Milesian.[2] Thus the Samian action should be seen as an example of a mother city's help for its colony in the early years.

Pouilloux is able to show (51–3) that Thasos probably had strong trading links with Egypt in the sixth and fifth centuries. It is less certain, but possible, as he suggests, that the finds of Parian coins in Egypt indicate that the trade route from Thasos passed through Paros.[3] This hypothetical connection between colony and mother city is made likely by definite evidence for close connections at the end of the sixth century. For at this time Akeratos had inscribed his proud boast that he alone had been archon (or, more generally, held high office) in both Paros and Thasos.[4] His dedication runs:

'Ηρακλεῖ μ' ἀνέθηκεν 'Ακήρατος, ὃς Θασίοισιν   I
καὶ Π[αρίοι]ς ἦρχσεν μοῦνος ἐν ἀμφοτέροις·

[1] The problems and some modern theories are briefly and satisfactorily noted by Halliday, *Greek Questions of Plutarch* 212. In spite of the aetiological character of Plutarch's account and its chronological uncertainty, we need not go as far as Swoboda who dismissed it with the words 'die Nachricht . . . kann nicht datirt und überhaupt nicht für die Geschichte nutzbar gemacht werden' (*Festschrift O.Benndorf* (Vienna 1898)254).

[2] Beloch's conjecture (I², 1.359) that the Megarians were the Megarian colonists of the region goes against Plutarch and seems unnecessary, though the colonists may well have participated. On the probable co-operation of Megara and Miletus see Hanell, *Megarische Studien* 135 f.

[3] His argument from the coin hoards cannot be accorded probative force however; see Fraser's review, *AJA* lxi 1957, 99.

[4] *IG* XII. Suppl. 412. First published by M. Launey, *BCH* lviii 1934, 173–183, who dated the inscription on epigraphical grounds which seem cogent to c. 500. This date is confirmed by Akeratos' appearance in a list of archons of the second half of the sixth century; see Pouilloux no. 31, 14 (p. 269); cf. also his pp. 46 and 270 n. 2.

πολλὰς δ' ἀνγελίας πρὸ πόλεως κατὰ φῦλα διῆλθεν   2
ἀν[θρώπ]ων ἀρέτης εἵνεκεν ἀϊδίης.[1]

We thus have an individual who held high office not only in his own city but also in his metropolis. What exactly does this imply about the relationship of the two cities?

The most extreme interpretation has been that Akeratos' dedication shows that there was sympolity between Thasos and Paros.[2] But since Thasos and Paros were clearly independent states in the fifth century,[3] the earlier merging of sovereignty which such an assumption implies[4] seems unlikely.

A less extreme view is that the inscription provides a very early example of isopolity or double citizenship.[5] This is a possible but not a necessary conclusion. Akeratos stresses that he alone had had this distinction, and the rest of the dedication shows that he was an outstanding individual. His distinguished career[6] makes him a bad example from which to generalize.

[1] 'I was dedicated to Heracles by Akeratos, who alone was magistrate both at Thasos and at Paros. He also travelled among the races of men and completed many embassies on behalf of his city, because of his unfailing virtue' (I follow Launey's interpretation 178–80).

[2] This was suggested by Robert BCH lix 1935, 500.

[3] The independent existence of Thasos in the fifth century is beyond question; cf. Launey op. cit. 179 n. 3. All the evidence may be found in Pouilloux' chapters III and IV.

[4] For a definition see E. Szanto, Das griechische Bürgerrecht, 104 f. There was sympolity between two or more states when they not only shared their citizenship but also had the same sovereign power, i.e. assembly, council, magistrates etc. For a detailed account see RE. s.v. συμπολιτεία, especially 1172–84.

[5] This is Launey's suggestion, 179. If Pouilloux is right in thinking (16 f) that there was a considerable Thracian element in the population of Thasos this might make it less likely that Paros would share her citizenship with the colony. His main argument is prosopographical. But P. Devambez notes (Journal des Savants 1955, 73–6) that these non-Greek names are always associated with a Greek name (father or son), so that they can hardly reveal a racial difference. He therefore calls them artificial and suggests that they are to be explained as showing pride of ancestry, as a reminiscence of early intermarriage by the first colonists only. Pouilloux' other argument for a large Thracian element (27) is that the colony could not have grown large enough to fill the great rampart of the end of the sixth century without it. But Malthus noted that the evidence from the North American colonies proved that a human community can double itself in less than a generation, if there is no check to its growth; see Principle of Population etc. 4th edition 1807, 6. This argument can therefore also be rejected and there is no reason to assume a large Thracian element, which would complicate the question of mutual citizenship with Paros.

[6] Which even enabled him to make his tomb a lighthouse; see IG XII.8.683; cf. Pouilloux 46.

This is a period in which outstanding individuals could apparently overstep the normal limitations of citizenship. Miltiades the Younger could be tyrant of the Chersonese and yet return to be *strategos* at Athens.[1] Men of distinction would naturally be more likely to move beyond their city, and go from colony to mother city. Thus Androdamas of Rhegium went as lawgiver to the Chalcidians of Thrace, presumably through Chalcis, the mutual mother city.[2] But if Akeratos was a special case and cannot be used confidently to prove isopolity between Thasos and her mother city, he still provides clear evidence of the very close relations between the two cities.[3] A great man in one was a great man in the other. It is over a hundred years since Archilochus, but mother city and colony have not lost the close connection that his poems suggest.

The next important information about the relations between Paros and Thasos comes from an inscription[4] about a century later than Akeratos' dedication. The inscription is seriously incomplete, so that any interpretation is bound up with the supplements made by editors. It was understood by its first editor[5] as the record of a treaty of alliance between Paros and Thasos. Since it is an agreement on oath[6] this was a natural explanation of the occurrence in it (8;16) of the name Thasos (Thasians) and the fact that it was a Parian document.[7] Within the limits fixed by the character of the writing the most likely occasion for an alliance between Paros and Thasos seemed to be the year 411, when both came under oligarchies hostile to Athens.[8] The document was therefore read as an agreement between colony and mother city to help each other in identical policies of hostility to Athens.[9]

[1] For references see Chapter IX where his position is discussed.

[2] See Arist *Pol.* 1274 b 23 and Dunbabin 75, who suggests a seventh-century date on the analogy of other early lawgivers.

[3] This close connection lends some support to Ehrenberg's conjecture that Miltiades' Parian expedition had as its final aim the control of Thasos and the Thraceward Region; see *Aspects of the Ancient World* 137 ff; but unfortunately definite evidence is lacking.

[4] *IG* XII.5.109.   [5] O. Rubensohn, *AM* xxvii 1902, 273–88.

[6] That the document is the record of such an agreement is proved by the word ὅρκο (14) and the first person singular verb in line 9, not to mention the other formulae common to such agreements which the fragments imply.

[7] Cf. Pouilloux 187.

[8] See Rubensohn 280 ff, where the evidence is given.

[9] This interpretation was accepted by C. Fredrich; see *IG* XII.8 p. 72.

This reconstruction was inevitably hypothetical, given the state of the inscription, and it has since been shown to be unsatisfactory. Partly using the criticisms of earlier objectors, Pouilloux[1] has built up an apparently unanswerable case against the theory of an alliance between Paros and Thasos. In the preserved part of the inscription the names of Thasos, Neapolis and Delphi occur, but not that of Paros.[2] This could perhaps be chance if it stood alone, but it takes on a different significance when combined with the fact that the decree is concerned with reconciliation. The words $τ]ῶν$ $παρικότων$ (12 f) imply that the parties to the oath swear to forget the past, and the negative clauses from the beginning suggest the formulae of peace treaties rather than those of alliances, as Pouilloux (185) remarks.

If we have a peace treaty, and the parties to it were Paros and Thasos, their history in the years at the turn of the fifth and fourth centuries should show serious disagreements. While Pouilloux (184) rightly admits that our knowledge is too incomplete to draw definite conclusions from the absence of such disagreements from the historical record, he is also right to stress that the participants actually named in the text had had such hostile relations at exactly this period. Neapolis and Thasos had been at war over the years 411–407, and there is other evidence to show that they made up their quarrels in the last years of the fifth century. This highly important material for the relations of Thasos as metropolis with her colony Neapolis will be fully discussed below; here it need only be said that Pouilloux (184) has good reason to suggest that the document under discussion is more likely to be a peace treaty between Neapolis and Thasos than between Paros and Thasos.

The appearance of Neapolitans in the text was explained by Rubensohn[3] as referring to Neapolitans resident on Thasos. In the detached fragment of the inscription[4] occur the words $ἐ]ν$ $Θάσωι$ $οἰκέοσι$; it was easy to add $τοῖς$ $Νεοπολίτηις$ before these words, and interpret the other occurrences of Neapolitans in the same sense. The Neapolitans included in the alliance were thus those living on Thasos. This was necessary in any case, because

---

[1] For his full discussion, with an account of earlier work, see 178–92.
[2] Cf. Pouilloux 183.   [3] See *AM* xxvii 1902, 276 f.
[4] See Pouilloux 188 n. 5.

Neapolis remained loyal to Athens in 411,[1] so that the state of Neapolis could hardly be made to take part in an alliance hostile to Athens. It may be doubted that the Neapolitans resident on Thasos would be sufficiently numerous or important to be parties to a treaty between Paros and Thasos. Such an explanation is, therefore, unsatisfactory, even if the supplement is accepted. Pouilloux' explanation (190 n.) is made in accordance with his general view of a reconciliation between Neapolis and Thasos, and seems reasonable; these were perhaps Neapolitan refugees living on Thasos whose status needed to be regulated in the peace treaty.

There remains the fact that one copy of the document was to be set up at Delphi (4). This was the main internal support for the theory of an alliance between Thasos and Paros in 411; for Delphi was a supporter of the Peloponnesians. Pouilloux criticizes this view and follows Robert in suggesting that the arrangement may rather mirror Delphi's close connection with Paros and Paros' colony, and with colonization in general.[2] He then uses this interpretation to answer the question why a peace treaty between Thasos and Neapolis was apparently arranged by Paros. The exhibition of a copy at Delphi shows that the decree was concerned with the affairs of colonies and mother cities, and the analogy of Epidamnus is cited (191) in support of this explanation. Thus Paros is seen in the role of conciliator, settling the difference between her colony and her colony's colony.

This hypothetical reconstruction is possible, though the parallel adduced by Pouilloux is not sufficiently exact to close the gap between evidence and imagination.[3] On the other hand the decree of Argos about Cnossus and Tylissus, which forms the subject of a later chapter, seems a closer analogy for the action of Paros inferred by Pouilloux. According to the most probable view Argos there arranges the relations of her two Cretan colonies. Pouilloux' whole interpretation suits the evidence well and is in general attractive. If he is right, we see the effective intervention of Paros in the affairs of her colony, and the authority accorded by Thasos to her mother city. But since this is hypothetical it is worth noting the irreducible minimum

---

[1] See below pp. 84ff. [2] See Pouilloux 182 f.
[3] This is especially clear on p. 191.

which can certainly be concluded from the inscription about the relations between Paros and Thasos. This is that at some time about the end of the fifth century Paros organized an agreement concerning Thasos and Thasos' colony Neapolis.

The last significant evidence for Paros' relations with Thasos within the chronological limits of this enquiry is also epigraphical. The Athenian general Cephisophon was honoured by a decree recorded in a Parian inscription of c. 340,[1] which contains the following words: ὅ[τι ἐστ]ὶν [ἀ]νὴ[ρ ἀγ]αθὸ[ς περ]ὶ τὸν δῆμο[ν] τὸ[μ] Π[αρ]ίων καὶ Θασίων.[2] The restorations, though numerous, are not likely to be doubted, and the important phrase at the end is certain. The form of expression in this is most striking. If it was desired to say that someone had deserved well of two peoples, it was normal to write δῆμον twice,[3] or at least repeat the article.[4] There is thus formal justification for Rubensohn's view[5] that the Parians and Thasians were so closely connected at this time that they formed one demos. This amounts to the conclusion that they had some form of sympolity.[6] Robert[7] combined this evidence with that from Akeratos' dedication and concluded that both showed sympolity. But the difference in time and the obvious independent existence of Thasos in the fifth century[8] invalidate such a conclusion.

[1] *IG* XII.5.114; cf.*PA* I.8410 and *Addenda* II p. 469. Although there is no proof of the exact date assigned to the inscription, it seems very probable that Rubensohn (*AM* xxvii 1902, 198) was right to bring the decree into connection with Cephisophon's activity as general εἰς Σκίαθον and εἰς Βυζάντιον in c.340; cf. A. Schaefer, *Demosthenes und seine Zeit* II².424 n. 2; 512. The exact date of Cephisophon's *strategia* comes from the inscriptions *IG* II/III².1628.436 ff; 1629.957 ff; cf. 1623.35 ff; 1629. 484 ff; and Plut. *Phoc.* XIV.3.

[2] 'Because he is a benefactor of the people of the Parians and Thasians.'

[3] E.g. *IG* II².1202.4 f; 1214.3 f, though these are demes of Attica; but cf. Tod 156. 8 f.

[4] E.g. *IG*. II².107.17 f.

[5] *AM* xxvii 1902, 199.

[6] For the form of expression and its implication Rubensohn gave as the only parallel the forged decree in Dem. *De Cor.* 90. The forgery was exposed long since, and lacks verisimilitude since Demosthenes' words clearly refer to two separate crownings by separate states: λέγε δ'αὐτοῖς καὶ τοὺς τῶν Βυζαντίων στεφάνους καὶ τοὺς τῶν Περινθίων. Robert (*Villes d'Asie Mineure* 64 n.2.) adduces two other examples of the same form of expression, Ditt. *OGI* 453.5 f; 455.2 f. But they are from the second century A.D. and can scarcely be used for comparison with the inscription under discussion.

[7] In *BCH* lix 1935, 500.

[8] See above p. 75 n. 3.

G

Rubensohn,[1] on the other hand, looked for contemporary reasons to explain the sympolity apparently implied. His ingenious argument was based on the striking fact that Cephisophon was called a benefactor of the demos of the Parians and Thasians, but given the proxeny of Paros alone (11–15). Rubensohn therefore suggested that some refugees from Thasos, which has been thought to be in Philip's hands from *c.* 340/39, had come to Paros and formed a synoecism and sympolity with their mother city.

This explanation of the apparent sympolity is rejected by Pouilloux (431 f) who rightly objects that there is insufficient evidence for the assumption that Thasos was in Philip's hands before the Battle of Chaeronea.[2] But though Pouilloux has shown the lack of evidence in support of Rubensohn's hypothesis[3] his own explanation of the implied sympolity is not convincing. He sees no need for special circumstances but regards indirect evidence for common policies at Thasos and Paros in the preceding years[4] as sufficient to account for it. This does not seem to explain adequately either the merging of the two cities' sovereignty which the wording of the decree implies, or the notable fact that the benefactor of Paros and Thasos only receives Parian proxeny.

It is difficult to reconcile the evidence for Thasos' independent existence with sympolity with Paros, and it is worth noting that the records of the political institutions at Thasos show no sign of mingling with those of Paros.[5] Perhaps it is best to regard the wording of the inscription as an error, or at least a loose

---

[1] *AM* xxvii 1902, 286 f.

[2] The passage Dem. *De Cor.* 197 is the only evidence adduced, but it is too brief and allusive to admit of a single definite interpretation. It shows (as e.g. Schaefer, *Demosthenes und seine Zeit* III² 28 n. 2) that those in power at Thasos were hostile to Athens. But this is in 330, when the speech was delivered, and thus the passage reflects conditions at Thasos after the Battle of Chaeronea. We know that Thasos was independent of Philip as late as 340 from his letter [Dem] XII.2. Head states (*HN*² p. 265) that there are no autonomous Thasian coins from the time of Philip, Alexander and Lysimachus, but it is impossible to give an exact date to the beginning of this break in Thasos' coinage.

[3] His positive argument (loc. cit.) for Thasos' independence is however weak. It is true that Thasos participated in the League of Corinth (see Wilhelm *Attische Urkunden* I.26 ff; Tod 177.29) but so did Thessaly (Tod 177.25) which had long been in Philip's power.

[4] See Pouilloux 432.　　　　　　　　　　　　　[5] See Pouilloux 431 n. 7.

expression. If it is not taken to prove sympolity but merely to show that the Parians saw it as an extra qualification in Ceph- isophon that he had also helped their colony Thasos, there is no difficulty in understanding the inscription. It would then merely reflect close and friendly relations between Thasos and Paros. Otherwise we have an example of sympolity between colony and mother city, unlikely and unexplained though it seems to be.

To turn from Thasos as a colony to Thasos as a metropolis, she seems to have entered on this role soon after her own foundation. Her early interest in the mainland is implied by the fighting with the Thracians in which Archilochus took part, and her strife with Maroneia over Stryme, to which he also bore witness,[1] shows that this interest extended to attempts at colonization. It is thus a reasonable inference that the Thasian peraea, the extent of which is only known from later sources, was settled early.[2] By the time that Greek historiography began the area was regarded as Thasian. Herodotus (VII.118) de- scribes the Thasian colonies on the mainland as the Thasian cities on the mainland ($\tau\tilde{\omega}\nu$ $\dot{\epsilon}\nu$ $\tau\tilde{\eta}$ $\dot{\eta}\pi\epsilon\dot{\iota}\varrho\omega$ $\pi o\lambda\dot{\iota}\omega\nu$ $\tau\tilde{\omega}\nu$ $\sigma\varphi\epsilon\tau\dot{\epsilon}\varrho\omega\nu$ (sc. $\Theta\alpha\sigma\dot{\iota}\omega\nu$)), and he calls Stryme a city of the Thasians ($\Theta\alpha\sigma\dot{\iota}\omega\nu$ $\pi\dot{o}\lambda\iota\varsigma$).[3] Thucydides records (I.101.3) that when Thasos capitu- lated to Athens she gave up $\tau\dot{\eta}\nu$ $\ddot{\eta}\pi\epsilon\iota\varrho o\nu$ $\varkappa\alpha\dot{\iota}$ $\tau\dot{o}$ $\mu\dot{\epsilon}\tau\alpha\lambda\lambda o\nu$. It may be concluded in broad terms that Thasos had colonized the opposite mainland in such a way as to make it her possession. We must examine further evidence before we can make more precise statements about the status of the colonies and the extent of Thasos' control.

Thasos received large revenues from her mainland posses- sions. These are described by Herodotus (VI.46.2 ff) though his figures have been thought unreliable.[4] His information may be set beside inferences from the Athenian tribute lists. The ten- fold difference between the 30 talents paid by Thasos from 446/5 and the 3 talents of the preceding years has been regu- larly explained by reference to Thucydides' information, noted above, that Thasos lost her mainland possessions after her revolt

[1] See Harpocration s.v. $\Sigma\tau\varrho\dot{\upsilon}\mu\eta$.
[2] On the peraea and its settlement see Pouilloux 32 f.
[3] VII.108. Cf. Pouilloux 109 n.1, who is perhaps overcautious when he says that this might only signify that it was founded by Thasos.
[4] See Pouilloux 110.

from Athens. Three talents is a quite inadequate figure for a city of Thasos' earlier prosperity, and a tenfold increase could only be justified by a sensational change in her economic situation. The explanation regularly given is that she was given back her mainland possessions.[1]

In its simplest guise—that Thasos had the revenues of her mainland possessions again and this explains the tenfold rise—this view is attacked by Pouilloux (109 ff). He notes that the two certainly attested Thasian colonies whose tribute appears in the tribute lists, Neapolis and Galepsus, continue to pay tribute separately after 446. The former pays the same tribute consistently. Galepsus, it is true, has its tribute reduced by two-thirds in 445/4, which might be held to show that it had lost revenue to Thasos at this time; but when its tribute is later again greatly reduced, probably in connection with the foundation of Amphipolis, there is no change in the tribute of Thasos. Pouilloux argues (111 f) that Thasos' tribute should surely have been reduced too. Pouilloux (109 f) also follows Perdrizet in interpreting Herodotus' statement (VII.112) that the mines of Pangaeum were exploited at this time by Thracians as showing that the mine at Scapte Hyle was no longer controlled by Thasos,[2] and so could not contribute to her revenues. However, it follows from Thucydides' words quoted above that the Thasians had at least one important mine.[3]

Pouilloux' own view is that Thasos' greatly increased tribute is due rather to organized exploitation of commerce. He is able to show (37 ff) from an important inscription about the wine trade that she had a developed commercial organization in the archaic period, and suggests with reason that her great prosperity came largely from dues levied on trade. He restores and interprets two fragmentary inscriptions of the fifth century in this sense (121 ff) and concludes (129 ff) that it was control of a maritime zone and dues levied on commerce rather than direct exploitation of the peraea which allowed the Thasian renaissance[4] after her defeat by Athens.

---

[1] For the evidence and modern literature see Pouilloux 107 ff.

[2] See Pouilloux 109 f for the evidence and further controversy on this point.

[3] As Meiggs noted, *JHS* lxiii 1943, 21 n. 4. On this see Pouilloux 110 n. 2; however he is mistaken when he says that Herodotus expressly states that the mine of Scapte Hyle was exploited by the Thracians.

[4] On this see Pouilloux 114 ff.

Pouilloux' theory is well argued, but must remain a theory in view of the fragmentary condition of the important inscriptions. It is therefore necessary to suspend judgment on the exact nature of Thasos' revenues. But that they came directly or indirectly from her control of the mainland opposite seems undeniable. This is the basis for Pouilloux' assumption of a maritime zone under Thasos' control, just as it was the source of her revenues to Herodotus (VI.46.2.). It still seems right, therefore, to assume that so large a rise in tribute should be explained by a recovery of the control over her mainland possessions, even if we do not know for certain how this control was exploited for economic gain.

The nature and extent of Thasos' political control is now more precisely known owing to a recent epigraphical discovery. This is the stone recording two laws encouraging delation, first published and fully discussed by Pouilloux (no. 18, 139 ff). It is completely preserved, and belonging as it does to a rich series of inscriptions[1] can be assigned its place in the series with some confidence. Pouilloux' arguments both epigraphical and historical seem in general sound.[2] He regards the document as emanating from the oligarchy of 411, which intended, by providing rewards for informers, to discourage revolts against the new regime.[3] However, though this convincing interpretation greatly enhances the general significance of the inscription, it is not essential to be certain about the precise historical circumstances in order to use it as evidence for Thasos' relations to her colonies. For this purpose it is enough that it is a Thasian decree of the latter half of the fifth century.

[1] This great advantage is fully exploited by Pouilloux, building on previous work on the epigraphy of Thasos; see his Annexe I, *Evolution de l'Ecriture*.

[2] Note especially his conclusions (145) from the appearance of the Three Hundred (3; 10). In a long and detailed review (*REG* lxxii 1959, 348 ff) Chamoux makes many criticisms of Pouilloux' work, and in particular stresses the uncertainties of his hypothetical reconstructions of epigraphical documents; see especially 351–8. But on the laws encouraging delation he seems to offer captious criticism rather than solid refutation of the main lines of Pouilloux' interpretation. Cf. Robert, *Bull.* 1960.328 (*REG* lxxiii 1960, 190).

[3] However recent evidence on the Thasian calendar suggests that a longer interval separated the two laws than the four months assumed by Pouilloux. See Salviat *BCH* lxxxii 1958, 212–15. But a more lengthy troubled period than that envisaged by Pouilloux is perfectly intelligible.

The first decree offers rewards for informers who denounce revolutionary plots in Thasos. The second offers similar rewards to those who denounce plots in the colonies. The opening of the second decree reads:

ὃς δ᾽ ἂν ἐν τῆις ἀποικίηισιν ἐπανάστασιν βολευομένην κατείπηι, ἢ προδιδόντα τὴν πόλιν Θασίων τινὰ ἢ τῶν ἀποίκων, καὶ φανῆι ἐόντα ἀληθέα, διηκοσίος στατῆρας κτλ.[1]

So the rulers of Thasos were able to offer rewards for information about plots in the colonies, and about traitors to the city whether Thasians or colonists, in just the same way as they could legislate about plots in Thasos itself.

The immediate conclusions are clear. Firstly, Thasos could legislate for her colonies; secondly, the colonies could revolt against her and their citizens could be traitors to her. This is control so close that it might be thought to imply that the colonies were part of the state of Thasos. More evidence must be considered before so extreme a conclusion could be accepted, but here a further implication of the law may be noted. The simple description τῆις ἀποικίηισιν shows that there was no need to name the colonies concerned; they were well known. At this date the extent of Thasos' control was well-defined, both geographically and politically, and it was not something new.

One colony which followed a different policy from its mother city in 411 and the years immediately following was Neapolis. For this reason its history adds to our understanding of the relations between Thasos and her colonies. The evidence for Neapolis' action is provided by an Athenian inscription[2] containing two decrees honouring Neapolis for her loyalty and support against the Peloponnesians and Thasians (6–8; 39 f). The first decree can be dated certainly to winter 410/9, the second probably to 407 or later.[3]

The factual information from this inscription is that Neapolis remained a loyal ally to Athens even at the cost of fighting her

---

[1] 'Whoever shall denounce a plot to revolt in the colonies, or anyone betraying the city, whether a Thasian or a colonist, shall, if the information prove true (receive) 200 staters, etc.'

[2] *IG* I².108; Tod 84, republished with many new readings by Meritt and Andrewes in *BSA* xlvi 1951, 200–9, whose version is now printed as *SEG* XII.37.

[3] See Tod I p. 209.

mother city. Pouilloux (155 f) combines this with other epigraphical evidence for the events of this time.[1] First with the law encouraging informers just discussed; for here is a colony which did revolt from Thasos. And secondly with the record of those whose goods were confiscated on Thasos,[2] which can be shown to belong to 410.[3] The last two names on this are of Neapolitans. The three texts show Thasos' attempts in these troubled years to prevent revolts in the colonies, her failure in the case of Neapolis and her punishment of individual Neapolitans.

But the Attic inscription is not only valuable for the facts it provides; it also gives a precious indication of the Neapolitans' ideas about their relations to Thasos. In the second decree (49 f) the Athenians accede to the Neapolitan request for a change of wording in the first:

ἐς δὲ τὸ ψήφισμα τὸ πρό[τερον ἐ]πανορθῶσαι τὸγ γραμματέα τῆς βουλῆς [καὶ ἐς αὐτὸ μεταγράφ]σαι ἀντὶ τῆς ἀποικί[ας τῆς Θασί]ων Ϝότι συνδιεπολέμησαν τὸμ πόλεμον μ[ετὰ ᾿Αθηναίων.[4]

The present appearance of the first decree (7 f) shows that this change was carried out; (the Athenians praise the Neapolitans)

[πρῶτον μ]ὲν ὅ{υ}τι συνδιεπο[λέμη]σαν τὸν πόλεμον μετὰ ᾿Αθηναίω[ν καὶ πολιο]ρκούμενοι [ὑπὸ Θασίων] καὶ Πελο[πονν]ησίων οὐκ ἠθ[έλησαν κτλ.[5]

The original state of these lines has been reconstructed by Meritt and Andrewes (201) as follows:

πρῶτον μὲν ὅτι ἄποικοι ὄντες Θασίων καὶ πολιορκούμενοι ὑπ᾿ αὐτῶν καὶ Πελοποννησίων κτλ.[6]

---

[1] His very precise reconstruction is, however, more than the uncertain chronological indications allow; see above p. 83 n. 3.

[2] *IG* XII.8.263.　　　　　　　　　　[3] See Pouilloux 156.

[4] 'The secretary of the council is to amend the previous decree and write in it instead of "the colony of the Thasians" "because they fought the war through to the end together with the Athenians".'

[5] 'Firstly because they fought the war through to the end together with the Athenians and though they were besieged by the Thasians and Peloponnesians were not willing etc.' The version is that of Meritt and Andrewes op. cit. 203; the words underlined are the small letters in *rasura* of the stone. Kirchhoff (*IG* I suppl. p. 17) thought that the hand which wrote those letters was the same as that responsible for the second decree; cf. *SEG* XII p. 17.

[6] 'Firstly because although they were colonists of the Thasians and besieged by them and the Peloponnesians etc.'

In 407, therefore, when Thasos was back in the Athenian Empire,[1] the Neapolitans no longer wanted to be described as colonists of Thasos, but to have substituted for that phrase a general statement of their loyalty to Athens. It is easy to understand why Neapolis' origin was stated in the first draft; as Wilhelm says,[2] it was specially worthy of note that Neapolis had stood firm for Athens even though this had meant war with her mother city. The reason why the Neapolitans wanted the phrase removed in or after 407 is perhaps less obvious, and involves the Greek view about wars between colonies and mother cities.

It was seen above (pp. 10 ff) that Thucydides was not alone in regarding colonies and mother cities as natural allies and unnatural enemies. Wars between them were certainly known[3] but were regarded as shameful.[4] In general with colonies far apart from their mother cities such wars were unlikely. Only a general conflagration like the Peloponnesian War could produce the number of such conflicts that Thucydides records at Syracuse (VII.57). Neighbours had more opportunity for hostility. An example recorded by Thucydides (V.5.3.) illustrates this. In 423 Epizephyrian Locri was at war with Hipponium and Medma, cities which Thucydides expressly describes as neighbours and colonies (ὁμόρους . . . καὶ ἀποίκους). But even though neighbours had greater opportunity, it need not be doubted that shame would still be attached to such wars.

It is in the light of this attitude that one should consider the Neapolitan desire for a change of wording. Wilhelm's opinion was that the bitterness of the struggle left the Neapolitans so estranged from their mother city that they no longer wished to be described as colonists of Thasos.[5] He compared Corcyra in her hostility to Corinth. Tod (p. 210) follows him and cites Amphipolis' behaviour in repudiating the Athenian connection.[6] But neither of these examples is apt. Corcyra never tried to deny her Corinthian origin and Amphipolis was at war with Athens, whereas Neapolis was no longer at war with Thasos. So it is perhaps likelier than Neapolis, though she could not

[1] See Xen. *Hell.* I.iv.9; Diod. XIII.72.1; cf. Pouilloux 162 ff.
[2] *Gött. gel. Anz.* 165. 1903, 777.   [3] Cf. Plato *Laws* 754B.
[4] Cf. also Themistocles' message to the Ionians before the battle of Artemisium (Hdt. VIII.22.1).
[5] *Gött. gel. Anz.* 165. 1903, 777.
[6] See Thuc. V.11.

alter the fact that she had supported Athens by fighting her metropolis, was anxious that the express emphasis on the shameful aspect of that action should be removed.

This way of understanding the change of wording suits Pouilloux' interpretation of the Parian inscription[1] as the record of an act of reconciliation between Thasos and her colony. Another possibility, that the Neapolitans were asking for a correction of fact, because they were not colonists of Thasos, need not be entertained. Apart from the unlikelihood of such an error on an Attic decree, Neapolis' position in the middle of the Thasian peraea puts beyond reasonable doubt that she was a colony of Thasos.[2] The change of wording may therefore be taken to show in general the sense of shame attached to wars between colonies and mother cities, and in particular Neapolis' desire to forget the past and be reconciled with Thasos.

There is also the question of Neapolis' status *vis-à-vis* her mother city. It seems clear that the colony formed a separate community. It is true that in the act of resisting Thasos it would obviously appear particularly independent, but one can add the evidence that it paid tribute separately to Athens, that Athens clearly treats it as a separate community in the document under discussion, and that the Parian inscription shows Neapolitans as participants in an agreement with Thasos, whether or not one concludes with Pouilloux that it was a peace treaty between them. If one accepts Pouilloux' more tenuous reconstruction (206 ff) of the inscription *IG* XII.8.264,[3] the same conclusion follows, for he restores this document as one of the acts in the reorganization of Thasos in the first half of the fourth century, and identifies the people who are to be incorporated in some degree with the Thasians as Neapolitans. They would be given *ateleia*(1) and other privileges, and the sons of Neapolitans by Thasian wives would be Thasian citizens (8 f). Unfortunately there is no firm indication that the people involved are Neapolitans. No ethnic is preserved on the stone except that of Thasos. However, if he is right, we not only see further close relations between colony and metropolis, but also

[1] See above pp. 76 ff.
[2] Pouilloux (157 ff) easily dismisses the arguments advanced against this.
[3] Chamoux demonstrates the uncertainty of Pouilloux' suggestions; see *REG* lxxii 1959, 357.

clear evidence that Neapolis was not legally part of the Thasian
state at that time.

There is a little fourth-century evidence for Thasos' relations
with her colonies. The rare bronze and gold coinage bearing
the legend *ΘΑΣΙΟΝ ΗΠΕΙΡΟ* is connected with the foundation of Daton/Crenides by the Thasians under the leadership
of Callistratus in 360.[1] According to the most recent study, the
bronze coins of the first three years of the colony's existence were
struck in Thasos, while a gold issue and new types in the fourth
year showed that the colony had acquired monetary independence.[2] Thereafter the colony becomes Philippi and the
issue of the coins inscribed *ΘΑΣΙΟΝ ΗΠΕΙΡΟ* ceased. It is
not surprising that the first coins were struck in the metropolis,[3]
and as the settlement succeeded and began to exploit its gold
resources it produced coins of its own. The only point of special
interest is the legend. That the new colonists thought of themselves as Thasians in their early years and were so regarded in
Thasos is easily intelligible, but 'of the mainland' is a broad
and imprecise description of a new city, to say the least. Perhaps
we are to explain it simply by doubts about the name of the
new settlement, doubts which introduced the present confusion
into the tradition.[4] But it seems more probable that the far-
going implications of the inscription were intended, and reflect
the long tradition of Thasos' claim to control her peraea.

[1] The history of the foundation and early years of the colony, together
with the ancient sources and evidence for the exact dates, is well set out by
P. Collart, *Philippes, ville de Macedoine* (Paris 1937) 133–7. The coinage has
been treated recently by G. Le Rider in his study of Thasian coins of the
time in question; see *BCH* lxxx 1956, 16 ff. He maintains (against Pouilloux
218 f) that the traditional interpretation puts the coins in their correct
historical setting, which is difficult to deny in view of their similarity to the
first, autonomous, coins of Philippi.

[2] See Le Rider op. cit. His interpretation seems to provide a satisfactory
solution to the dilemma that the coins are clearly Thasian yet the series is
continued (apart from the change of legend) by the first coins of Philippi.
The latter point convinced Collart that the place of production must have
been Crenides (135 n. 4 on p. 136), while the former is part of Pouilloux'
justification for seeing them as coins of Thasos.

[3] As they were for some of the colonies of Corinth (see Chapter VII). The
new colony was presumably also like Corinthian colonies in using the silver
coins of the mother city. This seems an easier explanation of the lack of
silver coins than Pouilloux' conclusion that the coinage was not that of the
new colony (loc. cit.).

[4] See Collart op. cit. and *RE* s.v. *Philippoi* 2212 f.

In 361/60 there was further strife between Thasos and Maroneia about Stryme.[1] This was the most easterly point of the
Thasian peraea, where such struggles could be expected.[2] So the
evidence supports Pouilloux' conclusion (223) that in the fourth
century Thasos reasserted the control over her peraea, which she
had enjoyed in the archaic period, and in the fifth century
when undisturbed by Athens or by civil war.

The status of Thasos' colonies may now be examined. It was
seen that the law about delation could be held to show that the
colonies formed part of the Thasian state. The evidence against
this in the case of Neapolis is very strong. Galepsus may be
accorded a similar separate existence, because it too paid
tribute separately in the Athenian Empire. If these two colonies
are typical, then the rest must also be allowed this separate
status. They could, on the other hand, be regarded as special
cases, simply because they alone paid tribute. However, the
appearance of Neapolitans among those whose goods were confiscated by the oligarchs in 410[3] seems to show that Neapolis
came under Thasian jurisdiction, like the colonies to which the
decree encouraging delation referred.[4] This suggests that Thasos
included Neapolis among the colonies which she aspired to
control.

If Neapolis was so included her separate status may be used
to prove that of the others. But this is not the only indication.
The Athenians were able to make Thasos surrender her mainland possessions after the revolt,[5] just as Mytilene gave up her
mainland possessions after the Mytilenean Revolt.[6] It would
have been difficult to detach them if they had been legally in-
distinguishable from the state of Thasos, so that this action also
suggests they had a separate existence.

The control of Thasos over her continental colonies has been
seen to be very close, yet they were not simply part of the

[1] See Pouilloux 221 f, for evidence and discussion.
[2] Pouilloux (222 f) connects it with the foundation of Crenides, which is
possible.
[3] Cf. Pouilloux 156.
[4] Pouilloux, 157, even considered that the indeterminate plural τηῖς
ἀποικίησιν of that decree essentially referred to Neapolis; but his connections
seem too definite for the evidence; cf. above p. 85 n. 1.
[5] Thuc. I.101.3.
[6] See Thuc. III.50.2, IV.52, and ATL I Gazeteer s.v. 'Ακταῖαι Πόλεις.

Thasian state. This position of communities which were possessions of the metropolis and under her legal control, yet were
called *apoikiai*[1] and had a separate existence, was probably only
possible if the colonies were reasonably near to the mother city.
Thasos is some twenty miles from the mainland.

A number of other islands owned or controlled portions of the
adjacent mainland, but the evidence is generally far less good
than that about Thasos. Corcyra had land and forts on the
mainland opposite,[2] and Mytilene had considerable possessions
on the mainland which she lost after her revolt, as has been
mentioned. But in neither case are we informed that the possessions could be called colonies; Mytilene's included cities, but
they could have been hers by right of conquest rather than
foundation. The Rhodian peraea and the evidence for it are
rather too late for the present purpose; it is very doubtful if it
was established before the end of the first Athenian Empire.[3]
Only in the case of Thasos have we evidence of relevant date
referring explicitly to colonies on the adjacent mainland. However, other instances may be found in Greek history of colonies
near to the metropolis, which may be studied in order to throw
light on Thasos' position, and, more widely, on the general
phenomenon of colonization at a short distance.

An early example of control exercised by a mother city over
a colony at a short distance may be found, it seems, in the
relations between Epidaurus and Aegina. According to Herodotus (VIII.46.1.), Aegina was settled from Epidaurus, and
other ancient writers, with differences of detail, support him.[4]
The matter seems to be put beyond doubt by the fact that a
special religious festival found on Aegina also occurred at
Epidaurus.[5] Herodotus relates (V.83.1.) that the Aeginetans
were subject to the Epidaurians both in other respects and as
regards their lawsuits, which had to be conducted at Epidaurus,
but that later they built ships and revolted. The position described by Herodotus cannot be later than the seventh century,
for it must antedate Periander's conquest of Epidaurus,[6] and

---

[1] The appearance of the word in the decree on delation, Pouilloux no. 18,
makes literary references unnecessary.
[2] See Thuc. III.85.2.
[3] See G. E. Bean and P. M. Fraser, *The Rhodian Peraea and Islands*, 94 ff.
[4] See Strabo VIII.375; Paus. II.29.5.   [5] See Hdt. V.83.3.
[6] See Hdt. III.52.7; cf. How and Wells, commentary on V.83.1.

there are good reasons for putting it in the early part of that century.[1] Thus, if Herodotus' account is accepted, Aegina is a very early instance of a colony in a position of close dependence which successfully revolted.

Not unnaturally, doubts have been cast on Herodotus' information,[2] but the only serious difficulty is the statement that the colonists had to go to Epidaurus for their lawsuits. As Athens' allies were required to go to Athens for some of their legal cases,[3] Busolt objected[4] that this gave the form of dependence the stamp of Herodotus' own time. While he may be right, it is worth remembering that litigation was already an evil in Hesiod's day[5] and the administration of the law was the valuable possession of his 'bribe-devouring kings'.

It would be rash to assume that Herodotus' account is completely reliable, but there seems no good reason to reject it. If there is anachronistic contamination it may only be in the detail about lawsuits. The general picture of Epidaurus' control and Aegina's revolt may, with the necessary reserve, be accepted. Aegina's position close to the heart of Greece and at a very short distance from Epidaurus makes this by no means a typical colonial situation. Such a relationship at so early a date is hardly conceivable except where distances were small.

Sybaris seems to have won a considerable empire, which appears partly to have consisted of colonies which she controlled. Strabo writes (VI.263) that Sybaris ruled four races (ἔθνη) and had twenty-five dependent cities. These cities probably included Sybarite colonies, such as Laus and other lesser settlements.[6] Posidonia has been included[7] among these dependent colonies, but its earliest coins, which are on the Campanian, not the Achaean, standard, seem to point to independence.[8] It was the most distant of Sybaris' colonies, and lies

---

[1] See Ure, *The Origin of Tyranny* 165 ff; cf. *CAH* III.540.
[2] The paper devoted to the topic by C. D. Morris, *AJP* v 1884, 479–87, is too inaccurate and illogical to be helpful.
[3] See *CAH* V.94.
[4] *Griech. Staatskunde* I.217 n. 6. His other objection that Aegina's membership of the Calaurian League shows her early independence is less good; both the date and the character of this league are too little known (cf. *CAH* III.610, 650).
[5] *Works and Days*, 27 ff, 225 ff; 248 ff.   [6] See Dunbabin, 155.
[7] By Randall-McIver, *Greek Cities in Italy and Sicily*, 11, and by Rieman, *RE*. 2. Reihe IV.1, 1008.   [8] See Head, *HN*² pp. 80 f.

about a hundred miles from the mother city as the crow flies, while Laus, the most important of the colonies thought to be dependent, is about forty. The difference in distance may explain the difference in status. However, it must be remembered that the identification of the sites of Sybarite colonies is, in most instances, nearly as difficult as of that of the mother city itself.[1] The nature of Sybaris' control is quite unknown in detail, but the general conclusion that she expanded by means of dependent colonies at a short distance seems admissible, and Posidonia's presumed independence may be taken to show that such dependent colonies needed to be near the mother city.

Syracusan expansion seems to have been similar to that of Sybaris and was partly furthered by colonization. Her foundations were three: Acrae, Casmenae, and Camarina.[2] Acrae was founded in c. 663,[3] and there seems little doubt that the settlement was intended to secure to Syracuse the whole plain debouching at Syracuse itself.[4] Because Thucydides (VI.5.2.) names no oikist and the city struck no coins till the Roman period, Acrae has been seen[5] as an outlying part of the Syracusan state rather than a separate colony. Casmenae was founded in c. 643[6] on a site not certainly identified.[7] The same conclusion may be drawn about its status as about that of Acrae; it struck no coins and Thucydides (ibid.) names no oikist.[8] It is true that the place is described as a polis on its sole appearance in history, when it was the refuge for the Gamoroi of Syracuse, who had been expelled by the people allied with the serfs or Kyllyrioi,[9] but, as Bérard (132. n. 3.) acutely remarks, at precisely this moment it was in fact independent. In any case it would probably be wrong to press this description. It is a reasonable assumption that Syracuse spread her power over the surrounding countryside by establishing colonies so

---

[1] See Dunbabin, 155 f.   [2] See Thuc. VI.5.2 f.

[3] See ibid.

[4] Both Dunbabin (99) and Bérard come to this conclusion from the geographical position; see Bérard 132 f.

[5] See Dunbabin 105, 109, and Bérard 132.

[6] See Thuc. loc. cit.

[7] For discussions of the possibilities, see Dunbabin 103 f., Bérard 133. Modern Mount Casale is the most probable candidate; see Guarducci, *Ann. d.Scuol. Arch. d. Atene* n.s. xxi–xxii 1959–60, 255.

[8] See Dunbabin 105, 109, and Bérard 132.

[9] See Hdt. VII.155.2

subordinate as to be hardly distinguishable from the founding state.

The third colony, Camarina, was founded in *c.* 598 and had two oikists.[1] Some fifty years after its foundation[2] it revolted from Syracuse, fought an unsuccessful war of independence and was destroyed. This, at least is the natural interpretation of Thucydides' words (VI.5.3.), but Dunbabin (106 f) shows that there is evidence that Camarina was a prosperous city in the second half of the sixth century, and suggests that the true meaning of the Thucydidean account is that the inhabitants were expelled, and, by inference, that the city was resettled from Syracuse.

It seems to have been of some importance and in close connection with Syracuse at the time of Hippocrates' victory over the Syracusans in 492, when it was ceded to Gela.[3] Dunbabin (407 ff) assumes from various doubtful accounts that it was necessary for Hippocrates to take Camarina before advancing on Syracuse, and this seems quite probable. In any case, the fact that Syracuse could cede Camarina to Gela shows that the city was under Syracusan control, and Herodotus, if his words may be pressed, states expressly that this was so.[4] From this time onwards the city can no longer be called a Syracusan colony, so that its continuous enmity with Syracuse[5] is no longer relevant to this investigation.

So Syracusan control over Camarina in its first years was sufficient to induce a war of revolt[6] and the later repopulated colony was effectively a Syracusan possession. On the other

[1] Thuc. VI.5.3. The significance of the two oikists cannot be determined. One might have come from Syracuse and one from Corinth, as Dunbabin suggests (105); for this procedure Zancle provides an analogy (Thuc. VI.4.5). Bérard (135) considers that they represented two different ethnic groups, and on this inference builds the hypothesis that Geloans took part in the colony. But the only support for this theory is that Camarina lay between Gela and Syracuse. It might be thought that the presence of Geloans would account for the colony's revolt from Syracuse, but, if so, it is surprising that Gela refused to help Camarina in her war of independence (if it is right to attribute Philistus frg. 5, *FGH* III B p. 559, to this war, as Dunbabin 105 f, and Bérard 135). Bérard's hypothesis about the composition of the colony seems to be without support.

[2] For the date see schol. Pind. *Ol.* V.16. [3] See Hdt. VII.154.3.

[4] Ibid.: Συρηκοσίων δὲ ἦν Καμάρινα τὸ ἀρχαῖον.

[5] See Thuc. VI.88.1.

[6] Compare Thucydides' words δι' ἀπόστασιν (VI.5.3).

hand the oikists show that it was a properly constituted colony
and it was capable of independent action against its mother city.
Syracuse seems to have wanted to use Camarina, as she used
Acrae and Casmenae, to spread her own power, but was evidently not so successful. Acrae is some twenty miles from Syracuse, Camarina seventy.[1] If Acrae and Casmenae remained
virtually outlying parts of the Syracusan state, and Camarina
had a separate existence, although the Syracusan aims were the
same in the three cases, it is tempting to see the reason for the
difference in status in Camarina's greater distance from the
mother city.[2]

Mylae in Sicily, which was founded in the late eighth century
at a place some 25 miles from its metropolis Zancle, seems to
have been a completely subordinate settlement, yet a separate
community.[3] This status is no doubt to be attributed to the
comparatively short distance from its mother city.

It was seen earlier in this chapter that Epizephyrian Locri
had two colonies situated close at hand, Hipponium and
Medma. A third-century inscription from Delphi bestows proxeny and other honours on one Demarchus, who is described as
Δημάρχωι Φιλώτα Λοκρῶι ἐκ τῶν Ἐπι[ζε]φυρίων Ἱππωνιεῖ.[4] This
description is rightly taken by Dunbabin (165) to show 'double
nationality or rather . . . local qualification of nationality.'
Apparently Hipponium was then scarcely distinguishable from
the Locrian state. In view of the vicissitudes of the history of
Hipponium and Locri,[5] we may also follow Dunbabin in assuming that this position was established at latest before the fourth
century; for it is hard to see at what time in that century the
two cities could have arranged such a relationship. Thus it
seems legitimate to compare this evidence with earlier indica-

[1] For the sites see Bérard 132, 134.
[2] Cf. Dunbabin, 105. Although the discussion here has been about the
dependent colonies of Sybaris and Syracuse, this is not to deny that their
empires included settlements of the native population; cf. Larsen RE s.v.
Perioikoi 832 f. However, such settlements are irrelevant to the present
purpose.
[3] I give the arguments and evidence for this conclusion together with
relevant modern literature in Historia xi, 1962, 249 f. For the foundation and
dates see Bérard 97 f and Vallet, Rhégion et Zancle, 83 f.
[4] 'Demarchus the son of Philotas, a Locrian of the Epizephyrians, a
Hipponian.' Fouilles de Delphes III.1 no. 176; for the date, c. 280, see notes
to no. 168.
[5] See Head, HN² p. 100.

tions about the status of Hipponium. In the latter part of the sixth century the Hipponians dedicated at Olympia spoils won in a war against Croton, which they fought in alliance with their sister colony Medma and mother city Epizephyrian Locri.[1] This, like Thucydides' description of Hipponium as a colony (V.5.3.), suggests at least separate existence. Thus different pieces of evidence show us a colony separate from its metropolis, which could yet be regarded as virtually part of it. Such diverse indications are perhaps to be explained by the fact that Hipponium was only about thirty miles distant from Epizephyrian Locri.[2]

The island of Cythera[3] lies ten miles out to sea off the south coast of Laconia. There is no account of its settlement, but its historical population was presumably determined, like that of Laconia, by the invasions at the beginning of the Iron Age. Herodotus (I.82.2.) relates that it belonged to the archaic Argive empire, and the implication is that Sparta won it by the 'battle of the champions' in 546.[4] The fullest description of its political position from that time onwards, apart from brief periods of control by non-Spartan masters,[5] is given by Thucydides, who writes (VI.53.2.) that the inhabitants were Lacedaemonian *perioikoi*, and that a yearly magistrate was sent to the island from Sparta, together with a garrison. Cythera would seem from this description to be like a part of Laconia, Lacedaemonian territory inhabited by Lacedaemonian *perioikoi*. On the other hand Thucydides calls the people of Cythera colonists, *apoikoi*, of the Lacedaemonians in another passage (VII.57.6). In this passage Thucydides is drawing the island and its inhabitants into his large picture of the way in which the claims of kinship were ignored in the Syracusan campaign. In the former account he is giving a thorough description, which is for that reason much more likely to be precise and accurate. The people of Cythera were, therefore, Lacedaemonian *perioikoi*, yet Thucydides could think of them as *apoikoi*. The fact that Sparta sent

---

[1] See E. Kunze, *3. Bericht über die Ausgrabungen in Olympia, 1938/9*, 77–79 (plates 24 and 25).
[2] For the site see Bérard 212 f.
[3] The best collection of historical references to Cythera is in *IG* V.1 p. 176.
[4] See *CAH* III.569.
[5] E.g. by Athens in the Peloponnesian War (Thuc. IV.54.3); by the Confederates after its capture by Conon in 393 (Xen. *Hell.* IV.viii.8).

H

a yearly governor and kept a garrison[1] on the island also dif-
ferentiates it from Laconia proper. It thus seems that the legal
position of the island was in practice affected by the distance
from Sparta and the sea passage, so that Cythera was in an
intermediate position between a colony and part of the Lacedaemonian state.[2]

The evidence for the effect of distance on colonial relationships has shown that when colony and mother city were near to
each other their relations were sometimes so close that the
colony could almost be called an extension of the founding
state. Even when this was not so, the mother city was often able
to exercise very close control. It is notable that the examples
range from very early times, in the seventh century, to the
classical period. As a mother city of colonies at a short distance
Thasos too exercised a strict political, and possibly also an economic, control, to the extent that her colonies were at times
treated like parts of the Thasian state. Though these relations
are not certainly attested before the fifth century, the fact that
similar examples are found in earlier times suggests that Thasos
may have exercised such control from the time when she first
founded settlements on the mainland in the seventh century.

As a colony Thasos' relations with her mother city were seen
to be very close and friendly throughout her history. Although
it seems wrong to interpret Akeratos' dedication and the
honorary decree for Cephisophon as showing either isopolity
or sympolity for certain, they both reveal a far closer bond than
would be normal between two unrelated independent states.
Paros and Thasos show that where communications between
colony and metropolis were reasonably easy the lives of the two
cities could remain interrelated, not merely to the extent of

[1] The governor and garrison were presumably those sent back to Sparta
under truce by Conon; see Xen. loc. cit. Thucydides' words make plain that
both governor and garrison were regular; this against Maull in *RE* s.v.
Kythera, 216, who implies that the garrison was temporary, and Meyer,
Theopomps Hellenika, 269 n. 3, who explains the probable presence of a
harmost there in the fourth century (see *IG* V.1 p. 176) by suggesting that
Sparta was temporarily treating Cythera like other ex-allies of Athens.
The office of *Kytherodikes* (Thuc. IV.53.2) is attested as late as the time of
Hadrian; see Robert, *Hellenica* I.110.

[2] Other communities of *perioikoi* were regarded as originally settled from
Sparta; for a list and references see Niese, *Nach. Gött. Ges.d. Wiss.*, Phil-Hist.
Klasse, 1906, 133 f; but Cythera seems the most striking and significant
example for our purposes.

personal contacts, or wartime help, but even to the point where the legal division between the two states was slightly blurred. In this chapter we have discussed the many aspects of the relationship between colony and mother city on which the history of Thasos throws direct light, but it also raises, if indirectly, the question of mutual citizenship, which must be considered in the next.

CHAPTER VI

MILETUS AND THE QUESTION OF
MUTUAL CITIZENSHIP

*πολλὰ δὲ τῆς πόλεως ἔργα ταύτης, μέγιστον
δὲ τὸ πλῆθος τῶν ἀποικιῶν.*[1]

Strabo XIV. 635

JUDGED by the number of its colonies Miletus was the greatest of Greek mother cities. For though some of the more extravagant claims made in antiquity[2] have not been substantiated by modern investigations,[3] her colonies were far more numerous than those of any other Greek city. 'For', to continue Strabo's statement above, 'the whole Pontus Euxinus was colonized by them, and the Propontis and many other places.' Literary evidence for her relations with her colonies, however, barely exists, and though commercial links may perhaps be implied by the predominantly East Greek pottery found on the sites of her Pontic colonies,[4] as a great trading city Miletus' commerce was very widespread, so that these commercial connections need not be regarded as special relations with the colonies. The name, or nickname, of her great men in early times, the *ἀειναῦται*,[5] shows the interest of the aristocracy in overseas ventures, so that Glotz may not be going too far when he says that they directed colonization and trade.[6] It was no doubt always right to assume the existence of some relations between Miletus and her colonies, but precise evidence was lacking until it was provided by inscriptions.

---

[1] 'This city's achievements are many, but the greatest is the number of its colonies.'

[2] Miletus founded 75 colonies according to Seneca (*Cons. ad Helv. matrem* 7.2); 90 according to Pliny (*N.H.* V.112).

[3] Bilabel reaches the number 45, but not all these are primary or certain or exclusively Milesian.

[4] See R. M. Cook, *JHS* lxvi 1946, 82.

[5] Plut. *Q.G.* 32. The arguments about this word and suggested meanings are set out by Halliday, *Greek Questions of Plutarch*, 146, who thinks it most probable that it was a nickname coined in party politics; for this view and other examples cf. Busolt, *Griech. Staatskunde* I.211.

[6] *The Greek City* 68.

Some of this epigraphic evidence, being of the Hellenistic period,[1] is too late for the present purpose; but there are three inscriptions, which fall just within the chronological limits of this study and provide valuable information. The most important one concerns Olbia,[2] and states the position about mutual citizen rights and other privileges reciprocally enjoyed by the citizens of colony and mother city. Olbia was founded from Miletus in c. 645.[3]

The inscription was dated to before 323 by its first editor[4] for a combination of epigraphic and historical reasons. There is a group of inscriptions,[5] all of the same period, which show an independent foreign policy at Miletus, and are regarded as emanating from the time when Miletus was freed by Alexander from Persian rule. This approximate dating has never been doubted. An attempt at a more precise date was made by S. A. Zhebeliov,[6] on the following argument. Miletus was freed in 332.[7] In 331[8] Olbia repulsed an attack by Zopyrion, Alexander's general, and introduced revolutionary measures during the siege,[9] which included the extension of citizenship to metics and the cancellation of debts. Zhebeliov (435) therefore concludes that our document has its natural place at a time when the metropolis had just returned to independence and democracy, and the colony had just widened its citizenship and cancelled all debts. This ingenious argument yields the date c. 330, which is accepted by Tod.[10] It is, however, inevitably hypothetical,[11] so we should put the date of the inscription as certainly before 323 and perhaps about 330.

[1] See above p. 2 n. 2.   [2] Tod 195; *Milet* I.3 no. 136.
[3] This is the Eusebian date; the earliest archaeological material discovered at Olbia is a little later; see R. M. Cook, *JHS* lxvi 1946, 84. For the Milesian origin see Hdt. IV.78.3, with whom all the other ancient authorities agree; see Bilabel 23 f.
[4] Rehm, *Milet* I.3 p. 293.
[5] *Milet* I.3 nos. 135, 136, 137 and the decree for Istria, published by S. Lambrino, *Dacia* III–IV, Bucharest 1927–32, 398.
[6] *CR. Acad. des Sciences USSR* (Classe des Humanités) 1929, 429 ff.
[7] This is established by Berve, *Das Alexanderreich auf prosopographischen Grundlage*, II.201.
[8] The date is fixed by the fact that the news of Zopyrion's campaign is brought to Alexander just after the death of Darius (Justin. XII.1.4), and Darius died in July 330; cf. Berve II.128.
[9] See Macrobius *Sat.* I.11.33.   [10] See Tod II p. 270.
[11] The main objection seems to be that Miletus made a number of such agreements at the same time, for this could be held to show that circumstances

In a literal translation the agreement runs as follows: 'The following are traditional arrangements for the Olbiopolitans and Milesians. That the Milesian in the city of Olbia sacrifice like an Olbiopolitan on the same altars, and partake in the same public cults under the same conditions as the Olbiopolitans. That the Milesian have exemption from taxation as it was formerly. That, if he wish to become eligible for office,[1] he is to come before the Council and be entered on the rolls and be liable to taxation[2] as other citizens are. That they (i.e. the Milesians) have the right of privileged seats at public gatherings, of being announced at athletic contests and of praying at the festival of the τριάκαδες,[3] as they pray in Miletus. And that, if the Milesian have a law suit arising from a legal contract, the case shall be tried within five days at the public court. That all Milesians be exempt from taxation except those who in another city exercise citizenship, hold magistracies and take part in the courts. That, on the same terms, the Olbiopolitan be exempt from taxes, and the other arrangements apply in the same way to the Olbiopolitan in Miletus as to the Milesians in the city of Olbia.'

The first point to notice is the bald beginning. From this Rehm drew the conclusion that relations between the two cities must have been very close;[4] this seems likely to be correct. It is

---

at Miletus alone were sufficient reason for them all. We cannot say for certain, in the absence of any prescript, which state initiated our agreement. Danov's attempt (*Bull. Soc. hist. de Bulgare* xii–xxiv 1948, 180–202) to prove that it was Miletus from the analogy of the contemporary decree from Istria (see above p. 99 n. 5, headed ΜΙ [ΛΗΣΙΩΝ (restored by Robert, *BCH* lii 1928, 170 ff), fails. The heading could, it is true, indicate the origin of the decree (as Robert loc. cit.), but it could also show the state to which the decree referred (on the headings of decrees see Larfeld, *Griech. Epigraphik* 307). However, it is more probable that Miletus initiated all the agreements, if only because there were several at the same time, all involving Miletus. But the changes at Olbia could still have acted as an extra incentive for Miletus to confirm and publish the mutual arrangements as soon as possible, as Zhebeliov suggested (op. cit., 435).

[1] This seems to be the meaning of τιμουχίων μετέχειν; cf. Tod p. 271.

[2] ἐντελής is evidently here the opposite of ἀτελής (as Tod p. 272), though there appears to be no parallel for this significance (see Liddell and Scott s.v.).

[3] On this festival see Bilabel 138. Rehm (*Milet* I.3 p. 291) thinks that it is specially mentioned because it is a celebration in which kinship was important, and he may well be right. It was a festival of the dead; see Harpocration s.v.

[4] See *Milet* I.3 p. 290.

also noteworthy that the first matter to be arranged is the religious status of the Milesian in Olbia. A similar arrangement
also came first in the foundation decree for Naupactus.[1] There
the colonist's right to take part in cults was expressly limited.
Here there is perhaps an implied limitation in the phrase
'public cults', but it is easy to understand that the decree only
admitted the Milesian to the public cults of the city.

The position regarding citizenship is complex. Full citizenship in Olbia in the sense of eligibility for office was open to
the Milesian; to have this privilege he had to undertake also
the full duties of a citizen and became liable to taxation. On
the other hand, if he was willing to deny himself this full
citizenship, he had exemption from taxation and kept the other
privileges, as, for example, an equal position with citizens in religious matters and a privileged one on state occasions. The
only Milesians who could not claim exemption from taxation
were those who exercised citizenship in full in another city. The
concept of citizenship in the agreement is close to Aristotle's
definition of the citizen as one who had a share in justice and
office, or, more simply, a share in office.[2]

The treaty is also reminiscent of Aristotle in its legal arrangements, for among the definitions of the citizen which he rejects
(*Pol.* 1275 a 8 ff), is he who has the right 'to defend an action
and to bring one in the lawcourts.'[3] He objects that aliens
have this right when there has been a treaty about lawsuits
between the citizens of the two cities.[4] At Olbia too the Milesian
could have his legal privileges without being a full citizen.

On the other hand, the name of the court, δημοτικὸν δικαστήριον, has been taken to show[5] that it was the court for citizens
as opposed to aliens. The description of the court is thought to
imply, by contrast, a ξενικὸν δικαστήριον, one of the types of
court listed by Aristotle (*Pol.* 1300 b 24). This is not a necessary

---

[1] See Chapter IV.

[2] μετέχειν κρίσεως καὶ ἀρχῆς, *Pol.* 1275 a 24; κοινωνεῖν ἀρχῆς, 1277 b 34;
μετέχειν τῶν τιμῶν, 1278 a 36.

[3] δίκην ὑπέχειν καὶ δικάζεσθαι; the translation is Rackham's (Loeb).

[4] The nature of these cases, or δίκαι ἀπὸ ξυμβόλων, has been discussed
recently by Hopper in his paper 'Interstate Juridical Agreements in the
Athenian Empire', *JHS* lxiii 1943, 35–51, and St. Croix *CQ* n.s. xi 1961, 95 f.

[5] See *Syll.*³ notes to 286; Zhebeliov *CR. Acad. des Sciences USSR* (Classe des
Humanités), 1929, 427 n. 4; Tod II p. 272; Liddell and Scott s.v. δημοτικός,
II.4.

inference, however, especially as the normal word for a court
for citizens as opposed to aliens is ἀστικός.[1] The type of court
need not, therefore, be interpreted as showing the Milesian's
superior position to that of other non-citizens in Olbia. However, the legal arrangement also is to be compared with the
similar provision in the foundation decree for Naupactus,[2] the
important difference being that in the Milesian document it is
specifically cases arising from a legal contract that are provided
for.

The carefully detailed arrangements of the document show
that this was not an empty exchange of honours, but rather of
practical advantages expected to be used. The same conclusion
follows from the concentration on liability for taxes, since this
was no doubt the most important thing for ordinary citizens.
Not only is taxation mentioned three times in the arrangements
for the Milesians in Olbia, it is the only subject actually
mentioned in the arrangements for the Olbiopolitans in
Miletus.

In the final clause complete reciprocity between the two
cities is established. This was taken by Rehm[3] to show that the
two cities had equal status, and this is clearly true in a legal
sense regarding the privileges exchanged. On the other hand
the document looks 'at things primarily from the point of view
of the colony'.[4] It appears that many more Milesians were expected to reside in Olbia than Olbiopolitans in Miletus. But if
this represents a right of the mother city, not unlike that deduced from the study of foundation decrees,[5] the mother city
was prepared to grant the same right to its colony.

The decree is expressly a restatement of traditional practices:
τάδε πάτρια ᾿Ολβιοπολίταις καὶ Μιλησ[ί]οις (1 f); καθάσσα καὶ πρότερον ἦσαν (5 f). The dangers in general of using later material as
evidence for earlier times have been noticed above in Chapter I,
but in this instance the document's own statements and the
character of its contents justify, or rather impose, the attempt
to see what light it throws on past relations between Olbia and
Miletus. Its references to the past are compared by Tod[6] with
the frequent use of the phrase κατὰ τὰ πάτρια in the decree regu-

---

[1] See Liddell and Scott s.v.
[2] See Chapter IV.
[3] *Milet* I.3 p. 291.
[4] Tod II p. 271.
[5] See Chapter IV.
[6] II p. 271.

lating offerings to Eleusis. In arrangements concerned with religion past tradition had special sanctity.

Analogies and express statements are, however, not alone in showing that the document contains real earlier practices. This is also suggested by what it does not say. When somewhat later Miletus granted the request of the people of Cius and extended her citizenship to them, the reason for her action is carefully stated: ἐπείδη Κιάνοι ἄποικοι ὄντες τῆς πόλεως κτλ.[1] On that occasion new arrangements were made. In the decree about Olbia no reasons are given and there is no statement that Olbia is a colony of Miletus. We have seen that the tradition is quite clear that Olbia was founded from Miletus, and the references to traditional arrangements and the complete reciprocity of religious rights put it beyond doubt that this was the basis for the rights exchanged. The absence of statements to this effect therefore implies that they were unnecessary because the practices were traditional and the basis for them well known.

For all these reasons—the express statements, the bald beginning[2] and the fact that the basis for the agreement is not stated—the document may be confidently called a restatement of past practice.

Unfortunately the attempt to date these practices more closely is hindered by the paucity of evidence for Olbia's earlier relations to Miletus. Literary evidence is confined to Herodotus' statement (IV.78.3) that the people of Olbia 'say that they are Milesians'.[3] The question is whether this expression should be understood to mean anything more than that the colony's origin was Milesian. An example where the geographical principle determined the ethnic of people who could still be regarded as Samians has already been noted.[4] If this analogy were to decide the question the form of expression reported by Herodotus could be regarded as exceptional and might even be held to show that the people of Olbia had remained Milesian citizens. But there is other evidence on ethnics which suggests

[1] 'Since the people of Cius are colonists of the city (Miletus) etc.' *Milet* I.3 no. 141, 1 ff. The document is dated on epigraphical arguments to the third century.

[2] Cf. above p. 44.

[3] οἱ δὲ Βορυσθενεῖται (for the two names see Strabo VII. 306) οὗτοι λέγουσι σφέας αὐτοὺς εἶναι Μιλησίους.

[4] See above p. 5 n. 7.

that there was a fluidity in their use which means that the ethnic alone can hardly determine legal questions about citizenship.

Some of this evidence relates to colonists of the first generation, who are variously described by the ethnic of their old and their new home. One, Herodicus of Megara or Selymbria, has been mentioned already.[1] The most distinguished example is Herodotus, who is given in the sources the ethnic of either Halicarnassus or Thurii.[2] The sculptor Pythagoras, who emigrated from Samos to Rhegium and is called a Rhegine by Pausanias,[3] signed himself Πυθαγόρας Σάμιος on the monument of Euthymus at Olympia.[4] Micythus of Rhegium and Messene also described himself by his old ethnics at Olympia, even though he was living at Tegea.[5] Praxiteles of Syracuse and Camarina, who had lived previously at Mantinea, is punctilious in giving two ethnics on his dedication at Olympia.[6] Cleomenes, Alexander's satrap of Egypt, is called Ἀλεξανδρεύς in one source,[7] though in all the others the ethnic of his original city is used (Ναυκρατίτης). These are ethnics of individuals, who could have been too proud of, or simply too accustomed to, their old homes to take exclusively to the name of the new. But they seem to show a freedom from legal considerations in the use of the ethnic.

Examples more precisely analogous to Herodotus' passage can be found in Thucydides. In describing the foundation of Himera from Zancle (VI.5.1) he writes Χαλκιδῆς μὲν οἱ πλεῖστοι ἦλθον,[8] though there is a perfectly good ethnic from Zancle, Ζαγκλαῖος.[9]

[1] Above p. 66.   [2] See RE Suppl. II 205 ff., 224 ff.
[3] E.g. IV.iv.4.
[4] Inschr. von Olympia pp. 247 ff. The view of Seltman (Num. Chron. 6th series ix, 1949, 19 ff) that this Pythagoras was actually a grandson of the philosopher Pythagoras, not a first generation settler from Samos, and that the signature therefore reveals pride in ancestry, seems to involve too many hypotheses.
[5] Inschr. von Olympia no. 267 and notes; however, the expression ϝοικέων ἐν Τεγέῃ may show that he was not a citizen of Tegea.
[6] ... Συρακόσιος ... καὶ Καμαριναῖος· πρόσθα δὲ Μαντινέαι ... ἔναιεν; see Jeffery, Local Scripts of Archaic Greece, Arcadia no. 120, p. 215. His two Sicilian cities are apparently to be explained by the transplantation of the population of Camarina to Syracuse by Gelon; see Jeffery 160 f.
[7] [Arist.] Oec. II.33a. See Van Groningen's notes ad loc. in his edition (Leyden 1933).
[8] 'Most of the settlers were Chalcidians'.
[9] See e.g. Hdt. VI.23.1.

The reason why he chooses to say Chalcidians here is, however, clear. Himera was a mixed colony, and he is looking forward to his remarks about the Chalcidian customs and the mixture of Doric and Chalcidic in the dialect. So the general ethnic was more suitable for his particular purpose than that of the particular Chalcidian city. Another example where his motive is again clear is his description of the Corcyreans (VII.57.7) as not only Dorian but manifestly Corinthian (Κορίνθιοι σαφῶς) in his list of the forces at Syracuse. They were manifestly not Corinthians legally, but they were by origin, and it is racial connections in which Thucydides was interested here. So where origin was the important matter, members of an old and independent colony could be given the ethnic of their mother city.

These examples show that Herodotus could have been merely expressing origin by his wording. But while Thucydides' and the first generation settlers' use of the legally incorrect ethnic can be explained, there is no obvious explanation for Herodotus'. It is just possible, therefore, that his choice of words (or that of the people of Olbia themselves) was dictated by the close relationship between colony and mother city.[1]

If inferences from Herodotus' words are uncertain and other evidence for the relations of Miletus and Olbia is lacking, the only safe way of estimating the antiquity of the arrangements recorded in the inscription is to consider how recently they could have been in force.[2] It may be assumed that the treaty was necessary because these arrangements had been in abeyance. The most obvious reason for this would be the Persian control of Miletus.[3] From the time of Cyrus' conquest of Lydia, c. 546, to the time of our treaty, Miletus was free from Persia only during the Ionian Revolt and as an ally, first of Athens, and secondly, for a brief period, of Sparta.[4] In view of this the most recent period to which the document could be referring

[1] Bilabel (137) considered that it showed pride in origin and good relations.
[2] This seems better than simply to assume that they had existed since the colony's foundation, as Zhebeliov (CR. Acad. des Sciences USSR, Classe des Humanités, 1929, 428, 435).
[3] Cf. Rehm, Milet I.3 p. 293.
[4] See RE s.v. Miletos 1594–1602 for a useful summary of its history during these years.

seems likely to have been the second half of the fifth century, when Miletus belonged to the Athenian Empire and had recovered sufficiently from the Persian destruction of the city in 494.[1] But it may be argued that Athens itself would not have tolerated such connections.[2] If we accept this argument, we must suppose that the document restates arrangements of the time before the Persian conquest. It would not be totally unrealistic to put them so early, for the sixth and seventh centuries were Miletus' great days as a commercial centre,[3] and the provision regarding lawsuits refers especially to cases likely to arise from commercial relations.[4] But while it is not impossible that the document describes relations which existed more than two hundred years before, it is clearly much less open to objection to think of them as practices of the fifth century, the time when Herodotus reports that the people of Olbia say that they are Milesians. These would be sufficiently old to have become traditional arrangements in c. 330.

There is a theory that Scythians formed an important element in the ruling class at Olbia, which would make shared citizen rights with the mother city in the fifth century or earlier less easy to envisage. The theory is expressed in Russian literature on the subject[5] but the evidence for the classical period does not support it. The philhellene Scythian ruler Scyles, who had a house in Olbia, is quite obviously an exceptional figure,[6] and in any case he was not a member of the ruling class there. The fifth-century graves of local Scythian type[7] in the Olbia necropolis certainly show that there were some Scythians in Olbia, as one would expect, but the prosopographical evidence[8] removes the possibility that they were among the important

[1] See Röhlig, _Der Handel von Milet_, 61.
[2] It was Athenian policy to keep her allies isolated according to the Old Oligarch; see [Xen.] _Ath. Pol._ II.2 f.
[3] See _RE_ s.v. Miletos 1590 ff for this period.
[4] This is not to suggest that examples of arrangements for such cases are attested so early.
[5] See p. 54 of D. B. Shelov's general survey, _Antichni Mir v severnom Prichernomorye_, Moscow 1956.
[6] See Hdt. IV.78 ff.
[7] For a publication of one of these and references to analogous material see S. I. Kaposhina, _Sovyetskaya Archeologia_ XIII 1950, 205 ff.
[8] This is very usefully assembled by T. Knipovich, _Materiali i Issledovaniya po archeologi SSSR_ no. 50, 136 ff.

citizens.[1] Of the names preserved on inscriptions from the sixth to the fourth centuries, only four are non-Greek, and among the names of magistrates none.[2] The relations of Olbia with the Scythians do not therefore enter into the question of her relations with Miletus.

The decree of the same period regulating relations between Miletus and Cyzicus[3] is unfortunately incomplete. Cyzicus was a Milesian foundation[4] of great antiquity; Eusebius records its foundation against two dates, 757 and 675, which may be reconciled by regarding the later expedition as a reinforcement. The earlier date has been indirectly supported by recent excavations which show that there were Greeks inland at Dascylium by c. 700.[5] The preserved part of the decree contains two provisions about relations between Miletus and Cyzicus: firstly (10 f) that the cities are to be friends for ever according to the traditional laws,[6] and secondly that there should be full isopolity between them.[7] This isopolity is also stated to have existed in the past, if the restoration καθότ[ι καὶ πρότερον ἦσαν is correct; it is a regular formula[8] and fits the sense well.

We thus have another restatement of past practices between Miletus and one of her colonies. The arrangement that the cities should be friends for ever is a little less clear in its meaning and value than that about citizenship. Colonies and mother cities were expected to be friends, not enemies, as has been seen;[9] this seems merely to provide for such a relationship.[10] However, Cyzicus and Miletus were not so far apart that international relations of war and peace were out of the question

[1] There is naturally no evidence that they were citizens at all. One wonders if they might have been mercenaries, for the graves are poor and simple and seem to belong to warriors; see Kaposhina op. cit. 207, 212 f.

[2] This is pointed out in refutation of Shelov by A. S. Kotzevalov in his review; see *Vestnik Instituta po Izucheniyu SSSR* 2 (30) (Munich) 1959, 116.

[3] *Milet* I.3 no. 137.

[4] For the evidence see Bilabel 46 f.

[5] See Akurgal, *Anatolia* I 1956, 24; cf. my remarks in *Bulletin of the Institute of Classical Studies* v, 1958, 32.

[6] τὰς μὲν πόλεις φίλας εἶναι ἐς τὸν ἅπαντα χρόνον κατὰ τὰ πάτρια.

[7] εἶναι δὲ τὸν Κυζικηνὸν ἐμ Μιλήτωι Μιλήσιον καὶ τὸν Μιλήσιον ἐν Κυζίκωι Κυζικηνόν (13 ff).

[8] Cf. the similar phrase (6 f) in the treaty with Olbia.

[9] See Chapter V.

[10] The meaning of φίλος is shown firstly by its being coupled with σύμμαχος; see e.g. Dem. IX.323; a friend was less than an ally. And secondly by Xenophon's use of it as the antonym of πολέμιος (*Hell.* VI.v.48).

(with Olbia they presumably were), and circumstances unknown to us may have urged them to make their friendly
relations a matter of legal provision. The isopolity here is complete and unconditional, so that in this respect too there is a
contrast with the Olbian arrangements.

In some respects, however, the treaties are more closely comparable. Once again there is no mention of the tie between
colony and mother city, but the reference to tradition and the
fact that Cyzicus was well known to be a Milesian colony
justify the conclusion that this relationship was the basis for the
mutual rights and there was no need to mention it. The arguments which were applied to the question of the date of the
arrangements said to have existed in the past in the agreement
with Olbia also apply here. At latest in the fifth century, and
possibly considerably earlier, Milesians had citizen rights in
Cyzicus and vice versa. The treaty with Cyzicus is less detailed
and practical than that with Olbia, and thus seems less convincing in its statements about the past, but detailed conditions
may have been included in the part now lost. It is permissible
to speculate whether there appeared among these a provision
for the regular offerings which we find Cyzicus making to
Apollo of Didyma in Hellenistic times.[1]

The decree referring to Istria[2] is much less informative, for
only parts of the opening lines are preserved. These belong to
the introduction, so that the purpose of the decree is not certainly known. Istria was a Milesian colony founded according to
the tradition in 657/6.[3] This fact and the analogy of the other
Milesian decrees led Robert[4] to interpret the whole document
as a decree of isopolity between Miletus and Istria, and to restore the opening lines accordingly. This interpretation seems
plausible, though it cannot be called certain. If Robert is right,
it is interesting that much more justification was necessary in the

---

[1] See Haussoulier, *Milet et le Didymeion*, p. 200, no. 2853, 8 f; p. 202, no.
2855, 18 f; p. 203, no. 2858, 8 f; p. 206, no. 5, 10 f; p. 209, no. 10, 17 f. The
offerings are always the same and always 'from the Cyzicenes'. We know
too that such offerings were imposed as a regular duty on Cius from the
third-century inscription *Milet* I.3 no. 141; cf. p. 315.

[2] See above, p. 99 n. 5.

[3] The earliest literary reference is Hdt. II.33.4. The sources are given by
Bilabel (19).

[4] See *BCH* lii 1928, 172.

opening lines than in either the Olbian treaty or that with Cyzicus: 'since the Istrians are friends and kinsmen of the people and preserve the formerly existing . . . friendship towards the people'. Just because it is more full this introduction implies that relations between Miletus and Istria had been less close. The reference to friendship may be compared with the arrangement for friendship in the treaty with Cyzicus.

The evidence about Olbia and Cyzicus shows that Miletus had arrangements of isopolity with these colonies at latest in the fifth century and possibly earlier. Does this suit the character of Milesian colonization? Herodotus calls the Greek cities of the northern Pontus *emporia* on several occasions.[1] He was therefore very conscious that they were trading centres. As we saw at the beginning of this chapter, Miletus' trade with these cities may be attested by the archaeological finds. The importance of the trade between Greece and the hinterland of the north Pontic coast is well known from the fifth century onwards,[2] and it is noteworthy that Miletus' colonization of this coast comes comparatively late in the Greek colonizing movement.[3] Her single much earlier foundation in the Black Sea,[4] Sinope, was situated on the south coast at a place not very suitable for trade,[5] and should be regarded as a colony of the normal Greek type, in which the settlers could hope to support themselves from the natural resources.[6] By the mid-seventh century Greek commerce was sufficiently developed for a leading city like Miletus to be conscious of trading possibilities, so that scholars are probably justified in seeing the colonization of the north Pontic coast as a clear example of colonization for commercial ends.[7] Roebuck's conclusion that Ionia needed to import grain from the

[1] E.g. IV.17.1; 20.1; 24; 108.2. Cf. above p. 5 n. 3.
[2] Cf. Herodotus' description (VII.147. 2 f) of the corn ships passing through the Hellespont seen by Xerxes. For the fourth century see Rostovtzeff, *Social and Economic History of the Hellenistic World* I 105–111.
[3] I discuss the dates of Greek colonies in the Black Sea in *Bulletin of the Institute of Classical Studies* v 1958, 25 ff.
[4] See ibid. Trapezus also has a high foundation date, but it is a colony of Sinope.
[5] Cf. Magie, *Roman Rule in Asia Minor* I. 185 ff, where it is noted that Amisus has better communications with the interior.
[6] Sinope was especially famous for fish; see Magie I.184; II.1076.
[7] See, e.g., Gwynn, *JHS* xxxviii 1918, 95; E. G. Minns, *Scythians and Greeks*, 439 ff.

early seventh century[1] supports this interpretation. The mother city thus had a strong interest in maintaining close relations and it would not be surprising if mutual citizenship and other privileges were arranged early between Miletus and her colonies.

We may now turn to the evidence about mutual citizenship and allied topics which comes not from Miletus but from other Greek cities. We have already noted[2] that it seems to have been common practice for mother cities to be able to send in further settlers to their colonies. This right to reinforce implies, where it existed, that citizens of the mother city were considered entitled to citizenship in the colony if they settled there.

The right of colonists to return to citizen rights in the mother city also emerged from the study of foundation decrees.[3] Apart from Hesiod's father,[4] the earliest event recorded which throws light on the exercise of this right is the refusal of the Eretrians to allow their colonists to return after they had been driven out of Corcyra.[5] We do not know how long they had been settled in Corcyra, so it is impossible to say whether they had a limited right of return which had become invalid, or no right of return, or some right of return which the men of the mother city violated. At least the account shows either that there was not an unlimited right of return, or that the mother city was not prepared to acknowledge such a right.

In the Cyrene decree[6] the colonists were allowed a grudging right of return even though the settlement was intended to relieve dangerous overpopulation at home. But in such cases the metropolis would be unwilling to respect the right in practice, and at Cyrene we are expressly told that the colonists were not allowed to land when they tried to return.[7] In the easy circumstances of the colony to Naupactus very generous conditions were laid down for the colonists' return, but an unconditional right to return was still withheld. It is also a probable assumption that the right of return was limited to the first settlers.

[1] *Ionian Trade and Colonization* 21.   [2] In chapter IV.
[3] See chapter IV.
[4] *Works and Days* 630–40; but the passage cannot be used as evidence for an actual relationship between a colony and mother city; the uncertainties are too many: e.g. Cyme's relationship to Boeotia (Strabo, XIII.621, says that Aeolic Cyme was founded from the Locrian mountain Phrikios, above Thermopylae), and the standing of Hesiod's father in Cyme and in Ascra.
[5] Plut. *Q.G.* XI. See Appendix I.   [6] See Chapter IV.
[7] Hdt. IV.156.3.

This was obviously so at Cyrene, and is implied at Naupactus by the wording of the decree.[1]

This evidence suggests that the colonist did not retain any automatic or permanent right to citizenship in the mother city. It is also unlikely that all colonies were in all circumstances bound to receive the citizens of the mother city. The right of the mother city to reinforce the colony must have been physically impracticable in many instances, where the land of the colony was strictly limited.[2] However, if mother cities and some colonies possessed the right to exclude the citizens of the other community, evidence for the reception of fugitives and exiles suggests that they might be prepared to waive it in case of need.

The earliest instance is the reception by Corcyra of the Bacchiad exiles from Corinth, who were expelled by Cypselus when he became tyrant in the middle of the seventh century.[3] This is an example where the exiles were political enemies of the government of the metropolis, so it is possible that political motives lay behind the action of the colony, which would make this instance a special case. But without further information it is vain to conjecture precise motives.

Next in time comes the reception by Massalia and Alalia of refugees from their metropolis Phocaea. The assumption that refugees from Phocaea were received by Massalia is made to explain the discrepancy between Massalia's well-attested foundation date, c. 600, and the tradition[4] that it was founded by those who fled after Phocaea was captured by Harpagus in c. 545. As both accounts are well-supported, the conclusion has been generally accepted that the colony was founded in 600 but reinforced by fugitives in 545, and if this is right we see a colony receiving fugitives from its metropolis. It is surprising, however, that Herodotus says nothing about it in his full account of Phocaean wanderings (I.164 ff), especially as he provides the evidence for their reception at Alalia, a colony founded twenty

[1] See Tod 24, 7 ff.
[2] Cf. the limitation of the right at a settlement in West Locris; see Chapter IV.
[3] Nic. Dam. frg. 57.7 (FGH IIA p. 357). The relations of Corinth and Corcyra are discussed below in Chapter VII.
[4] See e.g. Isoc. VI.84; Arist. frg. 549, (apud Harpocration s.v. Massalia); Timagenes frg. 2 (FGH IIA p. 320). The discrepancy is fully treated by Wackernagel; see RE s.v. Massalia 2130 f.

I

years before (I.165.1). In this instance the small gap in time
would mean that ties of blood and sentiment would still be
strong, and the numbers of the fugitives may have been too large
for the colonists to keep out, but they were certainly received on
friendly terms and lived with the previous settlers for five years,[1]
until the Etruscans and Carthaginians forced the abandonment
of the colony.[2]

Not much later than these events[3] some fugitives from Cyrene
were probably received by Thera. When Arcesilaus III regained power at Cyrene he sent his enemies to Cyprus to be
destroyed; but they were rescued by some Cnidians and sent to
Thera.[4] Herodotus' silence about their subsequent fate may be
taken as an indication that they were received into their mother
city.

An inscription found at Olympia,[5] containing a decree of
Selinus, not only testifies to the reception of exiles from the
metropolis,[6] but also shows some of the regulations made for
their status. It is unfortunately incomplete, but that this was its
purpose is clear.[7] The inscription is to be dated to the turn of
the sixth and fifth centuries, over 100 years after Selinus'
foundation from Megara Hyblaea in c. 628.[8]

The arrangements that can be identified in the decree refer
to financial[9] and legal matters.[10] These provisions are also made
to apply to the descendants of the exiles.[11] It appears that one of
the financial provisions arranged for some guarantee to safeguard the city if the exile returned to his homeland.[12] It also
appears that at least two waves of exiles had arrived, and the

[1] Hdt. I.166.1.   [2] Hdt. I.166.2.
[3] Chamoux, *Cyrène sous la monarchie des Battiades*, 151, calculates that
Arcesilaus' exile and recovery of power fall between 530 and 525.
[4] Hdt. IV.164. 1 f.   [5] *Inschr. von Olympia*, 22.
[6] Whether Megara Nisaea or Hyblaea is uncertain, though the latter
seems more likely; see Dunbabin 417 f, who notes that quarrels between
the rich and the people are reported in Megara Hyblaea by Herodotus
(VIII.156.2). It is also more probable that the number of exiles apparently
postulated by such a decree would come from the Sicilian city, as the editors
suggested in their notes to the inscription. But the example is even more
striking if the exiles were from the distant Megara Nisaea.
[7] Cf. Dunbabin's discussion, loc. cit.   [8] Thuc. VI.4.2.
[9] Frgs. *ab* 5 ff, 11 f; *def* 4 ff.   [10] Frgs. *ab* 8; *def* 5.
[11] Frgs. *ab* 12, 14 f.
[12] Frgs. *ab* 11, 9. This depends on the restorations of the editors. Of these
ἐπ]ανίτω is certain, so that the possibility of return seems definitely to have
existed.

firstcomers were not bound by oath regarding several of the matters arranged by the decree.[1]

We note that special arrangements for the exiles' status were necessary; they do not simply take up citizen rights in the colony. This is the more surprising since the residence envisaged for them may be long; provisions are made to apply to the second generation. The exiles seem to be condemned to a position different from that of citizens for a very long time. However, the reason for this may have been the possibility that they might return to their original city. They may have constituted a group separate from the citizens of their new city.

This may also explain the striking fact that a decree regulating domestic affairs should be set up at Olympia. Treaties of international importance were often displayed there,[2] but they are hardly comparable. However, another Sicilian city, Zancle, set up a decree there in the sixth century,[3] and another inscription contains exactly similar local regulations concerning the reception of exiles in some Chalcidian city.[4] Our decree is thus not without parallel. The reason why such a decree should be exhibited at Olympia may be that the exiles, if they belonged fully to no city, felt their position to be more secure if it was established by a decree set up at a Panhellenic religious centre.

The need for such legal provisions about the status of the exiles might suggest that the ties between colony and mother city had grown looser during the comparatively long time since the colony's foundation, though it may be that the first wave of immigrants were received more freely on an *ad hoc* basis, which the decree replaced.[5] But this is all conjecture. The value of the document, however uncertain its exact contents, is that it is the only primary evidence that has been preserved of the way in which the status of exiles from the metropolis could be regulated in a colony.[6]

---

[1] Frgs. *def* 5 ff.

[2] See Gardiner, *History and Remains of Olympia*, 112.

[3] *Inschr. von Olympia* 24.   [4] *Inschr. von Olympia* 25.

[5] If it is right that the first group was not bound to observe some of the provisions of the decree, as may be inferred from frgs. *def* 5 ff.

[6] A second example might be seen in the fragmentary bronze plaque of uncertain Sicilian provenance which mentions the Gamoroi (Jeffery, *Local Scripts of Archaic Greece*, 268 (no. 15)). But it is uncertain whether, as has been suggested (see Dunbabin 415; Guarducci, *Annuario d. Scuol. arch. d. Atene*, n.s. xxi–xxii 1959–60, 254–258), the document is to be connected with the

When Sybaris was destroyed by Croton in 511/10,[1] Herodotus relates (VI.21.1) that the fugitives went to Laus and Scidrus. The first of these was the chief Sybarite colony after Posidonia.[2] Scidrus was a less important city and is assumed, almost certainly rightly, to be a Sybarite colony.[3] They were probably both dependents of Sybaris,[4] and the large number of fugitives from the dominant mother city could, no doubt, insist that place be made for them in their subject colonies. These are, in consequence, not very good examples of colonies receiving fugitives from the mother city.

Posidonia, however, was probably independent of its mother city.[5] Early in the fifth century the coinage of Posidonia changes to the Achaean standard, and the bull, the traditional badge of Sybaris, appears regularly as the type on the reverse of its coins. Macdonald suggested[6] that the reason for this was that a sufficient number of Sybarite refugees had been received there to form a sort of synoecism, and this seems very plausible. There are some further coins of Sybaris or Posidonia[7] which could be held to show that the result of the synoecism was something like sympolity. Some have the types of Posidonia but the legend of Sybaris, others are similar but bear both Sybarite and Posidoniate inscriptions. The interpretation of numismatic evidence standing alone like this is bound to be uncertain,[8] but these various coins seem to reflect an unusual mingling of mother city and colony.

---

expulsion of the Gamoroi from Syracuse and their refuge in Casmenae (Hdt. VII.155.2). In any case Casmenae, as a dependent of Syracuse (see Chapter V), had presumably no choice in the matter.

[1] Full account in Dunbabin 362 ff.
[2] See Strabo VI.253; Dunbabin 155 f.   [3] See Dunbabin loc. cit.
[4] See Dunbabin 82 f, 155 f, and Chapter V above.
[5] See Chapter V.   [6] *Coin Types* 115.
[7] For these see Head, *HN*[2] p. 85.
[8] Thus Head explained the latter group as alliance coins, which proved that Posidonia helped in the recolonization of Sybaris. The late Dr. Charles Seltman, who kindly discussed the coins with me, objected to this that an alliance coinage should contain large denominations, while the examples extant are very small. Seltman's own explanation, however, by the analogy of Pyxus, which would make them coins of Posidonia (see *Num. Chron.* 6th series, ix, 1949, 2) is unsatisfactory, because the analogy is not exact. The attractive suggestion that the small bird on one of these coins is a Blue Stone-thrush and commemorates the help given to Sybaris by Laus, whose emblem it was (see *JHS* lxxxi 1961 47 f) implies that the coins are commemorative in purpose.

Neapolis (Naples) was considered a colony of Cumae,[1] and when Samnites took the latter city in *c.* 420, the inhabitants fled to Neapolis where they met a friendly reception.[2] They were very near to their colony, and also sufficiently numerous, it appears, to form a new settlement,[3] but in spite of these special factors, this seems a valid example of the reception of fugitives from the metropolis by the colony.

While it is true that it was generally recognized in Greece that it was a pious and praiseworthy act to receive fugitives,[4] these examples concerning colonies and mother cities show the way in which the relationship between the two communities made it possible for citizens of one to transfer to the other. They are thus comparable with the examples discussed above of the colonists' right to return and the right of the metropolis to reinforce in being evidence of practices related to isopolity. At Posidonia the reception of a large number of fugitives may even have produced a fifth-century example of sympolity, but this is uncertain. Within the time limits of the present study there remains one further example of isopolity between colony and mother city.

Epizephyrian Locri was founded by the Locrians of Greece in *c.* 673.[5] Polybius states (XII.5 ff) that the colony was founded by thieves, vagabonds, etc., and cites Aristotle as support, but Dunbabin finds reasons to prefer Timaeus' account that it was a properly established colony of respectable people. Timaeus' account, as Polybius (XII.9) has reported it, included the information that he was shown among the Locrians of Greece decrees establishing isopolity between colony and metropolis (καθ' ἃ πολιτείαν ὑπάρχειν ἑκατέροις παρ' ἑκατέροις).

Polybius thought that Timaeus was simply lying about these matters, but his reasons are slight. He suggests that Timaeus' failure to specify the Locrian city in which he saw the decrees shows that he had fabricated them. But, as Bérard pointed out (204), if Timaeus did not distinguish the Locrians to which he was referring, it was because he agreed with Aristotle on this

---

[1] See Strabo V.246; Livy VIII.22.5.
[2] Dion. Hal. *Ant. Rom.* XV.6; cf. Strabo V.243, Diod. XII.76.4.
[3] See *RE* s.v. Neapolis, 2115; *CAH* VII.594 f.
[4] Cf. Eur. *Suppl.* the thought behind 112 ff, 184 ff; *Heraclidae* 329 f; Soph. *O.C.* 261 f.
[5] Full account and sources in Dunbabin, 35 ff.

point; for we know from Polybius that Timaeus was criticizing
Aristotle's account; and Aristotle implies that the colony was
founded from Opuntian Locris.[1] A positive reason for believing
that Timaeus did see these decrees is that he was famous for
finding and copying such documents.[2]

There is a more serious objection in Polybius' statement that
he had been told that there was no memory or record of such
treaties in Epizephyrian Locri.[3] Memories on matters of this
sort were not short in Greek cities. A convincing explanation is
to hand, however. A particularly ferocious revolution took place
in Epizephyrian Locri in c. 346 after its rule by Dionysius the
Younger.[4] In the revolution it seems that the records and fundamental laws of the earlier, aristocratically-ruled, city were
destroyed or perverted.[5] This attempt by the revolutionaries to
discredit the rule of their predecessors, and to cut off the city
under its new constitution from its history under the old, may
well have included the destruction of the records of relations
established in the earlier period between the city and its metropolis.

If accepted, this suggestion provides the *terminus ante quem* of
346 for the decrees.[6] Probably it should be as early as 356,
when Dionysius fled from Syracuse and became tyrant of
Locri,[7] since treaties of isopolity between the colony and its
metropolis seem unlikely to have been made under his rule. If,
on similar reasoning, they are thought to precede the reign of
Dionysius I at Syracuse, during which the relations between
Syracuse and Locri became close,[8] the date of the decrees is put

---

[1] See Bérard 204. Opus is said to have been the metropolis of Epizephyrian Locri by Ps-Scymnus (316f), and Pausanias' information (III.19.12)
that the Italian Locrians appealed for help in war from Ajax, son of Oeleus,
'owing to their kinship with the Opuntians' is, if not decisive, further support for this view.

[2] See Polybius XII.11, especially the words καὶ μὴν ὁ τὰς ὀπισθοδόμους
στήλας καὶ τὰς ἐν ταῖς φλιαῖς τῶν νεῶν προξενίας ἐξευρηκὼς Τίμαιός ἐστι.

[3] XII. 6: συνθῆκαι δὲ πρὸς τοὺς κατὰ τὴν Ἑλλάδα Λοκροὺς οὔτ' ἦσαν οὔτ'
ἐλέγοντο παρ' αὐτοῖς γεγονέναι.

[4] A full account of this is given by Oldfather; see *RE* s.v. Lokroi 1336.

[5] For instance, Oldfather considers that the unlikely story of the origin of
the Hundred Houses was then invented in order to discredit the rule of the
aristocracy; see *RE* loc. cit.

[6] The date of the decrees is not recorded, but Timaeus' lifetime, c. 346–
260 (see *OCD* s.v. Timaeus), provides a certain, if approximate, *terminus
ante quem*.

[7] See Oldfather, 1335.   [8] See Oldfather, 1335 ff.

back into the fifth century. These arguments are at best only probable, but it is not unreasonable to say that the decrees which Timaeus saw show that isopolity existed between Epizephyrian Locri and her metropolis not later than the first half of the fourth century.

In the previous chapter it was seen that there was no un-equivocal evidence for sympolity or isopolity between Thasos and her mother city or Thasos and her colonies. Some evidence, however, especially Akeratos' dedication,[1] suggested at least relations close enough to approach such shared citizenship. Miletus certainly had isopolity with her colonies of Olbia and Cyzicus, which, though only definitely attested rather later, should probably be dated to the fifth century or even earlier. Colonies close to the mother city sometimes occupied an ill-defined position between separate communities and outlying parts of the founding state. Various arrangements for citizens of one community to transfer to the other are found early, and are signs that even in early times there was no rigid barrier against opening the citizenship of one community to citizens of the other. The precise statement of the Naupactus decree that the colonist should lose his old citizenship,[2] and inferences from the evidence about the right to return, seem to show that shared citizenship was not normal in ordinary colonization. But the evidence about Miletus, Thasos, the colonies at a short distance, and the practices which approximate to shared citizenship, shows that isopolity was an easy development in the relations between colonies and mother cities, once the concept had been evolved.

[1] See Chapter V. His magistracy at Paros might be compared with the Milesians' right to become magistrates at Olbia.
[2] See Chapter IV.

CHAPTER VII

CORINTH AND THE COLONIAL EMPIRE

αἱ γοῦν ἄλλαι ἀποικίαι τιμῶσιν ἡμᾶς (sc. τοὺς Κορινθίους)
καὶ μάλιστα ὑπὸ ἀποίκων στεργόμεθα.[1] Thuc. I. 38.3.

CORINTH's relations with her colonies are more fully documented than those of any other Greek city apart from
Athens in the fifth century. This is, no doubt, partly due to the
chances which have determined what sources are available for
Greek history, but it also shows the importance of these relations in Corinthian affairs. The colonies with which these important relations were maintained were the foundations of the
tyrants and the two great pre-tyrant colonies of Syracuse and
Corcyra.[2] We have already seen[3] that the colonies of the tyrants
were established as dependent colonies of the mother city. Now
the subsequent relations between Corinth and these colonies
need to be examined in order to see how far Corinth maintained
a colonial empire and what status the colonies enjoyed. To this
subject most of the present chapter is devoted. After that
Corinth's relations with Syracuse and Corcyra and Corcyra's
relations with her colonies will be discussed in two further
sections, as both are important for our understanding of
Corinthian colonial practices and Greek colonial empires.

The Corinthian colonial empire[4]

The colonies which seem relevant to a discussion of the
Corinthian colonial empire are the four whose foundations have
been treated above, Leucas, Ambracia, Anactorium and

[1] 'At least the other colonies honour us (i.e. the Corinthians), and we are
especially beloved by colonists.'
[2] Corinth's relations with Megara might also appear to be relevant; I
discuss these in Appendix IV.
[3] In Chapter III.
[4] I follow the traditional dating of the Cypselids (*c.* 655–*c.* 582). A
defence of these dates against Beloch's drastic lowering (*Griech. Geschichte*
I.2,274 ff) was given by Wade-Gery (*CAH* III 764 f), and Will's additional
arguments in favour of Beloch's hypothesis (*Korinthiaka* 406–420) are not
convincing.

Potidaea, Apollonia in Illyria which was founded jointly with the Corcyreans,[1] and three lesser settlements, Sollium, Chalcis (in Aetolia) and Molycrium. Information about these last is meagre, and is almost confined to brief descriptions by Thucydides. Sollium is called Κορινθίων πόλισμα (II.30.1), Chalcis Κορινθίων πόλιν (I.108.5) and Molycrium τὴν Κορινθίων ἀποικίαν (III.102.2). The site of Chalcis at the western end of the Corinthian Gulf is known,[2] and Molycrium, whatever its exact position, was in the same region,[3] but Sollium can only be conjectured to have been on the mainland opposite Leucas.[4] There is no information about the dates at which they were settled, but modern scholars have regularly included them in the same expansion of the Cypselids, which established the better known Corinthian colonies in the area.[5]

The very phrase Corinthian colonial empire recalls Kahrstedt's study[6] of these eight dependent colonies. In this he assembled the main evidence on the topic and advanced the bold theory that the colonies were no more than outlying parts of the mother city, their citizens no different from citizens of Corinth. His work has strongly influenced and still dominates the views of some ancient historians. Thus Hampl used some of his arguments to reach a different conclusion: the colonies were separate states but Corinth owned their land;[7] and he is followed by Gschnitzer.[8] Without occupying such extreme positions Will merely cites Kahrstedt's arguments and accepts in principle his main conclusion.[9] My own discussion is therefore necessarily often concerned with the refutation of Kahrstedt's mistaken conclusions.

The evidence about the status of the colonies is of three kinds: express information of a political nature from ancient sources, coins, and the expressions used by Greek authors to describe the colonies. Not all Kahrstedt's arguments from this evidence need

---

[1] The sources are given and discussed below pp. 130 f.
[2] See Gomme, Commentary to I.108.5.
[3] See Gomme, Commentary to II.84.4.
[4] See Gomme, Commentary to II.30.1.
[5] See e.g. RE s.v. Sollion 932; Gomme, Commentary to III.102.1; Will, Korinthiaka 520.
[6] Das korinthische Kolonialreich in Griech. Staatsrecht I,357 ff.
[7] Klio xxxii 1939, 39 ff.
[8] Abhängige Orte im griech. Altertum ch. 23.
[9] See La Nouvelle Clio vi 1954, 413 ff, especially 414 f; Korinthiaka 522 f.

to be reconsidered, for several are either quite mistaken or in-
sufficiently considered. For example the passage Thuc. I.55.1
(καὶ τῶν Κερκυραίων ὀκτακοσίους μὲν οἳ ἦσαν δοῦλοι ἀπέδοντο
(sc. οἱ Κορίνθιοι) κτλ.) is understood by Kahrstedt (359) to show
that the Corcyrean settlers in Anactorium had kept Corcyrean
citizenship, from which he infers that the Corinthian settlers
there possessed Corinthian citizenship. But this passage does
not refer to inhabitants of Anactorium at all, but to Corcyrean
prisoners taken at the Battle of Sybota, as is perfectly clear if
the sentence is read in its surrounding context. Kahrstedt's
treatment of the evidence from the coins of the colonies may
also be left on one side. It is clear that in the fourth century the
Corinthian pegasus was adopted as a coin type very generally in
the West for commercial reasons, even by cities with no political
connections with Corinth.[1] So the fourth-century use of the
pegasus coin type cannot be taken, as it is by Kahrstedt (363),
to show relations between the colonies and Corinth. It is also
perhaps sufficient to indicate the absurd conclusions to which
Kahrstedt is forced by his thesis in order to discredit it in
general. Thus he has to maintain that Molycrium and Potidaea
were in theory rebels from Corinth because they were allies
of Athens (362), and that Corcyra had given up its existence as
a separate state because Corcyreans took part in Timoleon's
expedition (363). His use of the expressions with which the
colonies are described by ancient authors cannot, however, be
dismissed quite so summarily. It is especially in this part of his
work that Kahrstedt has been followed by other scholars.[2]

These expressions describe some of the colonies as 'a city of
the Corinthians' or the like, and were taken by Kahrstedt to
show that the colonies were simply part of the Corinthian state.
There are four instances, one from Demosthenes (IX.34) and
three from Thucydides: IV.49, II.30.1, and I.108.5, referring
severally to Anactorium, Sollium and Chalcis. Although exact
parallels to these expressions are not found in Thucydides, a
detailed study of his terminology (which may be assumed to be
more exact than Demosthenes') seems to show that confident
generalizations about the legal status of all Corinthian colonies

[1] See Head, *HN*[2] pp. 406 f, for all the cities which issued pegasi; and
Macdonald, *Coin Types*, 83, for their commercial significance.
[2] As Will, *Korinthiaka* 522 f.

should not be made from the three descriptions. They show that the three cities were, in an undefined way, in Corinth's power, but the analogies provide no justification for the conclusion that they or the other colonies were legally part of the Corinthian state.[1]

Outside Thucydides' own work, the most illuminating analogy of the right date for his expressions is Herodotus' description of Stryme as a city of the Thasians (Θασίων πόλις; VIII.108). The status of the mainland colonies of Thasos has been described already.[2] They were under very close political control by the mother city, but were apparently not simply parts of the Thasian state. But before further analogies are applied, other evidence on the status of the Corinthian colonies must be considered.

Any discussion of the relations between Corinth and her colonies must include the evidence from coins, for some of the colonies struck coins identical in weight and type with those of the mother city, and distinguished from them only by the different ethnic.[3] As has been seen, coins with the Corinthian pegasus as their type were widely issued in Western Greece, Sicily and Magna Graecia in the fourth century. The reasons for this can be shown to have been purely commercial,[4] so that no conclusions about connections with Corinth can be drawn from the fact that a city adopted the pegasus in the fourth century. We must therefore confine our attention to the three Corinthian colonies which issued pegasi from early in the fifth century: Leucas, Ambracia and Anactorium.

In his very detailed study of the coins of Ambracia,[5] which must be the basis for any conclusions about the coins of these colonies and their significance,[6] Ravel has shown (20 ff) that the first pegasi of Ambracia were issued about 480, and (82 f)

---

[1] For a detailed study of these and analogous expressions in Thucydides see my paper *Historia* xi 1962, 246 ff.

[2] In Chapter V.   [3] See Head, *HN*[2] p. 406 f.

[4] See especially Macdonald, *Coin Types*, 83.

[5] *The Colts of Ambracia*, New York 1928, in the series *Numismatic Notes and Monographs*.

[6] It is therefore unfortunate that Will has not seen Ravel's book (*see La Nouvelle Clio* vi 1954, 416 n. 4 and *Korinthiaka* 524 n. 3); as a result he simply includes the evidence from the coins in his accounts of the Corinthian colonies, without discussing exactly what this evidence means; see *La Nouvelle Clio* vi 1954, 416 and *Korinthiaka* 524.

that among these earliest coins there are some which were struck from dies also used for coins of Corinth. As Ravel rightly concludes (ibid.), these coins must have been struck at Corinth. Thus the earliest coins of Ambracia were not only, except for the initial A, identical with those of the mother city, but some at least were actually made there. When this information is combined with the fact that the early coins of Ambracia are very rare,[1] it is natural to infer that Ambracia used Corinthian coins before 480, and to a great extent for a considerable time after that date. The question raised by the coinage of Ambracia (and, it may be assumed, of Leucas and Anactorium) has therefore two aspects: the use of the metropolis' coins, and the issue of coins identical with those of the metropolis.

Because of their character coins can have both commercial and political significance, and those under discussion can be interpreted from both these points of view. As the simpler the commercial aspect may be taken first. Throughout the history of Greek coinage, but especially in early times, it was not uncommon for the coins of one city to be used by others. The 'turtles' of Aegina were, for instance, the common currency of the Peloponnese in the early period.[2] In the archaic period, when mints were still comparatively few, the colonies in the North-West would naturally prefer to use the famous pegasi of Corinth than a less acceptable coinage of their own. It may be that Sollium, Chalcis and Molycrium never issued coins for the same reason.[3] Similar motives might also be expected to lead to the copying of an established coinage,[4] and it is notable that Ambracia was careful to distinguish her coins from those of Corinth by no more than a single letter, the initial A.

So the commercial significance of the coinage of the colonies seems easily understood. Their commercial connections were such that the currency most acceptable to them was that of Corinth. Ravel's discoveries make it possible to go somewhat further. If these colonies not only used Corinthian coins and

[1] See Ravel 82 f.
[2] See Head, *HN*[2] p. 395. Cf. also the 'owls' of Athens, which spread all over the ancient world; see Head, *HN*[2] pp. 373, 377.
[3] Though their small size would also partly account for it, as Kahrstedt 361.
[4] Though such copying by Greek states is not generally found.

copied Corinthian coins, but even had some at least of their first coins made at Corinth, it is reasonable to conclude that they had very close commercial and personal connections with the mother city.

The political interpretation of the colonies' coinage is more difficult. This is partly because no generally valid rules can be established for the political interpretation of Greek coins. Thus if the right to issue silver coins is thought to be an undeniable sign of autonomy,[1] these coins may be taken to show that the colonies were independent. If, on the other hand, identity of type and standard is interpreted as revealing a political connection, the coins show that the colonies were connected to Corinth in a subordinate position.[2] If generalizations lead to such an ambivalent interpretation of the coins, the basis for such generalizations must be examined.

It is not difficult to show that from the fifth century one of the restrictions which could be imposed on the autonomy of a Greek state was to prevent it from issuing its own silver coinage.[3] The clearest example is the famous Athenian currency decree,[4] which attempted to establish the coins of Athens as the sole silver coinage in the Athenian Empire. The corollary of this—that if a city issued silver coins it was autonomous—is probably true of the later Greek world. The issue of coins was a matter of political prestige, as may be seen from the agreement between Mytilene and Phocaea to issue coins in alternate years[5] (in this case of 'gold', i.e. electrum). This is a commercial agreement, involving the use of the same coins by two cities, but it is necessary to establish strict equality in the issue of the coins: otherwise, it may be presumed, their status as independent cities was thought to be impugned.

But this evidence is from the early fourth century.[6] Early in the fifth Leontini was reduced to subjection by Hippocrates of

---

[1] As Macdonald, Coin Types, 10.

[2] This has been the common interpretation; see e.g. Will, Korinthiaka 524; Kahrstedt 361.

[3] It is interesting to note that the evidence about the rights of coinage collected by Gardner (A History of Ancient Coinage 36 ff) all relates to restrictions of the right to issue coins.

[4] ATL II D.14. For a discussion of its date and effect see Robinson, Hesperia Suppl. VIII.320 ff. The date remains a matter of dispute, but does not affect the argument here.

[5] Tod II 112.   [6] See Tod II p. 34.

Gela.[1] It may be assumed that it continued to be subject to his successor, Gelon.[2] Yet Leontini was able to issue silver coins during this period inscribed with its own ethnic.[3] It follows that the issue of silver coins does not prove independence.[4]

The coins of Leontini are also relevant to the second generalization: that identity of type and standard, or of type alone, reveals a political connection; for one of the types on these coins, a quadriga, is the same as Gelon's own coins of Syracuse and Gela.[5] The type of a Greek coin was originally the symbol of the state that issued it like a seal or badge[6] so that the adoption of the same type by another city should imply a political connection. However, as coinage became common, and various motives influenced the choice of type, the immediate connection between a single type and a single state was often lost.[7] It is therefore wrong to argue *a priori* that the use of identical types by different states is politically significant. The coins of Leontini show that identity of type can reveal a political connection, but we have already seen that in the fourth century the Corinthian type was adopted by other states for commercial reasons.[8] This discussion of generalizations shows that they cannot be universally applied, so we must have recourse to more precise analogies for the coins in question.

Since the coins were issued by colonies, they should be compared first with Greek colonial coinage in general. The practice of Greek colonies regarding their coinages differed; some adopted the types of the metropolis, others did not. Gardner attempted to promulgate a general rule to account for this difference.[9] Of the colonies founded before the invention of coinage few, if any, adopted the types of the mother city, but those founded after the invention did so. The validity of this

[1] See Hdt.VII.154.2, where the word δουλοσύνη is used to describe Leontini's position. Dunbabin (383) shows that it was probably ruled by one of Hippocrates' officers as a subordinate tyrant.
[2] As Dunbabin 418.   [3] Head, *HN*[2] 148 f.
[4] Chantraine's interesting hypotheses about close personal connections between the rulers of Gela/Syracuse and Leontini do not affect this formal argument; see *Jahrb. f. Numismatik u. Geldges.* viii 1957, 7 ff.
[5] See Head, *HN*[2] p. 140.
[6] See Seltman, *Greek Coins*[2], 28.
[7] See Macdonald, *Coin Types*, 71 f.
[8] See above pp. 120 f.
[9] See *A History of Ancient Coinage*, 44 ff.

rule depends on a fairly high date for the earliest Greek coins,[1] but it is probably true in general.[2] The types of coins became part of the *nomima* which the colonists would take over from the mother city.[3] On this rule Gardner explained the difference between Corcyra and Syracuse on the one hand, which did not adopt Corinthian types, and the later colonies which did. There is perhaps some truth in this explanation. But the coins of Ambracia, Leucas and Anactorium do not merely bear a Corinthian type; they are as near as possible identical with the coins of Corinth. They seem to require, therefore, more explanation than Gardner's rule about colonial coinage provides.

Among actual coins there are two very close analogies to the coins in question. Some of the early coins of Dicaea, an Eretrian colony, are the same in type and weight as those of the mother city, and are only distinguished by a different inscription.[4] These coins are approximately dated to the first half of the fifth century.[5] However, at the same period Dicaea also issued coins with different types[6] so that her coinage is not exactly parallel to that of the Corinthian colonies in question. It is also, unfortunately, impossible to make any firm statements about Dicaea's relations with Eretria. Neither the site of Dicaea[7] nor its foundation date are known. It is only the evidence from the Athenian tribute lists that confirms that it was an Eretrian colony.[8]

Thus the coins of Dicaea, though exactly analogous to those

---

[1] A general lowering of the dates of the early silver coins of Greece was proposed by Brown (*Num. Chron.* 6th series, x, 1950, 177 ff, cf. *Schweiz. Münzblätter* iv 1953, 49 ff). However his arguments are often weak, especially those from historical probability, and those from stylistic parallels in other branches of art are inevitably uncertain. He is rightly criticized on these points by Will, *Korinthiaka* 489 n. 3.

[2] It is clearly not of universal application. Perinthus, for example, founded from Samos *c.* 600 (see *RE* s.v. Perinthos 805) does not use Samian types. However, it did not strike coins till the fourth century; see Head, *HN*[2] p. 270.

[3] See Chapter I.

[4] For descriptions of the coins see Head, *HN*[2] 213; the close similarity with those of Eretria is well shown by Seltman's illustrations, *Greek Coins*[2] Pl. XI 1, 2, 3.

[5] See Head loc. cit.; Seltman 67.   [6] See Head loc. cit.

[7] See *ATL* I Gazetteer s.v. Δικαιοπολῖται ᾽Ερετριῶν ἄποικοι on this point.

[8] See *ATL* I Register s.v. In order to distinguish its contributions from those of Δίκαια παρ᾽ ῎Αβδηρα, they are described in the earlier lists as from Δικαιοπολῖται ᾽Ερετριῶν ἄποικοι. Later the description was simpler: Δίκαια or

of the Corinthian colonies, contribute little to their interpretation. A second close analogy may be found in the sixth-century
coins of the Boeotian League.[1] The coins of the several cities
have the same type, the Boeotian shield, and are identical in
every other way, except that they bear different letters, the
initials of the various ethnics.[2] The coins are so alike that they
have been thought to emanate from a single mint.[3] In the fifth
century, after the Battle of Coronea, Thebes seems to have
monopolized the right to issue coins for Boeotia, and her coins
at that time also bore the Boeotian shield as their main type.[4]
From this it might be argued that the earliest, anepigraphic,
coins bearing this type were Theban,[5] and that in their slightly
later coinages the other cities of Boeotia were copying the coins
of Thebes, except for the initial letters of the ethnic. In this case
the parallel with the coins of the Corinthian colonies would be
exact. But as it is likely that the earliest Boeotian mint was at
Tanagra,[6] it may be that the earliest, uninscribed, coins bore a
common type of Boeotia, which Thebes later assumed as hers
alone. However this may be, the actual coins are so closely
similar in character to those of Corinth and her colonies, that
the political arrangements which lie behind the coins must be
considered.

Our certain knowledge of the early Boeotian League is
strictly limited.[7] The best indication of its nature is Herodotus'
account of the Corinthian arbitration in Thebes' dispute with
Plataea (VI.108.5). They laid it down that ἐᾶν Θηβαίους
Βοιωτῶν τοὺς μὴ βουλομένους ἐς Βοιωτοὺς τελέειν.[8] It may be
inferred from this that there was Theban hegemony but
the member states could theoretically decide for themselves

Δικαιοπολῖται Ἐρετριῶν. The temptation to regard the latter description as
parallel with Thucydides' terms for the Corinthian colonies discussed above
should probably be resisted. The earlier fuller description implies that the
later Δίκαια Ἐρετριῶν was shorter formula adopted for convenience only.

[1] For descriptions see Head, HN² pp. 343 ff, but Seltman's more recent
account, Greek Coins² 55 f, is slightly different.

[2] Some are illustrated in Seltman Pl. V.

[3] Cf. Seltman 55.   [4] See Head, HN² p. 349.

[5] As they are classified in Head loc. cit.

[6] See Seltman loc. cit.

[7] The evidence is given in Busolt/Swoboda, 1412.

[8] 'The Thebans are not to interfere with those of the Boeotians who do
not wish to count as Boeotians.'

whether or not they would belong to the league. It is not certain that they kept freedom and equality when they did become league members.[1] In two passages of Thucydides (II.2.4; III.66.1) it is strongly implied that there was a regular form of alliance traditionally laid down for the league states, and in a perhaps tendentious justification for their actions against Plataea (III.61.2) Thucydides makes the Thebans claim that it was laid down at the beginning, when they founded Plataea, that Thebes should have hegemony, and that the Plataeans were transgressing traditional laws when they turned to Athens for help. The Theban contention that it was an offence against traditional laws to make an alliance outside Boeotia, combined with the remark about Theban hegemony, may be taken to mean that Thebes claimed as a traditional right control over the foreign policy of Boeotian states.

Both the extent of Theban control and the date (and perhaps the existence) of the traditional laws on which it was based are uncertain. But the dispute with Plataea, probably in 519,[2] shows that Thebes was asserting definite control at that time. This is approximately the date of the coins under discussion. These coins were therefore issued by states closely connected in a league under the control of Thebes. If the coins have political significance,[3] these are the circumstances they reflect. As has been stated, the coins themselves are exactly analogous to those of the Corinthian colonies in being identical except for the initials of the different ethnics. They may even originally have been made at one mint, as the early coins of Ambracia were made at Corinth. It can therefore be said that if the only evidence for the status of the Corinthian colonies in question

[1] Ehrenberg notes that the constitution of the league of the fifth century (see *Hell. Ox.* XI) strangely and artificially combined Theban supremacy with the claim to equality of status of at least the most important other states; see *Der Staat der Griechen* I,94. The autonomy of the league states has been assumed because they had the right to issue coins; as, for instance, by Martin (*La Vie Internationale en Grèce des Cités*, 41) and Busolt/Swoboda (1411). It has been seen that this assumption cannot automatically be made from coins in the sixth or fifth centuries.

[2] The date is not certain; see *CAH* IV.78.

[3] It is possible that common origin and cults could lead to the adoption of a common coin type; cf. Busolt/Swoboda 1409 ff. But the other evidence for political, in addition to racial and religious, connections, suggests that the Boeotian coins should not be divorced from the political circumstances of the Boeotian states.

K

were their coins, they would be assumed, on the closest analogy available, to be connected in a political union under the control of Corinth.

Of the three kinds of evidence used to establish the status of these colonies two, the expressions employed to describe them and the coins, have now been discussed. There remains the express information of a political nature from ancient writers. In some of their statements the precise political implications are hard to establish. In the first place the word ἀπέλαβον in the passage Thuc. V.30.2, where the Corinthians want to receive back Sollium and Anactorium, was added by Kahrstedt (358) to the evidence which he interpreted as showing that the Corinthian colonies were part of the Corinthian state. The legitimate conclusions from the word may be found by comparison with other Thucydidean statements about exchange of territory at the same period.

In the Peace of Nicias territories to be given back (ἀποδόντων) to the Spartans include the island of Atalante, Pylus, Cythera, Methana and Pteleon.[1] Atalante was an island off Hypocnemidian Locris, previously uninhabited, but taken and garrisoned by the Athenians in 431.[2] It is clear that it is not legally part of Sparta's territory. Of the other places only Pylus and Cythera could be so described.[3] They are all territories which belonged in some way or other to the Peloponnesian side, and which Athens had captured in the war. Sollium and Anactorium were in the same category.[4] The word ἀπέλαβον is thus exactly comparable to ἀποδόντων and has the same general significance.

Other passages referring to Anactorium are not clear in their implications. We have seen that Kahrstedt was entirely mistaken in applying the latter part of the passage Thuc. I.55.1 (the phrases after ἐπ' οἴκου)[5] to Anactorium. But the preceding statements deserve attention. The Corinthians, as they sailed home after the Battle of Sybota in 433, took Anactorium by a trick and established Corinthian settlers in it. In explanation of their action Thucydides adds in parenthesis ἦν δὲ κοινὸν Κερκυραίων

---

[1] Thuc. V.18.7.   [2] Thuc. II.32.
[3] On Cythera see Chapter V. It is uncertain which Pteleon is meant; see Gomme Commentary ad loc.
[4] See Thuc. II.30.1; IV.49.
[5] The punctuation in the Oxford Text is questionable; a colon, or even a full stop, after οἴκου, would seem more appropriate than a comma.

καὶ ἐκείνων. If these genitives are like those noted above, Anactorium was in some degree a common possession of Corcyra and Corinth. The Corinthian capture of it turned it into a possession of Corinth alone, Κορινθίων πόλιν (IV.49). But the concept of a city which was a joint possession of Corcyra and Corinth is not easy, and is perhaps only to be understood by comparison with the situation in other states of the same area in the same period.

The most obvious analogy is Leucas. In no source is Leucas called anything but a Corinthian colony. Yet Plutarch relates (*Them.* XXIV.1) that Themistocles was called in to arbitrate between Corcyra and Corinth concerning their right to Leucas, and decided that Corinth should pay a fine of twenty talents and that they should own Leucas in common as a colony of both (Λευκάδα κοινῇ νέμειν ἀμφοτέρων ἄποικον). Plutarch's information may be accepted as reliable, for Thucydides apparently knew of the same event.[1] It could be assumed from Plutarch's passage that Leucas was a joint foundation of Corcyra and Corinth, for the fine shows that the Corinthians were legally in the wrong, so that Corcyra must have had some good claim to a share in the control of the island. The foundation of Leucas is attributed generally to Cypselus, as has been seen,[2] but Plutarch makes it a foundation of Periander (*de sera num. vind.* 552 E). This difference may be reconciled by making Periander's action a reinforcement.[3] If this is correct, the Corcyrean element could well have been introduced then, when Corcyra was under Periander's control.[4]

Whether or not this is the right way to explain Corcyra's rights over Leucas, it seems clear that the compromise arranged by Themistocles, whatever its exact arrangements,[5] did not last. Such shared rights of control or possession could hardly be

[1] See I.136.1, where Themistocles flees to Corcyra, ὧν αὐτῶν εὐεργέτης. It is true that the scholiast gives a different interpretation: Themistocles had prevented the league from sailing against those Greeks who had not fought against the Mede, who included the Corcyreans. But this is perhaps too general an action to make him εὐεργέτης of Corcyra.

[2] In Chapter III.　　　　　　　　　　[3] As in *RE* s.v. Leukas 2238.

[4] See Chapter III.

[5] Kahrstedt (358) took Plutarch's words to show the legal position that he postulates for the colonies. But it is probably wrong to press the words of an author like Plutarch, who is hardly likely to have had a precise idea of legal status in mind.

other than difficult in practice, and Corinth apparently suc-
ceeded in ousting Corcyra entirely; as will be seen, in the
Peloponnesian War Leucas was an enthusiastic ally of Corinth.
This Corinthian success may well account for the unanimity
of ancient writers in naming Corinth alone as the mother city of
Leucas.

Even though the details are unknown and the conjectures
may be wrong, it is reasonably certain that Corinth was trying
to gain sole control of Leucas in the early fifth century, and had
succeeded in doing so by the time of the Epidamnus dispute.[1]
Similar Corinthian behaviour may be observed at Apollonia in
Illyria. This colony was a joint foundation of Corinth and
Corcyra according to Strabo (VIII.316) and Ps-Scymnus (439).
Thucydides describes it (I.26.2) simply as Κορινθίων ἀποικίαν
and the note in Stephanus Byzantinus (s.v.) only mentions
200 Corinthians under their oikist Gylax. Pausanias on the
other hand makes Corcyra alone its metropolis (V.22.4). The
date of the foundation may be calculated as c. 600.[2]

Apollonia's first coins, which were issued about the middle of
the fifth century,[3] are as exactly like the coins of Corcyra, as
Ambracia's, for instance, are like those of Corinth.[4] Furthermore, the first coins of Corcyra to bear an inscription were
issued at the same time as these coins of Apollonia and the first
coins of Epidamnus, which are similar.[5] It appears likely that
the three cities had all used Corcyra's coins before this time, and
it was only necessary to put an inscription on Corcyra's coins
when the colonies began to issue identical coins for themselves.
The situation seems, therefore, to have been exactly parallel to
that of Corinth and her colonies. If it was right to attribute
more than commercial considerations to their coinage, it is also
legitimate to assume that Apollonia was closely connected to
Corcyra in the middle of the fifth century.

However, the other evidence about Apollonia suggests a connection with Corinth. This was worked out by Beaumont.[6] The

[1] When the Corcyreans attack it; see Thuc. I.30.2.
[2] See the convincing discussion of R. van Compernolle, *Antiquité Classique*
xxii 1953, 50–64.
[3] See Head, *HN*² p. 314.
[4] Compare e.g. *BMC* (*Thessaly*) Plates XXI, 14, 15 (Corcyra) and XII, 1
(Apollonia).
[5] See Head, *HN*² p. 315.   [6] *JHS* lxxii 1952, 65.

people of Apollonia dedicated at Corinth, in the second half of
the fifth century, some of the spoils taken at Thronium.[1]
Beaumont dated this to 435, and concluded from it that Corinthians had taken part in the campaign and that Thronium had
been reduced to secure the land route to the south, so that
Corinth would be free from Corcyrean interference in her
communications with Illyria. This is conjecture, and the offering of some of the spoils at Corinth does not prove that Corinthians had helped in the conquest of Thronium, but it seems a
reasonable suggestion and suits the fact that Apollonia was
clearly friendly to Corinth at this time, since Corinthian forces
were able to use the land route through Apollonia's territory on
the way to Epidamnus.[2]

As this last piece of information proves good relations between Corinth and Apollonia in 435, whether or not Beaumont's conjecture is accepted, and as the coins show that
Apollonia's relations with Corcyra were close at an earlier date,
it seems probable that in this mixed colony too Corinth had
succeeded in asserting her control. Such an assumption may
explain the fact that the early coins of Apollonia, in contrast to
those of Epidamnus, are very rare;[3] their issue may have ceased
shortly after it began, when the Corinthian connection became
dominant.

If Corinth did effectively oust Corcyra from her connection
with Apollonia, this may explain the discrepancies in the
accounts of Apollonia's foundation mentioned above. While it is
true that Thucydides should be given greater authority than the
other writers, the Corcyrean connection which they attest is so
strongly supported by the evidence of the coins that it seems
wrong to reject them. Beaumont, who does not mention the
coins, assumed that the colony was originally purely Corinthian,
and the Corcyrean element drifted in later.[4] This is unlikely in
general in view of the exclusiveness of Greek cities, and Apollonia's practice of expelling foreigners (ξενηλασία)[5] seems to
make it particularly improbable there. Altogether it is better to
conclude that the variations in the sources reflect Corinth's
success in asserting sole claim to the colony.

[1] See Paus. V.xxii.3 f; cf. *Inschr. von Olympia* 692.   [2] Thuc. I.26.6.
[3] See *BMC* (*Thessaly*) p. xxxix.
[4] *JHS* lvi 1936, 168 n. 66.   [5] See Aelian *V.H.* XIV.16.

If Corinth had successfully removed Corcyra from her footing in two mixed colonies at this period, the bitterness of the dispute about Epidamnus is easily intelligible. Although there had been Corinthian settlers at the foundation,[1] Corcyra was unquestionably the mother city,[2] so that it was even more intolerable for it to pass into Corinth's control than Apollonia or Leucas. The Corinthian action in acceding to the Epidamnian request and accepting the colony[3] would seem part of a general Corinthian plan to increase her control in the North West at Corcyra's expense.

It is in the light of these other instances that Corinth's treatment of Anactorium, and Thucydides' description of it, should be seen. Like Leucas the sources call it a Corinthian colony[4] but a Corcyrean element must be inferred; Thucydides alone, in the words under discussion (I.55.1), provides evidence of Corcyrean participation. As at Leucas, and on the same arguments,[5] it could be reasonably conjectured that Corcyreans were introduced by Periander, when he had control of Corcyra.[6] The early coinage has been discussed above, and may be taken to show, on the arguments there put forward, that Anactorium was closely connected to Corinth both commercially and politically.

While the coinage implies that Anactorium's position was similar to that of Ambracia and Leucas, the military assistance that they gave to Corinth suggests a considerable difference. For the Sybota campaign Ambracia supplied 27 ships, Leucas 10, and Anactorium one.[7] It is true that Anactorium was a lesser naval power tham Ambracia and Leucas. In Thucydides' list of the allies of the Peloponnesian League Anactorium is not one of those that supplied ships, unlike Leucas and Ambracia (II.9.2–3). Similarly Herodotus relates (VIII.45) that Ambracia supplied ships against the Persians, but there is no mention of Anactorium. Even so, Anactorium is worth mentioning as contributing to Cnemus' naval forces as well as to his

---

[1] Thuc. I.24.2.   [2] Ibid.; cf. above p. 31 n. 2.
[3] Thuc. I.25.2.   [4] See above p. 30 n. 3.
[5] See above p. 129.
[6] Gomme makes a similar suggestion (I.195 f); but his statement that Corcyra was under Corinthian control in the reign of Cypselus is unsupported by evidence.
[7] Thuc. I.46.1.

army in 429,[1] so it is at least possible that the very great difference between Anactorium's contribution at Sybota and those of Ambracia and Leucas reflects the fact that Corinth's connection was less firmly established with Anactorium.

Such a conclusion must in any case be drawn from the fact that there was a considerable anti-Corinthian party at Anactorium before and during the Archidamian War. In 435 the Corinthians had to capture the city. It has been suggested[2] that this shows that Anactorium had come over to the Athenian side, perhaps as a result of Phormio's expedition to the North-West, mentioned but not exactly dated by Thucydides (II.68.7). But this seems improbable. In such circumstances Anactorium could hardly have provided even one ship against Athens' ally, and Thucydides gives one reason only for the Corinthian need to capture the city (I.55.1), that it was a shared possession of Corcyra and Corinth. An anti-Corinthian party remained in Anactorium even after the Corinthians captured it, for in 425 the Athenians and Acarnanians took the city by treachery. The passage of Thucydides in which this is described, IV.49, was another piece of evidence used by Kahrstedt (358 f) to show that the inhabitants of Anactorium were Corinthian citizens.

It is unfortunate that the important sentence is textually corrupt. The general sense is that Acarnanian settlers occupied the place. The reading of the *OCT* is καὶ ἐκπέμψαντες [Κορινθίους] αὐτοὶ Ἀκαρνᾶνες οἰκήτορας ἀπὸ πάντων ἔσχον τὸ χωρίον. The scholiast read οἰκήτορας and is supported by some manuscripts, while the rest read οἰκήτορες. If οἰκήτορας is accepted on the evidence of the scholiast, it is governed by no verb; Dobree therefore excluded Κορινθίους and rendered the sentence logical. The variant on οἰκήτορας suggests strongly that Κορινθίους had come into the text, presumably from a marginal note, owing to a misunderstanding of the force of ἐκπέμψαντες in this sentence and a reminiscence of the passage I.55.1, where the Corinthians established Κορινθίους οἰκήτορας in the city; for the change to οἰκήτορες would make the sentence logical including Κορινθίους. If the reading of the *OCT* is correct, the passage IV.49 says nothing about the inhabitants of Anactorium, except that some of them were prepared to betray the city to the Athenians and Acarnanians. Kahrstedt's conclusion from the passage that the

[1] Thuc. II.80.3. [2] By Beaumont, *JHS* lxxii 1952, 62 f.

inhabitants of Anactorium were Corinthian citizens is thus at best based on an uncertain reading.

In general terms the examples of other colonies of Corcyra and Corinth in the same area have made Anactorium's position in 433 clear. It had connections with both Corcyra and Corinth and these connections were politically important. As at Leucas, Epidamnus and perhaps Apollonia, Corinth took the opportunity to gain sole control of the place at the expense of the Corcyrean connection. However, the degree of control and the legal status of Anactorium are not revealed by the evidence so far discussed. One further passage which Kahrstedt used to show Corinth's relationship to her colonies, and which, it might be thought, could be used as an analogy for Anactorium's status, remains to be considered.

When the Corcyreans suggested to the Corinthians that their dispute about Epidamnus should be decided by arbitration, their offer is expressed by Thucydides in these words (I.28.2): ὁποτέρων δ' ἂν δικασθῇ εἶναι τὴν ἀποικίαν, τούτους κρατεῖν. Kahrstedt (358) used this passage to show that the Corinthian control over the colonies in question, indicated by other expressions, was the consequence of their status as colonies, for the right to κρατεῖν over Epidamnus belongs to those whose colony Epidamnus is adjudged to be. Since κρατέω is used of Athens' control over her allies,[1] it might also be urged that Corinth's control over colonies was like that of Athens over her empire. In which case the analogy of Athens' better known control could provide a basis for conjectures about the detailed position of the Corinthian colonies.

Both these arguments depend on understanding τούτους κρατεῖν to mean 'they should possess (own, control, etc.) it'. Nearly all the English translators, whose rendering is close enough to show their opinion, do, it is true, take the phrase as meaning 'they should have it' (Loeb) or the like.[2] Gomme writes (I.162 f) ' "that side should possess it", Epidamnos, as though Epidamnos was not an independent state which might

[1] See e.g. Tod 72.6 and the inscriptions cited by Meiggs, *CR* lxiii 1949, 9 f.
[2] e.g. Hobbes (corrected edition 1676), Crawley (London 1874), Loeb editor (1919). A recent Italian edition also translates in this sense, and follows the same line in the notes; see Thucydides I, ed. Maddalena (Florence 1951) 100, 16.

have some say in the matter itself'. This shows that he felt some difficulty, but he does not suggest that there is any doubt about his translation.

This is a formidable array of modern interpreters, but a comparison with Thucydides' other uses of the word κρατεῖν suggests that they are mistaken. It is a very common word in Thucydides,[1] of which the primary meaning is 'to win' or 'prevail'. In this sense it is often used absolutely. It also frequently means 'to possess'. In this sense it takes an object in the genitive case. When it is used in this latter significance the word in the genitive is never left to be understood—unless in the passage under discussion. Bétant himself, whose special study was Thucydides' language, included the passage among the examples of the first meaning: 'praevalere, superare, vincere'. If he is right, the passage must be literally translated 'that, of whomsoever the colony be adjudged, they should be the winners (i.e. of the dispute)'. It certainly seems better to translate thus rather than to render the sentence in a way which demands supplying an object, a usage unexampled elsewhere in Thucydides.

If Bétant's interpretation of the phrase is correct, κρατεῖν has the same significance as νικῆν in the record of an arbitration by the Argives.[2] The judgment is expressed in these words: ἐδίκασσαν (sc. οἱ Ἀργεῖοι) νικῆν Κιμωλί[ο]υς; which are to be translated 'the Argives adjudged that the Cimolians win (the dispute)'. No one suggests that they mean 'the Argives adjudged that the Cimolians conquer (the islands in dispute)'. If κρατεῖν is understood in the sense proposed, nothing can be deduced about the legal status of the colonies from the sentence under discussion, and it does not add to our knowledge of the exact position of Anactorium with regard to Corinth and Corcyra.

The remainder of the evidence for the status of the Corinthian colonies in question comes from passages in ancient authors where the meaning of the words is hardly in doubt. The close connection with Corinth in war is well attested. Leucas and Ambracia were present, like the Corinthians, at Salamis,[3] and at Plataea there were contingents from Leucas, Anactorium and Potidaea, as also from Corinth.[4] Leucas and Ambracia played

---

[1] See Bétant, *Lexicon Thucydideum*, s.v.   [2] Tod 179.12–14.
[3] Hdt. VIII.45.   [4] Hdt. IX.28.3,5.

a very considerable role on Corinth's side in the war against Corcyra which preceded the Peloponnesian War, and in the latter too.[1] Further, when Potidaea was coerced by Athens in 432, the Corinthians organized a force to go to the help of the colony,[2] and they regarded the attack on their colony as a reason for war.[3]

Kahrstedt noted (359) that we are not told of any formal alliance between Corinth and her colonies. While it is wrong to make too much of an argument from silence, it is true that the regular help in war given between Corinth and her colonies is not thought to need explanation by ancient writers. The only time that Thucydides accounts for the connection, he says that the forces from Leucas and Ambracia came κατὰ τὸ ξυγγενές (VII.58.3), and we need not doubt that this relationship was either the basis for a formal alliance or the reason why such an alliance was unnecessary. Kahrstedt's conclusion (ibid.) that the contingents of the allies could be mobilized by Corinth as if they were Corinthians is not, however, necessary, nor do Corinthian garrisons in the colonies[4] reflect anything more than the practical need to defend her allies in war.

But if the mutual help in war does not necessarily show Corinth's control over colonies, clear evidence for such control is to be seen in the fact, reported by Thucydides (I.56.2), that Corinth sent magistrates (ἐπιδημιουργοί) each year to Potidaea. Pericles' demand that they should be dismissed makes improbable Kahrstedt's view (364) that they were no more than a survival and had no power in practice.[5] If Pericles was afraid that they would exert influence on Potidaea to encourage her to revolt from Athens, their position can hardly have been purely formal. It must be confessed, however, that we have no evidence for their exact position and duties.[6]

---

[1] The references in Thucydides for their activity are: (Ambracia) I.26.1; III.114.4; IV.42.3; VII.7.1; 58.3.; (Leucas) I.26.1; 30.2; II.9.2; 80.2; 81.3; 91.2; III.7.4; 61.1; 81.1; 94; VII.7.1; 58.3; VIII.106.2.

[2] Thuc. I.60.   [3] Thuc. I.66; 67.1.

[4] See Thuc. III.114.4; IV.42.3.

[5] Will follows Kahrstedt in this view; see La Nouvelle Clio vi 1954, 416; Korinthiaka 524 n. 1.

[6] The idea that they were eponymous magistrates (as de Sanctis, Storia dei Greci II,264) is presumably based on Thucydides' information (ibid.) that they were sent κατὰ ἔτος ἕκαστον, but there were plenty of annual magistrates who were not eponymous. It is possible that the name implies

Two opinions are equally possible on the question why we hear of these officials in distant Potidaea and in no other Corinthian colony.[1] It may be sheer chance,[2] since if Corinth sent officials to Potidaea, she might be expected *a fortiori* to send them to the more closely connected colonies in the North West. On the other hand it may have been Potidaea's distance from Corinth which made it necessary to send officials to that colony alone.[3] But both opinions assume, no doubt rightly, that Corinthian control over the relevant colonies in the North West was at least as close as that attested by the ἐπιδημιουργοί at Potidaea.

None of the evidence on the status of the colonies has been seen to support Kahrstedt's thesis that they were simply parts of the Corinthian state, but it has all tended to the conclusion that Corinth had a position of political supremacy with regard to her colonies. This is necessarily an undefined expression, as there is no evidence to allow a very precise description; however, the limits of this supremacy can be discovered by investigating whether the colonies had independence in foreign policy.

Before the Peloponnesian War two colonies of Corinth, Molycrium and Potidaea, were joined to Athens. Potidaea was a regular tribute-paying ally,[4] and Molycrium was subject to Athens but did not pay tribute.[5] It is not certain how Moly-crium became subject to Athens,[6] but there is no need to doubt that Potidaea did so voluntarily and did not regard the alliance as incompatible with her position as a loyal colony of Corinth. The events of 433 and the following years show that her

---

that they had powers of survey over the other magistrates (cf. Gomme, Commentary to I.56.2), but the other uses of the word suggest that it was simply one among the many names of Greek magistrates; see Pomtow, *Klio* xviii 1923, 285 ff. However, these instances are much later in date, and so can hardly be considered illuminating parallels for the ἐπιδημιουργοί at Potidaea.

[1] After the Battle of Olpae the Corinthians sent a garrison to Ambracia and Ξενοκλείδαν . . . ἄρχοντα (Thuc. III.114.4), but he is probably to be regarded as a special official sent because of the emergency at Ambracia after her terrible losses (see III.113.6).

[2] As Kahrstedt 361.

[3] As Will, *La Nouvelle Clio* vi 1954, 416 n. 2; *Korinthiaka* 524 n. 1.

[4] Thuc. I.56.2.   [5] Thuc. III.102.2.

[6] It is suggested in *RE*, s.v. Molykreion 37, that Molycrium was taken by the Athenians when they captured Naupactus; Naupactus too paid no tribute.

relations with Corinth were still very good. However, it could be argued that an alliance with Athens, when Athens and Corinth were at peace, does not necessarily prove that Potidaea could conduct her foreign policy independently of Corinth. It is also arguable that Potidaea's distance from Corinth would make any Corinthian aspiration to control her foreign policy impracticable,[1] and so Potidaea is not a good analogy for the position of the North-Western colonies.

It is therefore extremely fortunate that we have evidence about the foreign policy of Ambracia, one of the colonies most closely connected to Corinth, for the period of the Peloponnesian War. After great losses at Olpae and Idomene Ambracia concluded a peace treaty and alliance with the Acarnanians and Amphilochians, the terms of which are given by Thucydides as follows (III.114.3):

ὥστε μήτε 'Αμπρακιώτας μετὰ 'Ακαρνάνων στρατεύειν ἐπὶ Πελο-
ποννησίους μήτε 'Ακαρνᾶνας μετὰ 'Αμπρακιωτῶν ἐπ' 'Αθηναίους,
βοηθεῖν δὲ τῇ ἀλλήλων, καὶ ἀποδοῦναι· 'Αμπρακιώτας ὁπόσα ἢ χωρία
ἢ ὁμήρους 'Αμφιλόχων ἔχουσι, καὶ ἐπὶ 'Ανακτόριον μὴ βοηθεῖν
πολέμιον ὂν 'Ακαρνᾶσιν.[2]

This treaty shows that Ambracia could negotiate for itself in a treaty which was more than a local affair.[3] It was also, both in general and particular, a treaty against Corinth's interests. Their great losses may no doubt have inclined Corinth to forgive the Ambraciots for giving up the struggle against Corinth's enemies; but in their weakness they even had to agree specifically not to help Anactorium, which duly fell to Athenian and Acarnanian attackers the following year.[4] The treaty must therefore be accepted as unequivocal evidence that even a

[1] As, for example, in the Persian wars; see Hdt. VIII.126.2 f.
[2] 'That neither shall the Ambraciots make war together with the Acarnanians against the Peloponnesians, nor shall the Acarnanians make war together with the Ambraciots against the Athenians. But they shall help in defending each other's territory, and the Ambraciots shall give back such land or hostages of the Amphilochians as they possess, and they shall not help Anactorium, which is an enemy of the Acarnanians.'
[3] Kahrstedt (361 n. 3) tried to escape the necessary conclusions from this evidence by asserting that while the colonies could not conduct their own foreign policy, the parochial relations with the tribes of the interior were an exception. But the relations of Ambracia and her neighbours had become part of the Peloponnesian War.
[4] Thuc. IV.49.

colony so closely connected to Corinth as Ambracia could conduct an independent foreign policy.

It also, by itself, demolishes the two extravagant theories about these Corinthian colonies advanced by Kahrstedt and Hampl. If the colonies were simply extensions of the Corinthian state and their inhabitants Corinthian citizens, not only would it have been impossible for Ambracia to make a treaty against Corinth's interests, she could not have made a treaty at all. The treaty would have had to be made by Corinth. If, on the other hand, Ambracia was one of Hampl's putative 'Poleis ohne Territorium',[1] a separate community on Corinthian territory, she could hardly have made a treaty which bound the Acarnanians, Corinth's enemies, to support her if her (i.e. Corinth's) territory was attacked. Nor, if she had no territory, could she have agreed to give back territory taken from the Amphilochians.

This lengthy discussion of Corinth's dependent colonies was partly necessary for the negative purpose of removing false doctrine. It is now time to assess the positive conclusions to which the evidence points.

The general tendency of all the evidence discussed is towards the conclusion that Corinth not only maintained a very close relationship with these colonies, but that she had to some degree political supremacy over them. On the other hand, the evidence of some independence in foreign policy, if no other,[2] proves that the colonies had a separate existence from the mother city. In the fifth century, therefore, they should not be regarded as different in kind from other Greek colonies.

The necessity of making this point must not obscure the fact that in degree their relations with the metropolis were probably exceptionally close. All the evidence discussed suggests this; the Corinthians claimed it,[3] and incidental statements in Thucydides put it beyond doubt. For example, after the battle of Olpae the Peloponnesians were withdrawing according to their separate secret agreement with Demosthenes, which was

[1] See above p. 119.
[2] Other evidence for the independence of the colonies has been seen in the existence of their ethnics and in their separate contingents in war. But such evidence is not, by itself, proof of political independence, as Kahrstedt's arguments (360) showed.
[3] See the quotation at the beginning of the chapter.

designed to isolate the Ambraciots (III.109.2). These observed
the withdrawal and joined in, and the Acarnanians attacked
under the impression that they were all escaping without an
agreement. When they learnt that this was only true of the
Ambraciots, they turned their attention entirely on them, but
with some difficulty because ἦν πολλὴ ἔρις καὶ ἄγνοια εἴτε
᾿Αμπρακιώτης τίς ἐστιν εἴτε Πελοποννήσιος.[1] The Ambraciots were
thus very hard to distinguish from the Peloponnesians; presumably they had kept their Corinthian characteristics unimpaired
because of frequent intercourse with the mother city.

The easy way in which Corinth moved settlers into these
colonies, as at Anactorium[2] and, more notably, at Epidamnus,
when she invited volunteers from Leucas and Ambracia to join
her own,[3] may well suggest that the citizens of Corinth could
take up citizenship in the colonies.[4] It was suggested in Chapter
IV that this is the way to understand Corinth's behaviour regarding Epidamnus, and such immigration would also explain
why the soldiers of Ambracia were hard to distinguish from
those of Peloponnesian cities. However, there is no more certain
evidence on this point.

The removal of over-formal legal concepts about the colonies'
position allows proper emphasis to be given to the close personal contacts which probably made legal arrangements superfluous. When Potidaea was threatened by Athens, and Aristeus
was sent from Corinth with a force of Corinthian volunteers and
mercenaries from the other Peloponnesians, the volunteers went
with him largely because he was popular, and Thucydides
(I.60.2) adds, presumably to explain the choice of Aristeus as
leader, ἦν γὰρ τοῖς Ποτειδεάταις αἰεί ποτε ἐπιτήδειος.[5] If the relations between Corinth and these colonies were largely a matter
of personal connections rather than legal arrangements, it is not
surprising that the Corinthian complaints against Corcyra's be-

[1] 'There was much dispute and ignorance as to whether a man was an
Ambraciot or a Peloponnesian.'
[2] Thuc. I.55.1.   [3] Thuc. I.26.1.
[4] Though Gschnitzer would argue, following Hampl, that it shows that
Corinth disposed of the colonies' land; see *Abhängige Orte im griech. Altertum*,
133.
[5] 'For he had always been very friendly to the people of Potidaea.' As
Gomme notes, Commentary ad. loc., the explanation can hardly refer to the
immediately preceding remark about the reason why the volunteers joined
the expedition.

haviour as a colony[1] are not of legal nature. She wanted the
colonists to accord her general hegemony and to fulfil their
religious obligations.

If the colonies were not tied to Corinth by a strict legal
arrangement, it is probably wrong to imagine that they were all
in exactly the same position regarding Corinth. This would
explain the differences that can be observed in the way Thucydides describes them. The descriptions mentioned above[2] referred only to Anactorium, Sollium and Chalcis. To these he
applied the phrase Κορινθίων πόλιν, etc. On the other hand,
Leucas is called τὴν Κορινθίων ἀποικίαν (I.30.2), one of his normal ways of describing a colony, as are Ambracia (II.80.3),
Apollonia (I.26.2) and Potidaea (I.56.2). The status of Sollium
and Chalcis is unknown,[3] but Anactorium was in Corinthian
hands by capture at the time to which Thucydides is referring.
Perhaps the special control implied by his words is not universally applicable to all these colonies. Nevertheless a general
similarity between them may be accepted on the evidence of
their foundation,[4] coins and relations with Corinth in war.

The evidence for the position of these colonies which has been
discussed is not earlier than the fifth century. It has been seen
that the colonies were founded in such a way that they were
dependent on Corinth, and the fifth-century evidence at least
makes clear that this dependent position was not solely a consequence of the tyrants' ambitions for their family. However, it is
not so certain that the position revealed in the fifth century
should be assumed to have existed since the foundation of the
colonies. It has been seen that Corinth was trying to assert her
control over some mixed colonies at Corcyra's expense in the
fifth century, so that it might be argued that this was part of a
general Corinthian attempt to gain a stronger hold over her
colonies.[5] But this could be true, without necessarily implying
that relations had lapsed between the fall of the tyrants and the

---

[1] Thuc. I.25.3 f; 38.   [2] See pp. 120 f.
[3] See above p. 119.   [4] See Chapter III.
[5] Will ignores the evidence when he says (*Korinthiaka* 525) that there is no
indication that Corinth had been trying to establish an *arche* in the North
West. His further argument that, if she had established an *arche* in this way,
the colonies would have joined Athens against Corinth in the Peloponnesian War is clearly quite untenable. But his conclusion that the colonies
were closely dependent from the beginning is quite probable.

fifth century. It is much more likely that close relations had persisted and provided the basis for a Corinthian attempt to make her position even more dominant. Potidaea, which lies outside Corinth's geographical sphere, seems to be a decisive example. There could be no question of Corinth's enforcing a stronger hold on Potidaea in the fifth century, yet their relations were very close, and Potidaea accepted Corinthian officials, up to the Peloponnesian War.

So it may be accepted that in a general sense the position of the colonies in the fifth century is a guide to their status since their foundation. For instance, it would be surprising if the colonies had been legally parts of the Corinthian state at their foundation but had ceased to be so by the fifth century. The subsequent relationship agrees too well with the deductions from the way in which the colonies were founded for it to be regarded as unconnected with the aims of the founders.

There have been many attempts to conjecture precisely what these aims were. The view most commonly advanced is that the colonies were settled in order to secure Corinth's control of the route to the silver mines of Illyria.[1] This may be true, and would certainly explain why Corinth would want to keep up close relations with the colonies, but it is a conjecture only, so that it is not necessary for the present purpose to discuss the possibility in detail.[2] Here it is sufficient to state that there is good evidence to show that both at their foundation and in subsequent times the colonies were sufficiently closely connected to Corinth to be regarded as a means of extending Corinth's power abroad. It is therefore legitimate, so long as the phrase is not understood to imply special legal forms, to speak of a Corinthian colonial empire.

Corinth's relations with Syracuse and Corcyra

If a special legal status is assumed for the colonies of the tyrants, it is necessary to set the two pre-tyrant foundations entirely apart from them. So Kahrstedt (364 ff) naturally excluded Syracuse and Corcyra from a Corinthian colonial empire in

[1] Will (*Korinthiaka* 536 ff) follows Beaumont (*JHS* lvi 1936, 181 ff) in accepting that these mines were the source of Corinth's silver. J. M. F. May is more cautious; see *The Coinage of Damastion* pp. viii f, 2 f.

[2] On the basis of this assumption Will makes interesting suggestions about political reasons for the sites of the colonies; see *Korinthiaka* 529 f, 532 f.

which the colonies were part of the Corinthian state, and Will states[1] that it was a rhetorical device for the Corinthians to compare Corcyra to the other colonies,[2] since their juridical position was different. But as the juridical position postulated by Kahrstedt and accepted by Will is to be rejected, the colonies of the tyrants need not be considered to have been formally in a different legal position from Corcyra and Syracuse, and Corinth's relations with these two colonies should be studied for the sake of comparison, as well as for their intrinsic interest.

We have already seen that Corinth's commercial connections with Corcyra and Syracuse and her influence on them aesthetically show 'a constant interchange of men and ideas'.[3] Such relations between individual citizens of colonies and mother city provide the basis for their relations as states. In international relations Corinth seems to have regularly supported Syracuse, and on the first occasion recorded Corcyra was also concerned.

Herodotus relates (VII.154.3) that when Syracuse had been defeated by Hippocrates of Gela in 492, the Corinthians and Corcyreans intervened on Syracuse's behalf and settled the dispute on the terms that Camarina should be ceded to Gela. Possibly owing to the associations of the word used by Herodotus for the establishment of peace, καταλλάξαντες, this event has been thought to be an example of arbitration.[4] But it should be regarded, as Tod saw,[5] rather as an instance of mediation, for Hippocrates held the whiphand and had no need to seek arbitration. Corinth and Corcyra came to Syracuse's assistance in her emergency, and Hippocrates accepted the proffered settlement rather than oppose so formidable a combination.

It has been suggested[6] that the Corinthian and Corcyrean intervention was caused by a desire to protect their commercial interests. But such an explanation demands the assumption,

---

[1] *La Nouvelle Clio* vi 1954, 417 f; *Korinthiaka* 525.
[2] Thuc. I.38.   [3] Dunbabin 284; cf. above p. 13.
[4] Macan, for instance, although he notes that it may not be a true example of arbitration, suggested that the notorious enmity between Corinth and Corcyra would have ensured a fair judgment; see *Herodotus VII, VIII, IX with Introduction etc.*, 214 n. 1. This is not convincing; one chooses disinterested parties for an arbitration, not two possibly interested, but hostile, parties.
[5] *Greek International Arbitration*, 65; he is followed by Dunbabin (401).
[6] By Dunbabin (284).

which there is no reason to make, that Hippocrates would have
interfered with Syracusan trade. Furthermore, if interests were
at stake, it would be surprising to find Corinth and Corcyra
acting together. They were quarrelling over Leucas at about
this time,[1] and an explanation which implies long-term coincidence of Corinthian and Corcyrean interests conflicts with
Herodotus' statement (III.49.1) that they were virtually con-
tinually at enmity with each other. This statement may be
exaggerated, but Herodotus is hardly likely to have been
seriously mistaken about the fifth century. While Corinth and
Corcyra probably would not agree about interests, they were
both tied by relationship to Syracuse, and this may be regarded
as the reason why they both wished to protect Syracuse against
Hippocrates.

The Corinthian help for Syracuse against Athens in the
Peloponnesian War might be regarded as inspired as much by
hostility to Athens as good relations with her colony, but it is
notable that the Syracusan ambassadors sent to ask for help go
first to Corinth, and then, with Corinthian support, to Sparta.[2]

The next occasion on which Corinthian support of Syracuse
is recorded is the expedition of Timoleon. In 344[3] the aristo-
crats[4] in Syracuse appealed to Corinth for help against their
tyrant. The Corinthians voted to give assistance and Timoleon
was chosen to lead the expedition.[5] His force consisted of seven
Corinthian ships, two Corcyrean and one from Leucas.[6] After
the overwhelming success of his mission, Timoleon also arranged
for the reorganization and resettlement of Syracuse. He sent to
Corinth asking for settlers,[7] and Plutarch relates (*Tim.*
XXXVIII.4) that the Syracusans decreed that in any future
war against a foreign enemy they would employ a Corinthian
general.

As Plutarch tells the story, Corinth's position as a benevolent

---

[1] See above pp. 129 f.

[2] Thuc. VI.88 7–10. Note the phrase ἀξιοῦντες σφίσι κατὰ τὸ ξυγγενὲς
βοηθεῖν.

[3] See Plut. *Timoleon* II.1; Diod. XVI.65.1. For the date see Westlake, *AJP*
lxx 1949, 73. In this paper Westlake shows (65–75) that the expedition went
against the tyrants in Sicily, not against the Carthaginians, as Plutarch
states.

[4] See Westlake 74 and n. 28.   [5] Plut. *Tim.* III.1; Diod. loc. cit.

[6] Plut. *Tim.* VIII.4.

[7] Plut. *Tim.* XXIII.1.

mother city is strongly emphasized.[1] He remarks approvingly (XXXII.1 f) that Corinth did not make use of the opportunity for aggrandizement when asked to send in new settlers, and if his picture could be accepted as accurate Corinth would be seen as a supreme but helpful mother city. However, careful study of Plutarch's account by Westlake has shown that it and its sources make certain misrepresentations.[2] Among these must be set Plutarch's description of the attitude of Corinth. For Corinth showed in fact little interest in the expedition, and it is rather Timoleon's loyalty and propaganda that is reflected in the tendency of our sources to give the credit for the enterprise to the Corinthians.[3]

It is also true that the Syracusan decision to use a Corinthian general in future foreign wars may be rather an expression of gratitude, or possible safeguard against the danger of domestic tyrants,[4] than a recognition of any Corinthian right. On the other hand, this decision, the request for help in the first place, and the acceptance of new settlers from Corinth, are all finally based on the relationship of Syracuse and Corinth as colony and mother city. And the words of the dedication on Timoleon's victory monument at Corinth[5] show that this relationship was consciously in the minds of the participants in the events. The inscription is only partly preserved, but the allies named are, except the Sikeliots, Corinth and her colonies, and Corinth is called the founder ($\varkappa\tau\iota\sigma\tau\tilde{\eta}\varrho\alpha$).

It may be that the Spartan help given to Taras in 346 should be regarded as similar to Corinth's support of Syracuse. Diodorus (XVI.62.4 f) says explicitly that the appeal for help and its success were both due to Taras' position as a colony of

---

[1] E.g. II.1; III.1.

[2] The paper cited above showed one of Plutarch's misrepresentations. In *CQ* xxxii 1938, 65–74, Westlake showed that Plutarch's sources were two: Timaeus' history and a biography mainly interested in ethos. He therefore concludes that the main political events may be accepted as true, but the motives given by Plutarch must be treated more warily.

[3] See Westlake, *Camb. Hist. Jour.* vii 1942, 75 f. Wentker, *Sizilien und Athen*, (Heidelberg 1956), 11–14, takes Plutarch's account at its face value, and overemphasizes the effect of presumed family connections between the aristocracy of Corinth and Syracuse. Since both cities had been through many vicissitudes, and about 400 years had passed since the colony was founded, the effect of such family connections should not be exaggerated.

[4] The latter possibility was suggested to me by Sir Frank Adcock.

[5] See J. H. Kent, *Hesperia* xxi 1952, 9 ff; for the text, 13.

Sparta, but since Strabo (VI.280) equates the appeal with others to peoples unrelated to Taras, it is legitimate to ask whether the special motives given by Diodorus are not simply his own ideas. The rather mediocre support of Sparta's cause by Taras in the Peloponnesian War[1] does not imply specially close relations between the two cities.

Many of the aspects of Corinth's relations with Corcyra have already been touched on incidentally, but it is worth assembling all the material together, because Corcyra is the best documented example of a colony which was often hostile to its metropolis. We have seen that Herodotus (III.49.1) could state that Corinth and Corcyra had been hostile to each other since the foundation of the colony, and the first that we hear of their relations is that they fought a sea-battle in c. 664, the first Greek naval battle known to Thucydides (I.13.4). Thucydides himself gives no information about the causes or circumstances of the battle.[2] This has not deterred modern writers from assuming that it was a Corcyrean attempt to become independent of Corinth.[3] Such an assumption presupposes that Corcyra was established as a dependent colony of Corinth, though there is no evidence for such a conclusion.[4] In fact various slight indications suggest that the idea of a war of independence is out of place.

It is in the first place very unlikely that Corinth would have allowed a subject colony to build a navy capable of challenging her own, and if Herodotus' words are strictly accurate and Corcyra was refractory from the beginning, it is even more improbable. This argument is strengthened by the rarity of warships for naval battles in those days.[5] Secondly, the reception of

---

[1] It is true that Taras refused to allow the Athenian fleet even to anchor and take water (Thuc. VI.44.2), and gave Gylippus a friendly reception (VI.104.2), but these are passive acts, and the Tarentine ships mentioned in the Peloponnesian fleet sent to Euboea in 411 (VIII.91.2) are hardly significant. By that time Athens' weakness and the common Dorian stock would be sufficient reason for a modicum of support from Taras. Thus Thucydides does not differentiate Taras' support from that of other states which were unrelated to Sparta.

[2] The γάϱ of the succeeding sentence refers not to the sea-battle but to the implication in the previous two sentences that Corinth was the first Greek state to develop a navy.

[3] E.g. Dunbabin 56; Wade-Gery, CAH III.550.

[4] See below pp. 218 ff.

[5] Cf. Ure, The Origin of Tyranny, 321 f.

the Bacchiad exiles[1] at Corcyra not many years after the battle suggests that it had not been accompanied by the bitterness engendered by wars of independence, for these same men had been the rulers of Corinth at the time of the battle. Although these arguments are inevitably uncertain, when combined with the improbability that Corcyra was a dependent settlement at the beginning, they have a certain weight. If the cause of the dispute was not a Corcyrean attempt to win independence, it may be that Corinth's and Corcyra's interests were already clashing in North-West Greece, as they did in later times.

We have seen that the behaviour of Corcyra at the foundation of Epidamnus suggests that she was then on good terms with Corinth but independent of her.[2] There followed the period of definite Corinthian rule under Periander, when Corcyra's status was comparable to that of the colonies founded by the tyrants.[3] At this time Corcyreans may have joined various Corinthian colonies in the neighbouring region.[4]

It is clear from the next evidence for their political relations, which relates to the fifth century, that Corcyra had thrown off Corinthian control well before that time. The quarrel over Leucas[5] shows that she was then the fully independent state that we know better in the second half of the fifth century. Differences with Corinth over three colonies, Leucas, Anactorium and Epidamnus, are attested; it has been seen that there may have been a similar dispute over Apollonia. The details of their relations concerning three of these colonies are not known; but because of Thucydides' narrative the affair of Epidamnus is especially informative.[6]

The rebuff which Corcyra gave to the democrats of Epidamnus was countered by their appeal to Corinth. The way Corinth seized the opportunity may be seen as characteristic of her behaviour in the area under discussion; partly because of her bad relations with Corcyra, she vigorously accepted the task of protecting Epidamnus, and sent troops and further settlers to the city. Corcyra's protests and threats were ignored, and war followed. The defeat at Leucimme, and Corcyra's consequent success in imposing her will on Epidamnus and attacking

[1] See Chapter VI.
[2] See Chapter III.
[3] See Chapter III.
[4] See above pp. 129 ff.
[5] See above pp. 129 f.
[6] I.24–55.

Corinthian allies, only stimulated Corinth to greater efforts, but when she had almost succeeded in defeating Corcyra at Sybota the Athenian ships saved the day for their new ally. As some consolation the Corinthians took Anactorium on the way home.

Such a serious and lasting quarrel between Corinth and her colony might be expected to show a fundamental division. It is therefore surprising that the Corinthians hoped to influence their Corcyrean prisoners by good treatment so as to win the island over to friendly relations.[1] In 427 these hopes were temporarily fulfilled when the resulting pro-Peloponnesian party actually induced the state to decree that Corcyra should become friendly with the Peloponnesians as she had been in the past.[2] This shows that neither side regarded their hostile relations as inevitable and permanent, and, in fact, good relations at various times are attested. In addition to the period of Cypselus, they may be seen in Corcyra's contribution to Timoleon's expedition. Herodotus could not know the latter, but even so his words should not be accepted quite literally, for Corinth and Corcyra were not unceasing enemies from the time of the colony's foundation.

A comparison of Syracuse and Corcyra with the colonies of the tyrants reveals the following differences. Syracuse and Corcyra were probably not founded as dependent settlements; their coinage is quite distinct from Corinth's; and there is no evidence for Corinth's political supremacy over them except in the reign of Periander, when Corcyra was under his control. At this time Corcyra was in the same position as the colonies of the tyrants, which may show that the essential difference between these colonies and the pre-tyrant foundations was one of size and power. The colonies of the tyrants were never comparable with Corinth in these respects; both Syracuse and Corcyra were.[3] As a result political dependence was practically out of the question, and when their interests clashed a real quarrel could result, as on several occasions between Corinth and Corcyra. The difference is not less important for being one of practice rather than theory: Syracuse and Corcyra were obviously not part of Corinth's colonial empire. But if all the

---

[1] Thuc. I.55.1.   [2] Thuc. III.70.1 f.
[3] Cf. Corinth's resentment at Corcyra's wealth and strength; see Thuc. I.25.4.

colonies of Corinth were in principle similar, we can understand the character of the complaints against Corcyra, in
which she is unfavourably compared with the other colonies.[1]

Corcyra and her colonies

Corcyra's relations to her colonies seem to offer a close
parallel to the relationship between Corinth and her colonial
empire. As has been seen[2] Corcyra was the metropolis of
Epidamnus, though Corinthian settlers were among the
colonists,[3] and participated in the colonies of Leucas, Anactorium and Apollonia. Her relations with Leucas and Anactorium can only be conjectured from the information discussed
above that she had kept up relations with her colonists and it
was of interest to her that they should not fall completely under
Corinthian influence.

The coinage of Apollonia has been mentioned in an earlier
part of this chapter, where it was seen to imply that Apollonia's
connection with Corcyra was similar to that of Ambracia or
Leucas with Corinth. The same inference may be made about
Epidamnus' relations with Corcyra, for the first coins of
Epidamnus bear exactly the same relationship to the coins of
Corcyra as the first coins of Apollonia. The only difference is
that they are not so rare as those of Apollonia, which may be
explained by the possibility suggested above, that Corinthian
influence in Apollonia caused the first issue of coins to cease
soon after it began. But as inferences about political status
drawn from coins must always be uncertain, it is fortunate
that Corcyra's relations with one of these colonies, Epidamnus,
are more clearly illuminated by Thucydides' narrative.

Epidamnus' relations with the mother city are revealed particularly in the appeal to Corcyra and in Corcyra's reaction
when the colony handed itself over to Corinth. The ruling
democratic party appealed to Corcyra, as the mother city
(ὡς μητρόπολιν οὖσαν; I.24.6), to save them from destruction by
effecting a reconciliation between them and the exiled oligarchs and by bringing to an end the war with the surrounding
native population. This may be seen as an example of the kind
of intervention expected by a colony from its mother city.
Corcyra's rejection of the appeal is to be explained by reference

[1] Thuc. ibid. and I.38.   [2] In Chapter III.   [3] Thuc. I.24.2.

to the passage I.26.3, which describes how the oligarchic exiles from Epidamnus came to Corcyra, pointed to the tombs of their ancestors, appealed to the claims of kinship, and persuaded the Corcyreans to reinstate them. Presumably Corcyrean sympathies were with the oligarchs from the beginning.

The appeal of the oligarchs is a vivid illustration of the way in which kinship provided the fundamental basis for the relations between colony and mother city. It is probably right to see in the oligarchs of Epidamnus the descendants of the first settlers from Corcyra,[1] who had become the aristocracy of the colony and provided a close link with the mother city. But it should be noted that Corcyra was not so concerned with the affairs of Epidamnus that she felt the need to intervene to prevent the exile of the party she favoured.[2] She was prepared to let Epidamnus work out its own salvation, and to allow the oligarchs to fend for themselves, until the intervention of Corinth stimulated vigorous action, including a demand for their reinstatement.

Corcyra's reaction to Corinth's intervention is partly to be understood, as has been seen, by reference to the other colonies of the area in which Corinth had attempted to make her influence supreme. But it also shows that Corcyra considered that Epidamnus could be lost and won; to some degree, therefore, they regarded the city as under their control. The Corcyreans also felt that their title to Epidamnus would win the day, for they were willing to submit the dispute to arbitration; though this may show confidence in Spartan support[3] as well as a just cause, for both the arbitrators suggested, Delphi and cities of the Peloponnese, might be expected to follow Sparta's lead.

The way in which Epidamnus handed itself over to Corinth may also be seen as an illustration of the relations of colonies to mother cities, at least in this area. The question to Delphi, εἰ παραδοῖεν Κορινθίοις τὴν πόλιν ὡς οἰκισταῖς[4] (I.25.1), Delphi's reply, παραδοῦναι καὶ ἡγεμόνας ποιεῖσθαι[5] (ibid.), and Corinth's

---

[1] As Wentker, *Sizilien und Athen*, 11 f, though his reconstruction of the political developments in Epidamnus is more hypothetical than his language suggests.
[2] I owe this observation to the late Professor Gomme.
[3] See Thuc. I.28.1.
[4] 'If they should hand over the city to the Corinthians as founders.'
[5] 'Hand the city over and make them your leaders.'

subsequent actions to protect and reinforce the colony all show that real political supremacy was accorded the mother city. It is not unreasonable to add Corinth's claim that she founded the colonies ἐπὶ τῷ ἡγεμόνες τε εἶναι καὶ τὰ εἰκότα θαυμάζεσθαι[1] (I.38.2), and conclude that the position of the mother city here implied was hegemonial.[2]

To use such a word does not imply agreement with Wentker's theory that this hegemonial position was based on a connection of service between the nobility of the colony and that of the metropolis, by which the nobility of the colony became the 'Gefolgschaft' of the 'Adelsfamilien' in the mother city.[3] On the basis of this conception he assumes that Corinth's action in sending further settlers to the colony was intended to provide an aristocracy in the colony bound to Corinth in such a relationship. This somewhat far-fetched idea is made untenable by the fact that Epidamnus was under a democratic regime.

If Epidamnus provides a typical example of Corcyra's relations to her colonies, it may be said that Corcyra kept up a close connection with her colonies and that she regarded her influence over them as a matter of importance and justified by her position as mother city. On the other hand they were certainly not parts of the Corcyrean state, and their internal affairs at least were their own concern. Such relations justify the conclusion that the exact similarity in their coinage between two of Corcyra's colonies and some of Corinth's reflects a similarity of status. Corinth's relations with her dependent colonies were not unique.

The evidence about Corinth's relations with her colonies, and especially with those founded by the tyrants in the North-West, has shown that they were founded with imperial intentions and remained in close connection with Corinth and under her domination. Corcyra's colonies seem to have had a very closely similar status but these were in the same area and also closely

[1] 'In order to be leaders and receive reasonable respect.'
[2] As H. Schaefer, *Staatsform und Politik*, 225 f, who very justly compares Epidamnus' action with that of Plataea in seeking the protection of Athens. The words that Herodotus uses (VI.108.2–4) are very similar to those of Thucydides, and it is clear that Plataea delivered herself into Athens' power in return for Athenian protection.
[3] *Sizilien und Athen* 13 f.

connected racially to Corinth. It is, therefore, more important
to see if Corinth's relations with her colonies are markedly
different from the relations of other Greek colonies and mother
cities.

It has been seen that Athens founded colonies to further her
imperial aims,[1] but these were rather later than those of
Corinth, and their relations to Athens are still to be discussed.
However, in Chapter V several examples were noted of colonies
in a definitely subordinate position regarding their mother city,
such as those of Thasos, Sybaris and Syracuse. It was seen that
when the distance between the colony and metropolis was
small the colony tended to come under the mother city's close
control, so that in some cases its independent existence is in
doubt. The Corinthian dependent colonies were definitely
separate communities, but they too were so closely connected
with Corinth as to count in a general way as her possessions.

Except for Chalcis and Molycrium the colonies are not particularly close to Corinth geographically, but the same factor,
ease of communication, may have made their position similar
to that of colonies founded at a much smaller distance from
their mother cities. The character of Corinth's colonization is
to be understood in the light of Thucydides' information
(I.13.2, 5) that Corinth was very early a considerable naval
power. From the beginning frequent intercourse was possible
with her colonies, and this would allow her to control them.
This is the practical difference between Corinth and many other
mother cities to which we should attribute any special character
in her colonization, not the legal or formal differences postulated by some scholars, which have been seen to be unsupported
by evidence.

It has been seen that the colonists were not citizens of Corinth,
and there is no explicit evidence for mutual citizenship, as there
is in the case of Miletus. However, Corinth could send settlers to
her colonies, so that freedom of movement between colony and
metropolis also existed within this group.

The position of Corinth's colonies seems to have lain some-
where between autonomy and absorption in the state of
Corinth. Such a status is difficult to define, and the quarrel between Corinth and Corcyra partly sprang from this indefinite-

[1] See Chapter III.

ness. Corinth not only felt that she had political rights over Epidamnus because it was, they claimed, their colony just as much as Corcyra's, but she also hated Corcyra because Corcyrean independence and strength seemed an insult. These ideas, which Thucydides records, are particularly valuable, not only in themselves, but also because they can be tested against evidence for the practical position of the colonies. Just as the position was in practice neither freedom nor complete subjection so Corcyra could argue that colonies were sent out not to be the slaves, but to be the equals of those who stayed behind,[1] while Corinth maintained that she established colonies not to be insulted by them, but to be their leaders and receive reasonable respect (I.38.2).

Such generalizations go to the heart of the problem of a Greek colony's political position regarding its mother city. But the very fact that both Corinth and Corcyra discuss the relationship in such general terms suggests that political relations between Corinth and her colonies were not a matter of precise arrangement. On the other hand, religious relations evidently were. The only detailed complaints against Corcyra as an undutiful colony specify her failure to fulfil certain religious obligations to Corinth (I.25.4). But these obligations should be discussed in the light of the general religious relationship between Greek colonies and their mother cities, which forms part of the subject of the next chapter.

---

[1] οὐ . . ἐπὶ τῷ δοῦλοι ἀλλὰ ἐπὶ τῷ ὁμοῖοι τοῖς λειπομένοις εἶναι; I.34.1.

CHAPTER VIII

ARGOS, CNOSSUS, TYLISSUS, AND RELIGIOUS RELATIONS

IN THE early years of this century were found at Argos two large fragments of an inscription[1] dated by its script to *c.* 450, which concerned Argos and the two Cretan cities, Cnossus and Tylissus. At about the same time there came to light at Tylissus one large fragment and a few small ones of an inscription of similar import and date.[2] Although it was recognized that the documents found at Argos and Tylissus dealt with the same or similar matters,[3] they were regarded as separate until Vollgraff suggested, in the last full-scale treatment,[4] that they represented different parts of a single decree. Since the contents of the fragments found at Argos and Tylissus do not overlap,[5] it cannot be proved that they belong to a single document, but the subject-matter and treatment are so similar[6] that Vollgraff's view is highly probable, and even if he is wrong they cannot be separated in their historical significance. We shall therefore treat them as parts of a single decree.[7]

[1] Tod 33; *IC* I.viii.4.

[2] *IC* I.xxx.1. The two inscriptions are Argos 39 a and 39 b in Jeffery, *Local Scripts of Archaic Greece* (p. 165).

[3] Cf. Kirsten, *RE* s.v. Tylissos 1723 ff: *IC* I pp. 58, 308.

[4] W. Vollgraff, 'Le decret d'Argos relatif à un pacte entre Knossos et Tylissos', *Verhand. d. K. Nederl. Akad. van Wetenschappen* (Letterkunde), Nieuwe Reeks li 1948, no. 2. This book-length study supersedes all previous work, the references to which are given by Vollgraff in the notes to p. 1. I shall refer to the document in Vollgraff's notation, that is Roman numerals for the fragment, and Arabic for the line. It should be remarked that the inscription from Argos (Tod 33; *IC* I.viii.4) is Vollgraff's fragment VI, the large fragment from Tylissus (*IC* I.xxx.1) his fragment V. For his view that all the fragments from Argos and Tylissus contain parts of a single decree, see pp. 3, 17.

[5] Although Vollgraff (6) considers that fragment III (from Tylissus) contains parts of lines 33 f. of fragment VI (from Argos), this seems to be mistaken; see Jeffery loc. cit. (n. 2).

[6] Especially the mingling of political and military affairs with arrangements about cults; see Vollgraff, 17, who rightly says that this is the strongest argument in favour of his thesis.

[7] I print the text of the decree with a translation of the two main parts, V and VI, below in Appendix V.

The unusual character of the inscriptions found at Argos was immediately recognized.[1] Provenance, dialect, script and the dating by Argive officials (VI.43 f) all show that they record an Argive decree, yet the decree mostly concerns relations between two Cretan cities, is in many ways similar to Cretan treaties,[2] and even has occasional instances of Cretan dialect.[3] The inscription found at Tylissus was also recognized to be an Argive decree in spite of its provenance. Script, dialect and the similarity to the document found at Argos made this certain, not to mention the implications of the appearance of Argives in the text, and the probable conclusion from the small fragment I;[4] for this is recognizably the beginning[5] and contains the name Argive. The chief task in interpreting the documents has always been to explain why Argos should pass a decree of Cretan character about Cretan arrangements.

The most obvious explanation is that it is an example of arbitration. In his comparison with other Cretan treaties Vollgraff noted[6] that arbitration was quite common among them. But this cannot be an arbitration, to mention only one, quite incontestable, reason, because Argos is involved in the arrangements herself;[7] an arbitrator is not an interested party.[8]

Among the striking features of the document is the important religious element. For although the main subject of the decree is a peace treaty between Cnossus and Tylissus, there are

---

[1] The stones at Argos were discovered by Vollgraff, and published by him in *BCH* xxxiv 1910, 331 ff; xxxvii 1913, 279 ff. To distinguish Vollgraff's work I shall use the following abbreviations in this chapter: Vollgraff *Verhand.* for the work described above p. 154 n. 4; Vollgraff *BCH* 1910 and Vollgraff *BCH* 1913.

[2] As Vollgraff noted with examples, *BCH* 1913, 282 ff.

[3] See Vollgraff, *BCH* 1910, 353; 1913, 307; *Verhand.* 73. In the last place Vollgraff goes back on his earlier views, and says that the οἱ of οἱ Κνόσιοι (VI.33) is the sole 'créticisme' of the treaty. But his reasons for the exclusion of the other instances that he had collected earlier are rather weak.

[4] *Τύχα[ι*
Ἀρ[γ]ει[ο. The restorations of these opening lines by Vollgraff (see *Verhand.*6, 15 f) are inevitably uncertain.

[5] See Vollgraff, *Verhand.* 4.

[6] *BCH* 1913, 302 f.

[7] See, for the certain instances, V.8 ff, VI.37 f.

[8] Scholars have generally recognized that the document is not an example of ordinary arbitration; cf. Vollgraff, *BCH* 1910, 334 f, Kirsten, *Die Insel Kreta,* 16 f, *RE* s.v. Tylissos 1725. Tod cautiously says (I, pp. 62 f) 'mediation, or possibly arbitration, of Argos'.

several arrangements for sacrifices not only to Cretan, but also
to Argive deities, and the decree was passed by the assembly
for sacred matters.[1] Thus not only does Argos decree the detailed arrangements of a treaty of peace and alliance between
Cnossus and Tylissus, but her decree is a religious matter.

In seeking an explanation for a connection between Argos
and the Cretan cities which was bound up with religion, Vollgraff turned to the evidence that Argos was regarded as the
metropolis of Crete. Whatever the true facts about the origin
of the Dorian settlers of Crete in the period of the migrations,
both literary and numismatic evidence show that in the classical
period Argos was regarded as at least one of the centres from
which they came.[2] Vollgraff suggested that this belief was the
reason for the decree.[3] The two Cretan cities wanted to establish
peaceful relations, and turned to Argos as their mother city,
in order to have a higher, external guarantor of their arrangements.

According to this explanation Argos is in the background
and the basis for the document is an agreement between
Cnossus and Tylissus. The provisions which refer to two participants without naming them are taken to imply an earlier text
drawn up between Cnossus and Tylissus,[4] and the Cretan
character and dialect forms are similarly explained. The great
advantage of such an explanation is that it seems to cover all
the facts, and accounts for Argos' role and the religious character of the agreement. It is not surprising, therefore, that Vollgraff's thesis has been accepted by other students of Greek
inscriptions[5] and Cretan affairs.[6] It is not, however, capable
of final proof, which could only be provided by an explicit

[1] We may assume this, since the amendment was passed by that body:
ἁλιαίαι ἔδοξε τᾶι τῶν ἱαρῶν; VI.44 f. The assembly τῶν ἱαρῶν is well explained
by Vollgraff, Verhand. 89, who compares the Athenian arrangement that the
last two regular assemblies in a prytany had to deal first with sacred matters
(τὰ ἱερά); see Arist. Ath. Pol. 43.6 and Sandys' note ad loc. (Aristotle's Constitution of Athens², 173).
[2] The evidence is briefly collected by Kirsten, RE s.v. Tylissos 1725. For
a full discussion see Vollgraff, Verhand. 91–102, who also maintains from the
evidence for identical cults that these Cretan cities were in fact colonized
from Argos.
[3] First in BCH 1910, 334.
[4] Cf. Tod I p. 63; IC I p. 58.
[5] As Tod, if cautiously, I pp. 62 f; Guarducci, IC I pp. 58; 308.
[6] Especially Kirsten, Die Insel Kreta, 16 ff; RE s.v. Tylissos 1723 ff.

statement in the document itself that Argos was the mother city of Cnossus and Tylissus.[1]

Since Vollgraff's explanation cannot be proved right others must be considered. A very different interpretation of the decree was put forward by Kahrstedt,[2] who is followed by Gschnitzer in a recent discussion of the subject.[3] According to Kahrstedt the document represents a treaty between only two independent states, Argos and Cnossus. Tylissus is a foreign possession of Argos, and this accounts for Argos' interest in regulating the arrangements between Cnossus and Tylissus. This suggestion was not considered worthy of comprehensive refutation by Vollgraff,[4] but since the relations of Argos, Cnossus and Tylissus would not belong to the subject of the present study, if it were correct, I discuss the matter in detail in Appendix V below. There I show, firstly, that the provisions of the decree prove that Tylissus was an independent state, not a piece of Argive territory, and, secondly, that the document cannot be taken as an agreement between two states only, Cnossus and Argos. Each of these demonstrations destroys Kahrstedt's case. We have noted the advantages in Vollgraff's interpretation. Since the only other interpretation that has been proposed is clearly unsatisfactory, we may follow Vollgraff in regarding Argos' position as metropolis of the Cretan cities as the underlying reason for the decree.

On this interpretation the document represents one of the most important epigraphical additions to the evidence for the relations between colonies and mother cities. In the first place it shows that the two Cretan colonies acknowledged the general primacy of Argos, which gave the mother city the authority to establish the conditions for their agreement. It appears that the two cities had been at enmity,[5] and this may have been an

---

[1] It is true that Vollgraff restores $T[υλίσιον ἄποικον ᾿Αργε-$
$ίο]ν$
in lines 3 f of fragment I, but for a phrase which is not a formula too much has to be supplied for any suggestion to command much confidence.

[2] *Klio* xxxiv 1942, 72–91.

[3] *Abhängige Orte im griech. Altertum*, ch. 10.

[4] Cf. *Verhand.* 91, where he says, with some justice, 'Je considère les solutions de Kahrstedt comme infirmées par l'ensemble de mon commentaire.'

[5] See VI.25 ff and Vollgraff *Verhand.* 56 ff. These provisions about boundaries imply territorial disputes.

added reason for their recourse to Argos. If they regarded themselves as related by origin, their quarrel would have the shame
attached to strife between related cities, and their mother city
would be particularly suitable as a mediator. The situation
would be comparable to that of Neapolis and Thasos discussed
above,[1] where Paros may have arranged for their reconciliation.

The character of Argos' supremacy emerges fairly clearly
from the document. If it is right to interpret the provision that
Argos is to have a third of the votes in decisions about striking
new alliances (V.9 ff) as showing that Argos was to be the
guarantor of the agreement,[2] her position was not that of a
temporary mediator. Her authority over the affairs of Cnossus
and Tylissus was intended to persist. This suits the general implications of the decree. Argos' primacy seems to be something
accepted as normal by all parties, for, though the decree is
incomplete, it gives the impression that it was not necessary
to comment on the relationship of the three cities.[3] Another
general observation of importance is that there is no sign in the
document that Argos' actions were motivated by self-interest.
Apart from the offerings to her great deity[4] she appears to have
gained no advantage from the agreement. This is, therefore, not
an example of control exercised over colonies by a mother city
for her own imperial ends.

A possible parallel to Argos' relationship with Cnossus and
Tylissus may be found in the relations between Achaea and her
colonies in Southern Italy. Polybius relates (II.39 1–4) that
after the destruction of the Pythagorean Clubs there followed
every sort of disturbance in Magna Graecia. Embassies then
arrived from Greece offering their services as peacemakers, but
it was the Achaeans who won the confidence of the cities of
Magna Graecia and were entrusted with the task of ending
their troubles. Polybius' intention in telling this tale is to show
that the Achaeans possessed from an early date a very good
political system. He does not mention Achaea's position as
metropolis of many of the cities where the Pythagorean Clubs

---

[1] See Chapter V.   [2] As Kirsten, RE s.v. Tylissos 1725.
[3] The uncertainty of Vollgraff's restoration T[υλισίον ἀποίκον 'Αργείο]ν
is emphasised above, p. 157 n. 1.
[4] VI.16 f. Hera in the Heraeum is, of course, the great goddess of Argos;
see Appendix V.

are known to have flourished,[1] but it would have weakened his argument about the excellence of the Achaean political system, and it may be regarded as possible that the Achaean intervention was accepted because of the relationship between Achaea and her colonies.[2]

This seems all the more likely in view of Polybius' immediately subsequent information (II.39.5 f) that Croton, Sybaris and Caulonia formed a league modelled on that of the Achaeans, having the same league temple and god (Zeus Homarios), the same customs (ἐθισμούς), the same laws and the same constitution. All three cities were Achaean colonies,[3] but again Polybius does not mention this connection. However, the exact copying of the political arrangements of the mother country, and even more the choice of the same god, suggest that the cities were not only conscious of their origin, but also in contact with their metropolis. In view of this, the mediation of Achaea, which occurred some time before,[4] may be compared with Argos' supervision of the affairs of Cnossus and Tylissus. It seems to have been similarly disinterested, and to have been designed to bring about peaceful relations between quarrelling colonies.

The second important aspect of the relationship between colony and mother city illustrated by the Argive decree is religious. It provides for the colonies to make a joint sacrifice of a cow to Argive Hera before the Hyacinthia (VI.4 f).[5] Machaneus, on the other hand, (VI.29) seems certainly to have been a Cnossian god,[6] and Poseidon in Iutos (VI.15) is connected

[1] Notably of Croton, the centre of it all; see K. von Fritz, *Pythagorean Politics in Southern Italy*, especially ch. V.
[2] This possibility is noted by Walbank, *Commentary on Polybius* I.225.
[3] See Dunbabin 24, 27 f.
[4] Polybius gives no date, but only states (II.39.5) that the copying of the federal arrangements of the Achaeans occurred some time after (μετά τινας χρόνους) the Achaean intervention. The dates of both events are fully discussed by Walbank, *Commentary on Polybius* I 224 ff. It seems most probable that the Achaean intervention took place 'some time, but not very long, before the outbreak of the Peloponnesian War' (von Fritz 79), and the copying of Achaean institutions before 417, when the Spartans set up oligarchies in Achaea; see Walbank 224 f.
[5] τᾶι Ἥραι ἐν ’Εραίοι θύεν βõν θέλει[αν ἀμφοτ]έρον[ς κ]οινᾶι, θύεν δὲ πρὸ Ϝακινθ[ίον. . . .
[6] See Appendix V. He is, however, apparently in origin an Argive deity; see Vollgraff, *Verhand.* 59 f.

M

by Vollgraff[1] with Mount Juktas, which is near Tylissus. However, Poseidon was very important at Argos,[2] where there was also a cult of Ares and Aphrodite,[3] to whom offerings are also to be made (VI.34 f). But as some of these offerings were almost certainly to Cretan deities, and all may have been, it is advisable to regard the offering to Hera as the only definite example in the decree of sacrifices by colonies to the gods of the metropolis.

The sacrifice to the goddess of the mother city may mark, as Vollgraff writes,[4] 'l'étroite union des deux colonies et leur dépendance de la métropole', but it is worth noting that it occurs among several other arrangements for sacrifices, and it bears the signs of being an innovation. It is necessary, for instance, to specify the nature and the time of the sacrifice to Hera. It may be right to conclude that mutual sacrifices between allied states were common Cretan practice, and the colonies were making the offering at Argos for the first time. If that is so, the offering does not reveal earlier practices, but ideas current at the time. However, other examples of such religious connections show that they were a regular and important part of the relationship between colonies and mother cities.

We have already seen that when Thucydides describes (I.25.4) how the Corcyreans neglected their mother city the only precise shortcoming that he mentions is their failure to fulfil certain religious obligations. 'For they neither gave the customary offerings at the common festivals, nor did they give the first portion of the sacrifice to a Corinthian, as the other colonies did.' The second part of this sentence is the only evidence that it was normal at sacrifices in the colonies to give the first portion to a citizen of the metropolis, but evidence for such a practice could be expected to be rare, especially if it was traditional and generally accepted, so that it need not be denied general application. When the scholiast adds in explanation 'for it was customary to bring the chief priest from the metropolis', he gives away his misunderstanding of the phrase, and his information is therefore suspect. It too is unsupported by other evidence, and since it is a rather more striking practice

---

[1] *BCH* 1913, 296; *Verhand.* 49 f.   [2] See Paus. II.xv.5; xxii.4.
[3] See Paus. II.xxv.1.   [4] *Verhand.* 51.

than that recorded by Thucydides it seems dangerous to accept it on the evidence of a single late and doubtful passage.[1]

The exact meaning of the first phrase in Thucydides' sentence is not agreed. Thucydides' words are ἐν πανηγύρεσι ταῖς κοιναῖς διδόντες γέρα τὰ νομιζόμενα, and the scholiast on the passage explained the γέρα as the rights of *proedria* and the like in the festivals of the colony. His explanation was accepted by the early writers about the colony–metropolis relationship,[2] and the fact that Thucydides is certainly referring to sacrifices in the colony in the second part of the sentence is in its favour. The practice would then be comparable with the privileges enjoyed by Milesians in Olbia.[3] However, Diesterweg explained the phrase as referring to gifts or offerings brought to the festivals of the metropolis by colonists.[4] The description πανηγύρεσι ταῖς κοιναῖς certainly seems more suitable for festivals of the metropolis in which the colonies took part. Since there are parallels to support both interpretations, it is perhaps impossible to choose with certainty between them, but the larger quantity of analogous instances is in favour of Diesterweg's view.

We have already noted[5] that arrangements were made in the foundation decree for Brea for the colonists to make regular offerings at Athens' great festivals.[6] Colonies of Miletus had similar obligations to Apollo of Didyma, though the evidence refers to Hellenistic times.[7] In these instances the evidence is explicit that the colonies were to make regular offerings as a duty, which is also the implication of Thucydides' words, on Diesterweg's interpretation. In view of this, individual offerings of which we have record may perhaps be regarded as part of a regular duty.

The earliest definite example of an offering by a colony to the gods of its metropolis is the seventh-century dedication by Gela to Athena of Lindus.[8] The words of the dedication Γελῶιοι

---

[1] It was accepted by the earlier writers; cf. de Bougainville, op. cit., 38; but Diesterweg, op. cit., 25, is already suspicious of it.

[2] As, e.g., by Raoul-Rochette 43; see above p. xviii n. 1.

[3] Tod 195.11 f; see above Chapter VI.

[4] Op. cit., p. 24.   [5] See Chapter IV.

[6] Tod 44.10 f.   [7] See above p. 108 with n. 1.

[8] See *Lindian Chronicle* XXV, in *Lindos, Fouilles d'Acropole, II, Inscriptions*, by Chr. Blinkenberg; cf. Dunbabin 113. On the question of the chronicle's reliability see above, p. 20 n. 4.

τᾶ[ι] ᾽Αθαναίαι τᾶι Πατρωίαι . . .[1] show both that the offering
came from the state of Gela and that the goddess was expressly
regarded as a deity of the fatherland.[2] The offering of Deino-
menes, the father of Gelon, to Athena Lindia[3] in the middle of
the sixth century is rather different, as coming from an individual Geloan, but the offerings of Acragas to the same
goddess in the latter half of the sixth century are, like the early
one from Gela, from the whole community.[4]

Pausanias (III.xii.5 f) mentions a statue of Athena at Sparta,
which was said to have been dedicated by the colonists of Taras,
but his words (ὅ τοὺς ἐς ᾽Ιταλίαν τε καὶ Τάραντα ἀποικισθέντας
ἀναθεῖναι λέγουσι) make it possible that it was supposed to have
been dedicated by the first settlers.[5] If that is so it is unlikely
that the tradition was correct, as an ἄγαλμα of Athena of the end
of the eighth century[6] would have required rather more careful
description by Pausanias.[7] It may, therefore, be assumed either
that the attribution to Taras was incorrect, or that Pausanias'
wording is simply a description of the inhabitants of Taras at
some period considerably after the foundation.[8]

A large and expensive dedication to Hera of Samos by two
Perinthians is recorded in an interesting archaic inscription.[9]
At first sight it seems to be a dedication by private individuals,
but M. Guarducci contends that we should regard it as emanating from the state of Perinthus.[10] Apart from a new reading,

[1] 'The Geloans to Athena of the fatherland. . . .'
[2] As Blinkenberg remarked in his note ad loc. in *Die lindische Tempelchronik* (Bonn 1915).
[3] See *Lindian Chronicle* XXVIII, and Dunbabin 483.
[4] *Lindian Chronicle* XXVII, XXX. One (XXVII) is from Phalaris, but,
as ruler, he represented Acragas.
[5] This view of the phrase's meaning is taken by Jones (Loeb), who translates 'which is said to have been dedicated by those who left for Tarentum
in Italy'.
[6] The traditional date of the foundation of Taras is 706. It is accepted as
approximately correct by Dunbabin (31) and Bérard (169 f).
[7] Cf. his remarks about the wooden statue of Hermes Cyllenius in Arcadia,
VIII.xvii.2 f. Frazer's note ad loc. mentions the many other places where
Pausanias remarks on wooden statues; see *Pausanias' description of Greece*
IV,245 ff.
[8] As Frazer translates, I p. 151.
[9] First published by Klaffenbach in *Mitt. d. deutsch. arch. Inst.* vi 1953,
15–20; cf. Jeffery, *Local Scripts of Archaic Greece* 365 (no. 35). Klaffenbach
argues for a date in the decade 580–570, but Jeffery would put it 'c. 525'
(p. 371).
[10] *Studi in onore di Aristide Calderini e Roberto Paribeni* I (Milan 1956) 23–27.

which cannot be accepted,[1] she argues from the analogies of colonies which made offerings to the metropolis as a regular duty and from the most unusual statement of the exact cost of the dedication. She envisages an agreement by which the colony was obliged to make a dedication of this value, and the delegation of the task to the two men named. This seems a possible hypothesis, though it is without specific support in the text itself. At the least we have a clear and fairly early example of a dedication by colonists to the great deity of the mother city.

There is a fourth-century inscription concerning the relations of Epidaurus and its colony Astypalaea,[2] which provides for the colonists to make offerings at the mother city. As the wording of the decree is striking it deserves to be quoted in full:

Θεός. Τύχα ἀγαθά. ἔδοξε τοῖς
᾿Επιδαυρίοις ᾿Αστυπαλαιεῦ-
σιν ἀποίκοις ᾿Επιδαυρίων
ἐοῦσιν καὶ εὐεργέταις ἀτέ-
λειαν εἶμεν πάντων καὶ ἀσυ-
λίαν καὶ ἐν ἰράναι καὶ ἐν πο-
λέμωι καὶ κατὰ γᾶν καὶ κατὰ
θάλασσαν, καὶ τὰ ἰαρ[ε]ῖα τὰ
τῶν ᾿Αστυπαλα[ι]έων πεμπέσ-
[θ]αι σὺν τᾶ[ι τῶν] ᾿Επιδαυρίων
[πο]μπᾶι καὶ θύεν τοῖς θεοῖ[ς]
[τοῖς] ἐν ᾿Επι[δαύρωι . . .[3]

The express statement that Astypalaea was a colony of Epidaurus contradicts the information of Ps-Scymnus (551)

[1] The enigma of lines 3/4, where the two dedicators are described as ο[ἰ]κηιηιοι (sic) Περίνθιοι, is perplexing; see Klaffenbach 17 f and Robert *Bull.* 1959 no. 320 (*REG* lxxii 1959, 225), who dismisses Guarducci's attempted emendation. I suggest elsewhere in a detailed discussion of the crux that we should read ο[ἰ]κήι{ηι}οι with Klaffenbach and Robert, and understand the word as referring to the tie of kinship between colonists and mother city; see *JHS* lxxxiv 1964.
[2] *IG* IV².1.47 and commentary.
[3] 'Gods. Good Fortune. Decreed by the Epidaurians. Because the people of Astypalaea are colonists and benefactors of the Epidaurians, they shall have complete immunity from taxation and be inviolable both in peace and war both on land and sea; and the sacred offerings of the Astypalaeans shall be sent in the procession of the Epidaurians, and they shall sacrifice to the gods of Epidaurus. . . . '

that it was a colony of Megara, but the statement of the inscription is to be preferred, because there are other indications that Astypalaea was settled from the Argolid. The dialect of its inscriptions points to such an origin,[1] and the sanctuary of Asclepius on Astypalaea[2] suggests a connection with Epidaurus. It may be assumed that the island was a Dorian foundation from the Argolid of the migratory period, like Crete, Rhodes, Aegina and other islands.

Among the privileges granted to the people of Astypalaea on the grounds that they were colonists and benefactors of Epidaurus were the rights to send their offerings with the procession of the Epidaurians and to sacrifice to the gods of Epidaurus. There is little doubt that both were innovations, and it is interesting that the offerings decreed were privileges rather than a duty imposed on the colonists. In this the decree presumably reflects the special prestige of Epidaurus as a religious centre. The tone of the document and its express reference to Astypalaea's status as a colony of Epidaurus tell against any presumption that the relations were based on more ancient practices. But they reveal the way in which the relationship of colony and mother city was regarded in the fourth century, and the evidence from other colonies shows that the religious provisions were in accordance with much more ancient traditional practices.

The other privileges conferred on the people of Astypalaea, inviolability (*asylia*) and tax-immunity (*ateleia*), were commonly granted to foreign benefactors, either individuals or whole communities, though most of the evidence naturally comes from inscriptions of the fourth century or later.[3] The grant of *ateleia* is comparable with the arrangements between Olbia and Miletus,[4] while that of *asylia* implies strongly that Astypalaea and Epidaurus had not kept up close relations before the time of the decree.

These privileges are specific. The Argive decree about

[1] Cf. *IG* XII.3 p. 30 and Collitz and Bechtel *SGDI* III.1 p. 209 and notes to nos. 3459, 3472.
[2] See *IG* XII.3.167.6.
[3] These terms and the evidence for them are briefly discussed in Busolt, *Griech. Staatskunde* I 300; Busolt/Swoboda 1242 with notes 1 and 2; *RE* s.v. ateleia 1911.
[4] Tod 195.6, 17 f, 21 f; see above Chapter VI.

Cnossus and Tylissus shows that the people of Cnossus and Tylissus also had privileges in their mother city. For the amendment (VI.44 f), by which the Tylissians who came to Argos were to receive the same treatment as the Cnossians, presumably refers to exemptions from exactions on foreigners and the like, though the privileges are not specified in the parts of the decree preserved. They may have been specified, as Vollgraff suggests,[1] earlier in the decree, at the point where fragment V breaks off. He reads (V.34 f) αἴ κ᾽ ἔν θ[ει τις Κνοσίον ἐνς ᾽Αργος.[2] Whether or not this is right, the privileges enjoyed by the colonists who came to the mother city may be added to the aspects of the relationship for which the decree provides evidence.

The relations between Argos, Cnossus and Tylissus attested by the inscriptions discussed are at the same time unpretentious and surprising. Unpretentious in that there is no far-reaching claim to control or exploit the colonies; surprising because they show that there were in the fifth century effective bonds between a mother city and colonies settled in the migratory period. The relations do not depend either on special geographical proximity, like those of Thasos and her colonies, or on the ambitions of the mother city, like those of Corinth with hers; they are more to be compared with the kind of relations discussed in Chapter VI, where the citizens of colonies and mother cities had mutual privileges without the influence of these special factors. As such they have great value in showing how close the bonds could be even when the metropolis had no imperial ambitions regarding the colonies, and also in showing the kinds of relations which were maintained in such circumstances. The colonists had religious connections with the metropolis, they had privileges in the metropolis when they went there, and, finally, they recognized the general primacy of the mother city, which gave her the authority to settle their affairs.

[1] *Verhand.* 39 f.   [2] 'If [a Cnossian] comes [to Argos].'

CHAPTER IX

ATHENS AND LATE IMPERIAL COLONIES

A THENS is most noticeably absent from the mother cities of the great colonizing movement in the eighth and seventh centuries. Her colonies belong to later times and are different in character from most of those founded in the earlier period. Some have already been discussed in Part I, as their foundations provided evidence about the role of the oikist and foundation decrees.[1] The imperial ambitions which were discerned to a greater or lesser extent in these foundations may be compared in this chapter with the colonies' subsequent relations to Athens, to see how far they were actually realized. The relations in the same period between other mother cities and colonies of comparable character will need to be set beside the Athenian material, before general comparisons can be made with the colonial relationships already discussed.

But in addition to the colonies whose foundations were discussed in Part I there is a great deal of other Athenian colonial activity of relevance to the present subject. Much of this was by means of the settlement of cleruchies. And since any discussion of an Athenian colony begins with the question whether or not it was a cleruchy, the first part of this chapter must be devoted to the nature of the cleruchy and to its differentiation from other colonies. The place of the cleruchy in Greek colonization should also emerge from such a discussion.

The most far-going theory advanced in recent times about the relations between Greek colonies and their mother cities is Hampl's thesis that when a colony was founded by the state its land remained the territory of the mother city, even when the colony itself formed a polis 'im Rechtssinne'.[2] Such a city was therefore a 'Polis ohne Territorium'. This thesis appears to

---

[1] See Chapters III and IV.
[2] 'Poleis ohne Territorium', *Klio* xxxii 1939, 1–60. For the general statement about colonies see p. 6.

demand over-formal legal distinctions which did not exist in Greek political life.[1] Since the Greeks were advanced in political thought, a striking political concept supposed to explain Greek political circumstances, but not found in ancient writers, is inevitably suspect. However, it would not be justifiable in a study devoted to the colony-metropolis relationship to dismiss on general grounds alone so bold a theory about those relations. As Athenian colonies of the fifth century form the main examples on which Hampl's thesis is based, we may consider it in detail in this chapter with the colonies in question.

Cleruchies and doubtful cases

The cleruchy of the fourth century and later times is well defined by the ancient evidence.[2] It was a settlement of Athenian citizens living abroad, and was clearly described as such in inscriptions by titles like 'the Athenians living in Myrina' or 'the Athenian demos in Imbros',[3] and by similar phrases in literary sources.[4] In their local institutions the cleruchies copied Athens faithfully,[5] and in every way they can be regarded as an extension of the Athenian state overseas.[6]

However, this is not to deny that in practice the geographical separation from Athens made the cleruchy different from part of Attica. The effect of this separation is probably reflected in the variation in the ethnic applied by ancient writers to the

[1] Hampl is followed by Gschnitzer, *Abhängige Orte im griech. Altertum, passim,* but otherwise his ideas have not won wide acceptance. Kirsten, for instance (*RE* s.v. Tylissos 1727) objected that they ignored the personal character of Greek states and Will rejects his conclusions (*La Nouvelle Clio* vi 1954, 413 ff), though without, on the whole, criticism in detail. Cf. also Habicht, *Gnomon* xxxi 1959, 704 ff.

[2] The accounts of cleruchies in *RE* s.v. κλῆρουχοι and in Busolt/Swoboda 1271–9 are sound and thorough. Recently Gschnitzer has treated them fully and carefully, as we know them after 400, *Abhängige Orte im griech. Altertum* 98–112.

[3] For these inscriptions see Busolt/Swoboda 1277 n. 4.

[4] E.g. [Arist.] *Oec.* II. 1347 a 18, Ἀθηναῖοι δὲ ἐν Ποτειδαίᾳ οἰκοῦντες; [Dem.] VII.10, where the wording is similar; cf. also Dem. XXIII.103, where those inhabiting the Chersonese are called πολῖται.

[5] Thus a cleruchy was described by Gilbert as 'bis in die geringsten Details ein vollständiges Klein-Athen'; see *Handbuch d. griech. Staatsalterthümer* (Leipzig 1881) 423.

[6] The evidence to prove that cleruchies were regarded as territory of the Athenian state is given by Gschnitzer 99; it is not all of equal quality, but the conclusion is certain.

fourth-century general Athenodorus. Plutarch calls him an
Imbrian (Ἴμβριος) (*Phoc.* XVIII.4), as does Aeneas Polior-
cetes (24.10), but when Demosthenes wants to make a strong
debating point, he writes (XXIII.12) ὁ δὲ δὴ γένει πολίτης
Ἀθηνόδωρος.[1] As Athenodorus also appears without distinguishing epithet in an inscription from Imbros,[2] it seems right to
interpret this variation, with Foucart,[3] as showing that he came
from a family of Athenian cleruchs on Imbros. Thus he was
legally an Athenian citizen, but he could still be called Ἴμβριος
because of the locality of his origin.[4]

In spite of this concession to the practical separation of a
cleruchy from Athens, however, the legal position of the cleruchy
in the fourth century is not to be disputed. But the sources for
the cleruchies of the fifth century do not provide such un-
equivocal evidence.[5] Hence there are doubts not only about
the status of individual settlements, but also on the whole
question of the difference between a cleruchy and an *apoikia*.
This evidence, therefore, requires more detailed consideration.

The earliest cleruchy of which we have certain knowledge[6] is
that described by Herodotus (V.77.2), which was settled on the

---

[1] 'But he who is by race a citizen, Athenodorus. . . .'   [2] *IG* XII.8.48.9.
[3] See *BCH* vii, 1883, 161 f, where the ancient references to Athenodorus
are assembled.
[4] Note, by the way, that this is a further example to discourage modern
scholars from drawing conclusions about legal citizenship from ethnics,
Cf. Chapter IV.
[5] Gschnitzer notes this (98 f), and rightly stresses that the evidence of the
fourth century does not necessarily show the legal position of the fifth, when
the form of the cleruchy might not have been so fixed.
[6] The incomplete first Attic decree, *IG* I².1 (Tod 11, *SEG* X.1), has been
thought to concern an Athenian cleruchy on Salamis, founded either under
the tyrants or after their fall. However, this view was rejected in *CAH* IV.161
n. 2, and it must be confessed that the contents of the document remain too
uncertain for any definite conclusions; see my remarks in *Proc. Class. Assoc.*
liii 1956, 28 f, where I show that the date is probably early in the fifth
century and that it seems unlikely that it referred to cleruchs. On the other
hand Hammond concludes (*JHS* lxxvi 1956, 37 and n. 18) that Herodotus'
description (VIII.95) of some hoplites on Salamis as γένος ἐόντες Ἀθηναῖοι
shows that they were generally called Salaminioi. If he is right they could
be compared with Athenodorus and taken to show that there were cleruchs
on Salamis by 480. The whole question of Salamis is complicated, and it
does seem, owing to its geographical proximity to Athens, to have occupied
a unique position, expressed, for instance in the archon for Salamis (Arist.
Ath. Pol. 54.8), an office not paralleled among other Athenian possessions.
There is a long and full note on questions about Salamis in Busolt/Swoboda
871 f.

land of the Hippobotai of Chalcis in 506. In deciding the status of these cleruchs we should be chary of arguing from the ethnics used to describe them. For though Herodotus calls them Athenians when describing their part in the events of 490 (VI.100), it has been plausibly suggested that he called them Chalcidians before the Battle of Artemisium (VIII.1.2) and at Salamis (VIII.46.2).[1] In any case arguments from ethnics are weak, as has been seen. The cleruchs' position is illustrated more clearly by Herodotus' statement (VI.100.1) that when the Eretrians asked for Athenian support in 490, the Athenians replied that they could have the 4000 cleruchs. It seems likely that only Athenian citizens could have been used by the Athenian state in this way. If this conclusion is accepted, the most important characteristic of the cleruch, his retention of Athenian citizenship, is found in the first instance of which we know.

In this instance the relation between the terms used and the circumstances described is satisfactory by modern standards. In keeping their original citizenship the cleruchs were a special type of colonist, and Herodotus uses the words κλῆρουχος (V.77.2) and κληρουχέω (VI.100.1) to refer to them. It is also apparent that official language at Athens in the fifth century recognized a distinction between a cleruchy and an *apoikia*; for in the incomplete inscription *IG* I² 140 occur the words ταῖ]ς ἀποικίαις καὶ κλεροχία[ις. It is, therefore, legitimate to assume that Attic inscriptions observe the distinction in their language. However, this is unfortunately not possible with literary sources, and the confusion, or rather untechnical language, of ancient writers has led to great variety in modern interpretations of their words.

Plutarch, for instance, includes Thurii among the cleruchies (*Per.* XI.5), though this is obviously impossible in view of the mixed origin of the settlers. Andocides applies the word ἀποικίαι to Naxos, the Chersonese and Euboea (III.9), all of which contained cleruchies.[2] Demosthenes called the fourth-century

---

[1] The suggestion is made by Grundy, *The Great Persian War*, 320; see also Hammond, *JHS* lxxvi 1956, 37 n. 18, who argues the matter in detail.

[2] Plut. *Per.* XI.5 for Naxos; for the Chersonese XIX.1; Euboea, because, even if Hestiaea is left out of account, there was a cleruchy at Chalcis in the second half of the fifth century; see Aelian, *V.H.* 6.1. On this point see the convincing treatment in *ATL* III.296 f.

cleruchs of Potidaea ἄποικοι (*Phil.* II.20), although we know that
they were cleruchs from an inscription,[1] and this at a time when
the distinct form of the cleruchy was clear and fixed, and recognized by literary authorities, including Demosthenes himself
on other occasions.[2]

But the most serious difficulties arise with Thucydides. Ehrenberg has shown convincingly that Thucydides can use the words
apoikia and *apoikos* for cleruchy and cleruch. He employs the
technical term cleruch (κλήρουχος) on one occasion only, when
he describes the establishment of the cleruchy on Lesbos after
the Mytilenean Revolt (III. 50.2); and here he was clearly
interested in the procedure involved.[3] Ehrenberg's arguments
are strong, but he has not been universally followed,[4] and since
his thesis is of great importance for the present study the main
examples on which it is based must be considered here. The
settlements in question, yield, in any case, important information about Athenian colonization.[5]

When Thucydides describes the Athenian settlement of Hestiaea in 446/5, he writes (I.114.3) Ἑστιαιᾶς δὲ ἐξοικίσαντες αὐτοὶ
(sc. οἱ Ἀθηναῖοι) τὴν γῆν ἔσχον,[6] and in a passage referring to 411
(VIII.95.7) he describes the settlers at Hestiaea[7] as the Athenians themselves (αὐτοὶ Ἀθηναῖοι). However, when he lists the
Athenian allies at Syracuse he includes Ἑστιαιῆς οἱ ἐν Εὐβοίᾳ
Ἑστίαιαν οἰκοῦντες ἄποικοι ὄντες[8] (VII.57.2).[9]

[1] Tod 146.
[2] See above p. 167.
[3] Ehrenberg put forward his view first in *Aspects of the Ancient World*,
ch. IX, but the matter is fully argued in *CP* xlvii 1952, 143 ff.
[4] See *ATL* III.285 n. 46, though this antedates, indeed provoked, Ehrenberg's second study.
[5] The question of the status of Athenian colonies in the fifth century has
been discussed by Jones, *Athenian Democracy*, 169 ff, but as he bases his
work largely on the treatment of *ATL* III.282–97 (see p. 168), which has
been shown to be unsatisfactory by Ehrenberg (whose work Jones ignores),
his study does not make another discussion superfluous.
[6] 'Having expelled the Hestiaeans they themselves (i.e. the Athenians)
occupied the land.'
[7] For the use of the name Oreos as equivalent to Hestiaea see *RE* Suppl.
IV.749.
[8] 'The Hestiaeans who inhabit Hestiaea in Euboea, being *apoikoi*.'
[9] On the evidence of the words ἄποικοι ὄντες Hestiaea is taken not to be
a cleruchy in Busolt/Swoboda (1274 n. 1), although they recognize elsewhere (1276 n. 2) that the distinction between ἄποικος and κλήρουχος was not
strictly maintained in general usage. In fact they imply in this note that the

Fortunately Thucydides' phrase does not stand alone as evidence for the status of Hestiaea. The inscriptions *IG* I².40–43[1] contain Athenian regulations about Hestiaea passed after 446.[2] They are seriously incomplete, and cannot be restored with certainty. However, as Cary noted,[3] the preserved passages contain key words, so that the stones can be informative even if no complete restoration is possible. The inhabitants of Hestiaea seem to be described periphrastically as, for example, ὁ ἐξ Ἑστιαίας (I².40.7) or τῶν οἰκούντων ἐ[ν Ἑστιαίαι (?)[4] (41.14). These phrases are reminiscent of the later descriptions of cleruchs in inscriptions mentioned above,[5] even though they do not include the name Athenian, and they are also like Thucydides' words already quoted (VII.57.2). Since we know that the inhabitants of Hestiaea at this time were Athenians in origin,[6] it seems reasonable to conclude with Cary (248) that these periphrastic descriptions were used in recognition of the fact that the people described, although living at Hestiaea, were still Athenian citizens, that is cleruchs. But as the phrases are robbed of their context, the matter is not certain, and other indications in the texts must be considered.

The most important lines are I².42.18–24. Although the restorations on which Cary based his interpretation (243–5) are impossible with Meritt's much shorter lines, we still definitely have some arrangements about taxation. For in line 21 there are the words ἀτελε͂ ἔναι μ[εδὲ ἑ͂]να χρεμάτον, in 22 τε͂ι κυρίαι ἐκ[κλεσία]ι, and in 24 χρεμάτον ἐσφορ[ᾶς μὲ ἔ]ναι ἐπιφσε-. The

word ἀποικία occurs in the inscription(s) about Hestiaea, *IG* I².40/41, but this is not so.

[1] The latest texts of parts of these appear in Hill *Sources*² B.54, where it is noted that 43 (reverse) and perhaps 42 belong to 40, and 43 belongs to 41.

[2] The date is given as 'very soon after the Thirty Years Peace' in *ATL* III.301 n. 4.

[3] *JHS* xlv 1925, 243 ff. His rather confident conclusions about the documents are, however, to be treated with caution, for Meritt has since demonstrated that the earlier restorations are precluded by the fact that the lines were probably much shorter than was once thought; see *ATL* loc. cit. and Hill *Sources*² 302 f.

[4] 'the man from Hestiaea', 'those living in [Hestiaea]'. The restoration in the second passage seems likely and was generally made in earlier editions (e.g. *IG* I².41), but Meritt makes no supplement to the letters on the stone; see Hill *Sources*² 303.

[5] See p. 167.

[6] Cary (248 n. 15) lists the other sources for the events, all of which support Thucydides (I.114.3).

main question raised by these lines is whether the tax in question is the Athenian *eisphora*.[1]

It is clear from the literary evidence that the word εἰσφορά without χρημάτων but in combination with εἰσφέρειν had the technical meaning of war tax in the fifth century, and was so understood by all Athenians.[2] It is used with χρημάτων, as in the inscription, by Xenophon (*Hell*.VI.ii.1), and Jones translates '(worn out by) levies of war tax'.[3] Plato's use of the same wording (*Laws* 955 d), however, does not refer to the Athenian tax. In fourth-century epigraphical texts the word occurs regularly to denote the Athenian tax,[4] but in the fifth century it only appears as wholly, if reasonably, restored in the second of Callias' decrees, where it also has the technical sense.[5]

These analogies do not lead to a completely clear-cut conclusion, though they make it a reasonable assumption that in an Attic decree of the second half of the fifth century the words χρημάτων εἰσφορᾶς would refer to the Athenian war tax. This is supported by a further argument. Cary was surely right to conclude (245) that the κυρίαι ἐκκλησίαι must, in an Athenian document, be the Athenian assembly. If so, it was the main Athenian assembly which had to deal with exemption from the tax in question. This suggests that it was an Athenian tax, not, for example, some local payment in Hestiaea. It seems, therefore, that the words χρημάτων εἰσφορᾶς should be referred to the Athenian war levy. Such a tax was imposed on Athenian citizens, and so the settlers of Hestiaea should be regarded as cleruchs.[6]

Aegina and Melos are two other Greek states which the Athenians settled themselves after expelling the previous inhabitants.[7] The status of Aegina has been fully discussed by

[1] The tax, as it was in the fourth century, is discussed by Jones, *Athenian Democracy*, 23 ff; see Gomme, II.278 f, on the questions about *eisphora* in the fifth century.

[2] See Antiphon II.2.12; Lysias XXX.26; Thuc. III.19.1.

[3] See *Athenian Democracy*, 29.

[4] See *IG* II² 141.35 f; 237.27 f; 351.31 f; 505.14; cf. Jones, 23 ff.

[5] *ATL* II D2.17; Gomme argues (II.278) that the way it is mentioned here shows that it was a familiar levy.

[6] This interpretation explains Thucydides' description of the settlers as αὐτοὶ Ἀθηναῖοι (VIII.95.7) more easily than the view that he is only expressing their origin, as Jones, *Athenian Democracy*, 169.

[7] Thuc. II.27.1; V.116.4.

Ehrenberg,[1] who shows that the late sources which state or imply that it was a cleruchy should hardly be dismissed on the assumption that Thucydides' descriptions of the settlers as ἄποικοι or ἔποικοι[2] have a strict technical sense. It should be noticed that Thucydides describes these Athenian settlers in terms that recall his description of those at Hestiaea: Αἰγινῆται οἱ τότε Αἴγιναν εἶχον[3] (VII.57.2).

The words of Thucydides (V.116.4) in describing the settlement of Melos have also been taken[4] as evidence that it was not a cleruchy: τὸ δὲ χωρίον αὐτοὶ ᾤκισαν, ἀποίκους ὕστερον πεντακοσίους πέμψαντες.[5] If we leave on one side the word ἀποίκους, the only indication of the settlement's character in this sentence is the exact number 500. In Plutarch's list of Athenian cleruchies (*Per.* XI) many exact numbers of settlers are given, even down to 250 on Andros, while exact numbers of this sort are not reported for any undisputed Athenian *apoikia*.[6] This is not a sure indication that Melos was a cleruchy, since some limitation of numbers must have been necessary in any settlement where the territory was limited, but it points in that direction.

A funerary inscription found on Melos, which may be dated with some confidence to the period of the Athenian occupation,[7] is the only other evidence bearing on the question. In this one Eponphes (Ἐπονφής) describes himself first as an Athenian, and then of the phyle Pandionis and the deme Kytheros. As Homolle pointed out,[8] this formula is not normal. On Attic funerary inscriptions the name of the dead man is followed regularly by the name of the father and the deme, the latter being sufficient to indicate the man's quality as an Athenian.

[1] *CP* xlvii 1952, 145 f.
[2] II.27.1; VIII.69.3 and perhaps VII.57.2.
[3] 'The Aeginetans who then occupied Aegina.'
[4] As, surprisingly, by Ehrenberg loc. cit.
[5] 'The territory they settled themselves, sending out afterwards 500 colonists (*apoikoi*).'
[6] The identification of the 1000 settlers sent to the land of the Bisaltai (Plut. *Per.* XI.5) with the Athenian colony at Brea is conjectural; see Woodhead, *CQ* n.s. ii 1952, 60; and the numbers recorded of the settlers at Amphipolis and Thurii have not the same exactness as those relating to cleruchies; see above, Chapter III.
[7] *IG* XII.3.1187, first published by Homolle, *BCH* i 1877, 44 ff, whose dating has been followed by subsequent editors.
[8] Op. cit. 45.

The explanation of the unusual description offered by Hiller[1] is ingenious and plausible. The form of the name Ἐπόνφης is like that of Κλιόνφας, a known Melian name. The man is, therefore, taken to be a Melian who was given Athenian citizenship as a reward, it is conjectured, for betraying Melos to the Athenians.[2] It is known from the treatment of the Plataeans in 427 that the Athenians could grant citizenship to foreigners at this period,[3] and the natural reward for a traitor would have been to exempt him from the sentence of death and leave him in possession of his property on Melos. In order to allow the latter, if Melos became an Athenian cleruchy, it was necessary to make the Melian an Athenian citizen. It seems, therefore, that the probable conclusion from Eponphes' epitaph is that Melos was a cleruchy.

Melos, Aegina and Hestiaea were all settled by the Athenians in the second half of the fifth century after the expulsion of Greek inhabitants. The Athenian settlements on Lemnos, Imbros and Scyros were somewhat earlier, and followed the expulsion of non-Greek populations. But these too are doubtful cases, although there is more evidence bearing on the question of their status.

The three islands often occur together in fourth-century writers as overseas possessions of Athens.[4] At that time too there were cleruchies on all of them. Demosthenes, for example, when enumerating bellicose acts of Philip, says (*Phil.* I.34) οὐχ ... εἰς Λῆμνον καὶ Ἴμβρον ἐμβαλὼν αἰχμαλώτους πολίτας ὑμετέρους ᾤχετ᾽ ἔχων,[5] and Scyros is listed with Samos, Imbros and Lemnos as overseas possessions to which Athens sent officers.[6] But though the fourth-century and later evidence gives a clear picture of islands regarded as Athenian possessions and occupied by Athenian cleruchs, that from the fifth century is not so simple. Most of this evidence concerns Lemnos (though

[1] See notes to *IG* XII.3.1187.
[2] Cf. Thuc. V.116.3: γενομένης καὶ προδοσίας τινός..
[3] See [Dem.] LIX.104 ff.
[4] e.g. Aeschines II.76; Xen. *Hell.* V.i.3; Andocides III.14.
[5] 'Did he not invade Lemnos and Imbros and take away your citizens as prisoners when he left?' There was a cleruchy on Lemnos by 387/6; see *IG* II².30, with notes; this inscription is discussed below, p. 187.
[6] Arist. *Ath. Pol.* 62.2; cf. also *IG* XII.8.688.1 f, [δέδοχθαι τῶι δήμωι τῶν Ἀθηναίων] τῶν κατοικούντων ἐν Σκύρωι.

Imbros may reasonably be assumed to have had a very similar history),[1] so Lemnos must dominate any discussion of the three islands in the fifth century.[2]

The Athenian settlement on Lemnos in the early years of the fifth century[3] followed the expulsion of the previous Pelasgian inhabitants.[4] From that time on, unless all the literary evidence is rejected, the population of Lemnos was of Athenian origin. A Corinthian helmet of late archaic style found at Olympia is inscribed with the words Ἀθεναῖοι [τ]ὸν ἐγ Λέμν[ο], and it is a reasonable conjecture that it was a dedication from the spoils taken at the time of the island's capture.[5] In which case, as Kunze points out,[6] the wording implies that the capture and settlement of the island was an official Athenian venture.

The first evidence for its subsequent position relates to the Persian Wars. The Persians won control of the island, for Herodotus reports that there was a Lemnian contingent in the

---

[1] It is generally thought that Imbros had an identical history to that of Lemnos throughout, as it certainly appears to have had from the time of the Peloponnesian War onwards; see e.g. Busolt II.531.

[2] Will has a long note on the status of Lemnos (La Nouvelle Clio vi 1954, 442 n. 2), but it is doubtful if this is adequate for so complex a problem.

[3] The date is not recorded, but there are good reasons for attributing the occupation to the time of the Ionian Revolt; see Bengtson, Sitz. Bayr. Akad. 1937, 28 ff; D. Mustilli, 'L'occupazione ateniese di Lemnos' in Studi di antichita classica offerti da colleghi e discepoli a Emanuele Ciaceri (Rome, 1940); Seltman, Athens, its history and coinage, 141 f, and Wade-Gery (JHS lxxi 1951, 217). A much higher date for the arrival of Athenians on Lemnos was maintained by Segre, on the basis of a boundary stone of the temenos of Artemis, which he dated to c. 550; see Annuario della R. Scuola di Atene xv-xvi, 1932–3, 294 ff. His dating was accepted as certain by Robert, Bull. 1949, 135 (REG lxii 1949, p. 133), but it rests entirely on an out-of-date view of the significance of the form of M on Attic inscriptions (see 296 n. 1); for M with a shorter right hasta, which was thought to indicate a date before 550, occurs in the inscription IG I².1, which must be dated at the earliest to the first two decades of the fifth century; see above p. 168 n. 6, and, for a photograph, Kirchner, Imagines Inscriptionum Atticarum, 13. Other letters on the horos inscription are also like those of IG I.²1, as A, E, so it should most probably be dated to c. 500 or later.

[4] The literary references are given above p. 32 n. 5; cf. also Thucydides' description of the inhabitants of Akte (IV.109.4) τὸ δὲ πλεῖστον Πελασγικόν, τῶν καὶ Λῆμνόν ποτε καὶ Ἀθήνας Τυρσηνῶν οἰκησάντων. No trace of the Pelagasian inhabitants which postdated c. 500 was found by the Italian excavators; see Mustilli, op. cit. 158.

[5] 'The Athenians from the spoils from Lemnos.' The helmet is published and discussed by E. Kunze, Festschrift für Carl Weickert, 7–21; see especially 19 f.

[6] p. 20.

N

Persian fleet (VIII.11.3; 82). In the first of these passages he reports that in the sea-battle Antidorus the Lemnian alone of the Greeks with the Great King (᾽Αντίδωρος Λήμνιος μοῦνος τῶν σὺν βασιλέϊ ῾Ελλήνων ἐόντων) deserted to the Greek side. There should be no doubt that these Lemnians were the Athenian settlers. The population of Lemnos was of Athenian origin after Miltiades' capture and settlement of the island, and Herodotus' ῾Ελλήνων rules out any question of the earlier non-Greek population.[1]

The fact that the Persians treated the Athenian settlers in Lemnos as subjects, like other Greeks in Asia Minor, could be held to show that they were not Athenian citizens. For Athens was not offered the choice of submitting to the Great King.[2] But this argument, standing alone, cannot be pressed, as their place of residence could in practice have outweighed their legal citizenship. Slightly stronger arguments may perhaps be found in the Athenian treatment of Antidorus.

He was rewarded for his desertion by a grant of land on Salamis.[3] It is perhaps tempting to argue that this shows that the Athenians had no right of disposal over the land of Lemnos; but if the award was made immediately, not only had they no reason to assume that they would quickly clear the Persians from the whole Aegean, they were even prevented from giving him land in Attica by the evacuation following the Battle of Artemisium. Will makes another suggestion,[4] that the gift of land on Salamis 'en territoire clerouchique' (Will's italics) might show that they were establishing him in the same situation that he had occupied before. But it would surely be more likely that he was rewarded by an improvement in status. Further, if he ranked as an Athenian citizen, his desertion was not so much praiseworthy as his plain duty; and, though one hesitates to use the argument from silence, it seems doubtful that Herodotus

---

[1] Meyer suggested (*Forschungen zur alten Geschichte* I.14) that the Persians would certainly have brought the old inhabitants of Lemnos back, had they only recently been expelled. Busolt, however (II.531 n. 2) points out rightly that this is not only pure conjecture, but also unlikely in view of the fighting between the Persians and the Tyrsenian inhabitants of Lemnos of not long before; see Hdt. V.27, which suggests that a large part of the population was annihilated, and Diod. X.19.6, where the Tyrsenians are said to have forsaken their homes from fear of the Persians.

[2] Hdt. VII.32.   [3] Hdt. VIII.11.3.

[4] *La Nouvelle Clio* vi 1954, 441.

could have passed over this status, when he was making a special point of the desertion.

The tendency of all these arguments is against the idea that Lemnos was a cleruchy at this time, and though none of them is compelling, they gain in strength from Lemnos' position as a tribute-paying ally in the League of Delos. In the list of 452/1 the Lemnians (Λέμνιοι) pay nine talents,[1] and later the two cities of Lemnos, Hephaestia and Myrina, pay tribute regularly. It was suggested in the past, in the face of the consistent testimony of the literary sources, that this tribute was paid by the remnants of the pre-Athenian population,[2] but this attempt to avoid deciding either that cleruchs could pay tribute, or that the Lemnian settlers were not cleruchs, must be rejected; a very considerable number of Pelasgians would have had to remain to pay nine talents.

The payment of tribute by an Athenian settlement cannot be considered an automatic criterion of status, for it can be shown that no Athenian settlement founded after the Persian Wars, whatever its status, paid tribute,[3] and the only absolutely certain cleruchy founded earlier, that at Chalcis, did not survive into the time of the Athenian Empire. On the other hand it seems very improbable that cleruchs would pay tribute.[4] They remained Athenian citizens, as the evidence from the cleruchy at Chalcis shows, so that the payment of tribute to Athens, which implies the position of an ally of Athens, would be an extraordinary anomaly. The conclusion follows that the payment of tribute suggests very strongly that the first Athenian settlers on Lemnos were not cleruchs.

On the other hand, some inscriptions from Lemnos have been thought to prove the opposite conclusion. The first of these is a list of names arranged according to the Cleisthenic tribes, which was dated by its lettering to not later than the first quarter of the fifth century.[5] This has been taken to prove that the first settlers

---

[1] *ATL* II list 3, I.2.   [2] See e.g. *IG* XII.8 p. 3.

[3] See *ATL* III 285 ff. Although not all their examples are of equal weight, Potidaea, which disappears from the tribute lists after the Athenians occupied it, seems to be sufficient to prove their point; for its status seems assured by the inscriptions Tod 60 and *ATL* II D21, where the settlers are called ἔποικοι.

[4] It is assumed to be impossible in *ATL* III 290.

[5] The inscription is quoted under *IG* I².948; it was first published by Picard and Reinach, *BCH* xxxvi 1912, 331 ff.

were cleruchs.[1] However, as Berve rightly pointed out,[2] the retention of the Athenian tribes does not prove that the colonists kept their citizenship. The tribal divisions in the metropolis were regularly maintained in colonies.[3]

Two other inscriptions from Lemnos which have been thought to prove that there was a cleruchy there by at latest the early fifth century are records of legal encumbrances.[4] But only one is of sufficiently early date to bear on the status of the first settlement and it gives no indication that that settlement was a cleruchy.[5] As none of these inscriptions contradicts the other evidence, it may be concluded with some confidence that the first Athenian settlement on Lemnos was not a cleruchy.[6]

In the tribute list of 444/3 the island's tribute is recorded against the names of its two cities, Hephaestia and Myrina, and together they pay four and a half talents.[7] The tribute paid by the island was thus halved at some time between 452/1 and 444/3. Kirchhoff suggested that the reason for this was that cleruchs had been settled on the island,[8] and supported his conjecture by analogous cases. For instance, Pericles sent a cleruchy to the Thracian Chersonese at the same period,[9] and the tribute of the Chersonese apparently fell from eighteen talents to one talent between 452/1 and 442/1. Much of this enormous reduction is to be attributed to the fact that a former *synteleia* of the Χερρονησῖται was divided into the several cities of the area.[10]

[1] As, e.g., by Ehrenberg, *Aspects of the Ancient World*, 135 f, who is thus led to conclude that what he calls a 'municipal cleruchy' could pay tribute.

[2] *Militiades, Hermes* Einzelschriften 2, 1937, 51 f.

[3] See *RE* s.v. Phylai 1002.

[4] Published by M. Segre, *Annuario della R. Scuola di Atene* xv–xvi 1932/3, no. 11, 305 f, no. 12, 306 f.

[5] See my note in *Historia* xii 1963 127 f, where the inscriptions and their significance are discussed.

[6] Will seems to miss the significance of the payment of tribute, at least, when he concludes (*La Nouvelle Clio* vi 1954, 449) that we cannot decide if Lemnos was a cleruchy or not at the beginning; and this in spite of the fact that he seems to realize earlier (442) that the payment of tribute is hard to reconcile with the status of a cleruchy.

[7] *ATL* II list 11, V.30, 31.

[8] *Abhand. d. preuss. Akad.*, Phil. Hist. Klasse, 1873, 34.

[9] Plut. *Per.* XIX.1; the date is not certain but the modern inference that it was in the early forties is probable; see Gomme I.376–80.

[10] See Ehrenberg, *Aspects of the Ancient World*, 125 n. 1. The Χερρονησῖται of the lists from at latest 442/1 are almost certainly the people of a single city sometimes more precisely designated as Χερρονησῖται ἀπ' Ἀγόρας; see *ATL* I Register s.v. and Ehrenberg, 126.

But there was also a real drop in the tribute from the area, and the modern inference that this is to be explained by the arrival of Pericles' cleruchs seems likely to be correct.[1]

Although Kirchhoff's suggested explanation for the halving of Lemnos' tribute has not been effectively attacked,[2] it is true that there may have been other reasons for the lowering of tribute. At this time there were a number of reductions which were not connected with colonizing activity.[3] However, on the one occasion when Thucydides describes in detail the establishment of a cleruchy, its settlement is expressly linked with the tribute: ὕστερον δὲ φόρον οὐκ ἔταξαν Λεσβίοις, κλήρους δὲ ποιήσαντες τῆς γῆς κτλ.[4] (III.50.2). In view of this and the other analogies Kirchoff's explanation of the halving of Lemnos' tribute must be considered very reasonable, especially as some serious change is required for so large a reduction.

However, since the explanation is conjectural, it is necessary to consider other evidence for the status of Lemnos in the second half of the fifth century. Two lists of the fallen in the early part of the Peloponnesian War inscribed at Athens are relevant to this question.[5] The first (IG I².947) contains a list of names arranged by tribes headed by the title 'Lemnians from Myrina' (Λημνίων ἐγ Μυρίν[ης]). In the second (948) there is a list of names, headed by the tribal designation, under which comes, as a sub-title, the name Lemnians (Λήμνιοι). The literary evidence has shown that the ethnic cannot be taken as a certain criterion of citizenship,[6] so that the name Λήμνιοι in these inscriptions does not of itself preclude the possibility that the dead were Athenian cleruchs.[7]

In the second inscription the Lemnians are merely a section of a larger list of names of the same tribe. They were therefore

---

[1] Cf. Ehrenberg, 126.

[2] Picard's and Reinach's criticism of it (BCH xxxvi 1912, 333 ff) is almost entirely vitiated by their confusion of Myrina on Lemnos with the other Myrina later more specifically described as Μύρινα παρὰ Κύμην (ATL I Register s.v.).

[3] These are studied by Ehrenberg, Sophocles and Pericles, 124–9.

[4] 'After this they did not impose tribute on the Lesbians, but divided their land into lots, etc.'

[5] IG I².947, 948; they are dated by the lettering to not much later than the beginning of the Peloponnesian War.

[6] See above pp. 103 ff, 168; cf. ATL III.293.

[7] Against Will, who discusses these inscriptions in La Nouvelle Clio vi 1954, 444–7.

listed with members of the tribe at Athens, and it might be thought difficult to differentiate them from full Athenian citizens.[1] In the first inscription the Lemnians do not occur side by side with Athenians, so they are not subject to the same argument. These certainly need not have been cleruchs; for their retention of the Cleisthenic tribes, as has been seen,[2] does not prove that they had Athenian citizenship. The evidence of these two lists must be judged inconclusive,[3] though in the second it seems more probable that the Lemnians were cleruchs.

The second of the stones recording legal encumbrances mentioned above[4] is also relevant to this question. It is to be dated to the second half of the fifth century and one of the participants in the transaction had an Athenian demotic. It seems reasonable to conclude that this man, Euainetos, was an Athenian citizen and therefore that there was a cleruchy on Lemnos in the second half of the fifth century.[5]

If there was a cleruchy on Lemnos in the second half of the fifth century, and the original settlement was not a cleruchy, Kirchhoff's conjecture from the evidence of the tribute lists that a cleruchy was established in the forties seems very probable. In any case we know that about the time of the Peloponnesian War there were on Lemnos both cleruchs and non-cleruchs.[6] A surprising conclusion perhaps, but, on the evidence available, apparently inescapable.

It might seem strange to imagine two communities, both of Athenian origin but of different status, living on Lemnos,[7] and it would be easier if it could be assumed that the cleruchs, although they owned land on Lemnos, still lived at Athens. In order to explain the considerable rise in hoplite numbers at Athens in the second half of the fifth century, Jones has advanced the thesis that in the time of the Athenian Empire

---

[1] Jones' argument (*Athenian Democracy*, 173), that in a war memorial distinctions of citizenship might be considered unimportant, seems unconvincing.

[2] Above, p. 178.

[3] They have often been thought to refer to cleruchs, as, for instance, by the editors of *IG* I and I^2 and the authors of *ATL* (III.292).

[4] See above p. 178.

[5] For a full discussion of the inscription, its date and significance, see my note in *Historia* xii 1963, 127 f.

[6] This is the conclusion of the authors of *ATL* (III.292).

[7] The difficulty is played down in *ATL* loc. cit.

cleruchs did not leave Athens.[1] They let their allotments, and remained in Athens with hoplite status. There are attractive points in Jones' thesis, and it must be considered possible that cleruchs sometimes did not reside on their lots. But special pleading is required to discount all the evidence for cleruchs residing abroad,[2] and if the arguments about the status of Hestiaea, Aegina and Melos are accepted, cleruchs were sometimes sent to settle areas from which the previous population had been expelled.

With regard to Lemnos the only evidence of any clear value seems to be, once again, the *horos* of Euainetos. He was an Athenian citizen, and he had rights to property on Lemnos. The nature of his financial transaction, as Finley has rightly described it,[3] makes it improbable that he was at a long distance from the land involved. The system of recording the fact that land was encumbered by simply planting a mortgage inscription is a sign of fairly primitive arrangements, in which personal inspection of the property was normal. On Jones' thesis the cleruchs were ex-Thetes at Athens. It seems inherently unlikely that they all became absentee-landlords of property they did not know. Similarly Jones' objection about the cleruchy on Lesbos, that the cleruch would have no house to go to, if his lot was worked, as before, by the Mytilenean occupier, would only be valid if the houses of that period were big and complicated buildings. So that, in addition to the more definite counter arguments, there seems to be some inherent improbability in the idea that no cleruchs of the fifth century resided on their lots. It seems very difficult, therefore, to assume that there was a fixed rule that cleruchs did not reside abroad, and the question about the population of Lemnos after the cleruchy was established remains.

In the four references to Lemnians (and Imbrians) in Thucydides it is not perfectly clear whether they are cleruchs or not.

---

[1] *Athenian Democracy* 168–76.

[2] E.g. Thucydides' word ἀπέπεμψαν (III.50.2) regarding the cleruchs on Lesbos (one of the best examples for Jones' hypothesis), which Jones suggests may be 'a term of art' (175), not to mention other evidence for Athenians living on land abroad (176), of whom Jones can only say that they are not stated to be cleruchs. Thus it is not surprising that Jones' suggestion has not been well received; see Gomme *JHS* lxxix 1959, 64 and Calder *CP* liv 1959, 141.

[3] See *Land and Credit in Ancient Athens*, especially 13 ff.

In two, IV.28.4 and V.8.2, there is no indication of the status
of the Lemnians and Imbrians mentioned. At III.5.2. the words
Ἴμβριοι καὶ Λήμνιοι καὶ τῶν ἄλλων ὀλίγοι τινες ξυμμάχων,[1] if
pressed, show that the Lemnians and Imbrians counted as
allies, but the most important passage is VII. 57.2,[2] for here
there are other communities with which to compare them. The
sentence is difficult to punctuate and interpret with certainty,
but the way in which it should, in general, be understood, has
been shown by Ehrenberg.[3] The four communities, Lemnians,
Imbrians, Aeginetans and Hestiaeans, are very closely connected with Athens, and are distinguished from the subject and
tribute-paying allies. On the other hand they are also distinguished from the Athenians.

Gomme thought that the grouping together of the four communities should suggest identity or close similarity of status,[4]
but, as Ehrenberg noted, whatever their status, they are not
on the face of it identical, because two of the communities paid
tribute and two did not. He suggests, therefore, that the common
factor expressed in the words ἄποικοι ὄντες is sufficient to explain their special position in Thucydides' list. This seems very
reasonable, but to test it thoroughly it is necessary to see what
follows if Thucydides words are pressed.

Two of the communities, Aegina and Hestiaea, were most
probably cleruchies;[5] in strict theory, therefore, they should be
included with the Athenians. The other two paid tribute; in
strict theory they should belong with the tribute-paying allies.
The latter problem would be avoided if these Lemnians and
Imbrians were the cleruchs, not the tribute-paying settlers;
they would then be like the Aeginetans and Hestiaeans and
subject to the same theoretical objection. This possibility, how-

[1] 'Imbrians and Lemnians and a few of the other allies.'
[2] Ἀθηναῖοι μὲν αὐτοὶ Ἴωνες ἐπὶ Δωριᾶς Συρακοσίους ἑκόντες ἦλθον, καὶ
αὐτοῖς τῇ αὐτῇ φωνῇ καὶ νομίμοις ἔτι χρώμενοι Λήμνιοι καὶ Ἴμβριοι καὶ
Αἰγινῆται, οἱ τότε Αἴγιναν εἶχον, καὶ ἔτι Ἑστιαιῆς οἱ ἐν Εὐβοίᾳ Ἑστίαιαν
οἰκοῦντες ἄποικοι ὄντες ξυνεστράτευσαν. The punctuation here is that of the
Oxford Text. I offer a translation which does not conceal the ambiguities
in Thucydides' sentence: 'The Athenians, being themselves Ionians went
voluntarily against the Dorian Syracusans, and those who still used the
same dialect and customs as themselves, the Lemnians and the Imbrians and
the Aeginetans, who then occupied Aegina, and also the Hestiaeans who
lived in Hestiaea on Euboea, being colonists, joined in the campaign.'
[3] CP xlvii 1952, 147 ff.   [4] See I.375 n. 1.
[5] The arguments for this conclusion are set out above pp. 170 ff.

ever, would be excluded if Ehrenberg is right in assuming[1] that Thucydides' words τῇ αὐτῇ φωνῇ καὶ νομίμοις ἔτι χρώμενοι could only apply to the first settlers. He thinks that ἔτι must refer to a fair span of time, and the first settlers were established eighty years before, the cleruchs not more than thirty. On this view the Lemnians and Imbrians must be the tribute-paying allies; but it is not necessarily right.

In reading the sentence alone it is perhaps difficult to decide whether the phrase τῇ αὐτῇ φωνῇ καὶ νομίμοις ἔτι χρώμενοι is to be confined to the Lemnians and Imbrians or applied also to the Aeginetans and Hestiaeans. The latter interpretation, however, seems easier, and is that of the editor of the Oxford text, as his punctuation reveals. If so, Thucydides was ready to apply the words ἔτι χρώμενοι to the settlers on Aegina in 431. Although this seems unlikely at first sight it is not difficult to explain in the context of Thucydides' whole chapter. As has been seen,[2] he is stressing the origin of states in order to show how the war had cut across the alignments based on ties of kinship that he considered right. He is conscious of relationship at the expense of chronology. The Ionian allies were of Athenian origin (VII.57.4) and this was important to him, however many centuries separated them from Athens. Cretan mercenaries who fought against Geloans were also shocking to his ideas (57.7), although we may question whether they knew or cared that Cretan settlers had joined in the colonization of Gela two and a half centuries earlier. Colonial relationships are the theme of his chapter, and in such a context the position of the four communities under discussion was separate and special. Of those present these alone were not only of Athenian origin but still Athenians in customs and dialect. This view of the sentence not only accounts for the application of the words ἔτι χρώμενοι to colonists of at most eighty years standing, but also makes futile any attempt to force conclusions about legal status from Thucydides' words or arrangement. The Lemnians and Imbrians could be cleruchs, as the Aeginetans and Hestiaeans probably were, but the sole and sufficient common factor is that they were all settlements of Athenians abroad on land from which the previous population had been entirely expelled.

This long discussion has shown that Ehrenberg's view about

[1] Op. cit. 148.   [2] See Chapter I.

the lack of distinctions in Thucydides' language about cleruchies and colonies is correct. Just as Demosthenes and later writers,[1] so Thucydides also could embrace cleruchies in his general concept of colony and colonist expressed by the words ἀποικία, ἄποικος and ἔποικος. A study of the fifth-century evidence about Lemnos is sufficient to complete the argument for that conclusion, but for the significance of Lemnos, Imbros and Scyros in general in Athenian colonization the fourth-century evidence must also be considered.

As we have seen,[2] in the fourth century Lemnos, Imbros and Scyros were Athenian cleruchies, and generally recognized to be Athenian territory. In the fifth century some of the inhabitants of Lemnos were not cleruchs, though the islands were, in general terms, obviously Athenian possessions. It is not easy to understand how the fifth-century situation developed into that of the fourth. Any difference between them must have been the result of events between c. 404 and c. 394/3,[3] but before the happenings of those years are discussed we have still to consider the fifth-century status of Scyros.

Thucydides describes the Athenian settlement of Scyros in these words:

ἔπειτα Σκῦρον τὴν ἐν τῷ Αἰγαίῳ νῆσον, ἣν ᾤκουν Δόλοπες, ἠνδραπό-δισαν καὶ ᾤκισαν αὐτοί.[4]

In view of what has been said about Thucydides' wording it is wrong to look for any sure indication in his expression whether or not the settlement was a cleruchy.[5] But it is worth noting that the words ᾤκισαν αὐτοί were also used by Thucydides to describe the settlement of Melos (V.116.4) which, as we have seen, was probably a cleruchy.[6] Diodorus' use of the word κατεκληρούχ-ησε (XI.60.2) is also inadmissible as evidence; it need not imply

[1] See above p. 169 f.
[2] See above p. 174.
[3] Since the Athenians were in possession of the islands by the spring of 392, when Antalcidas went to Tiribazus (Xen. Hell. IV.viii.15), it is reasonably assumed that they recovered them some time after, and as a result of, the Battle of Cnidus in August 394; see, e.g., Bengtson GG².259.
[4] 'Then they enslaved the population of Scyros, the Aegean island, who were Dolopians, and settled it themselves.'
[5] Ehrenberg argues from Thucydides' usage that the word ᾤκισαν seems to imply that Scyros was an apoikia; CP xlvii 1951, 145.
[6] See above pp. 173 f.

a cleruchy.[1] However his information (ibid.) that Cimon set up a founder (κτίστης)[2] there might be thought to show that it was a regular colony rather than a cleruchy. But even this cannot be maintained, since we hear of oikists in connection with a cleruchy.[3] As has been seen, the fact that Scyros did not pay tribute is also no criterion. There is, in fact, no certain evidence for Scyros' status until the fourth century, when it was a cleruchy.

As Scyros was a cleruchy in the fourth century, it would be most natural to conclude that it had the same status in the fifth. Otherwise, unless there was a complete change of population in some way, one would have to assume that a people who had not had Athenian citizenship for two to three generations were suddenly made Athenian citizens, which seems improbable. On the other hand, if Scyros was a cleruchy in the fifth century, Andocides' account of its situation after Sparta's victory in the Peloponnesian War becomes difficult to understand. He is contrasting the provisions of the peace in 404 with those of the King's Peace, and says (III.12):

Λῆμνον δὲ καὶ Ἴμβρον καὶ Σκῦρον τότε μὲν ἔχειν τοὺς ἔχοντας, νῦν δὲ ἡμετέρας εἶναι.[4]

The words ἔχειν τοὺς ἔχοντας must be judged in the light of the Spartan treatment of Athenian settlers abroad. We know that Lysander resettled in their homes Greeks who had been expelled,[5] and he also sent back to Athens Athenian garrisons and εἴ τινά που ἄλλον ἴδοι Ἀθηναῖον.[6] Strictly interpreted these words would include all Athenian cleruchs abroad. Since there were no previous inhabitants to whom Scyros could be returned,[7] if the Athenian settlers were cleruchs and were sent to

[1] As Jones notes, *Athenian Democracy*, 169, 171 f.
[2] This word is a synonym for οἰκιστής, and its use increases in the later period. See Lampros, *de conditorum coloniarum Graecarum indole praemiisque et honoribus*, Diss. Leipzig 1873, 25, 30 ff.
[3] See Busolt/Swoboda 1272 n. 3.
[4] 'That Lemnos, Imbros and Scyros should belong to those who possessed them, but now that they should be ours.'
[5] Xen. *Hell.* II.ii.9.
[6] 'Any other Athenian whom he found anywhere,' Xen. *Hell.* II.ii.2.
[7] The Dolopian inhabitants were sold into slavery, see Thuc. I.98.2. It is suggested in Busolt/Swoboda, 1272 n. 3, that enough of the previous population remained to occupy the island after 404. But this involves rejecting

Athens, there would have been no one on the island to possess it. This is the dilemma: if the settlers on Scyros were not cleruchs, and so were left in possession in 404, how did they become a cleruchy in the fourth century? If they were cleruchs, who were Andocides' possessors after 404?

Lemnos' position at the same time is more complicated, but perhaps less difficult. If it is assumed that the Athenian settlers descended from the original settlers were not Athenian citizens and were therefore left in possession of the island, the cleruchs could have been sent home as Athenians without leaving the island deserted. Two inscriptions have been thought to confirm that this is what happened. An epitaph for a certain Nicomachus reads:

$$\textit{Λήμνο ἀπ' ἠγαθέας κεύθει τάφος ἐνθάδε γαίας}$$
$$\textit{ἄνδρα φιλοπρόβατον· Νικόμαχος δ' ὄνομα.}^{1}$$

The letter forms make it reasonable to attribute the inscription to the period in question, and it has been taken to refer to a cleruch who had to leave his land (or flocks) on Lemnos.[2] This is possible, but not certain, for the inscription cannot be dated sufficiently precisely and he could have died on a visit.

The second inscription is a decree of Myrina,[3] in which the demos of Myrina is mentioned but not that of Athens, as in later cleruchy decrees.[4] Partly because of this and partly from the script it has been dated to the period after 404.[5] If the dating is accepted, the inscription could perhaps be held to show that Myrina was independent of Athens. But the argument is dangerously circular, and furthermore, if the original settlers of Myrina were not cleruchs, they could presumably have produced such a decree, whether or not there was also a cleruchy on the island.

Thucydides' statement, and it is an attempt to avoid the difficulty, like that described above (p. 177) regarding the tribute of Lemnos. Their remark that Plutarch's account does not suit the supposition that all the previous population were removed seems hard to understand in face of Plutarch's words (*Cimon.* VIII.5) τοὺς μὲν Δόλοπας ἐξήλασε.

[1] 'The tomb here covers a man from the sacred land of Lemnos who loved his flocks; his name was Nicomachus,' *IG* II/III² 7180; Peek, *Griech. Versinschriften* 490.

[2] Cf. editor, *IG* ad loc.　　　　[3] *IG* XII.8.2.

[4] See above p. 167.　　　　[5] See *IG* XII.8, notes to no. 2.

Another inscription, unfortunately very fragmentary, seems to show at least that cleruchs were either sent to the island or already there in 387/6.[1] This refers expressly to cleruchs on Lemnos and makes arrangements about goods and land on the island. Disputes about land are provided for,[2] and a prohibition against letting may be confidently referred to land.[3] It is tempting to interpret the decree as arranging for the resettlement of a cleruchy on Lemnos after the island's recovery by Athens.[4] Given the state of the inscription, however, such an interpretation can be no more than a conjecture.

These inscriptions provide at the most very dubious confirmation for the view that the cleruchs left the island in 404, but that the descendants of the original colonists remained; and even so difficulties remain. The evidence about Lemnos in the fourth century and after seems to show that the island was completely a cleruchy by that time.[5] If that is so, how did the previous non-cleruchs become Athenian citizens? It is also at least doubtful that Lysander would have differentiated the cleruchs from the non-cleruchs among the Athenian settlers, if he was sending all possible Athenians back to Athens.

There is one explanation which would remove many of the difficulties both at Lemnos and Scyros. If Lysander sent home all the Athenian settlers whatever their status, when the Athenians recovered the islands, they could have resettled them entirely with cleruchs, and the difference between fourth-century and fifth-century status would be explained. For this explanation to be correct it is necessary to ignore the doubtful inferences from the inscriptions just discussed, though that is not difficult. It is also necessary either to assume that Andocides' words ἔχειν τοὺς ἔχοντας are merely a loose way of saying that the islands ceased to be Athenian, and do not imply definite possessors, or that some unknown squatters took over the vacated islands. While neither of these assumptions is impossible, it must remain uncertain whether the Spartans would have expelled Athenian colonists from these three islands. There was no Greek population with a right to them, and at an

---

[1] See *IG* II².30, with notes.   [2] See fragment *a*.23.

[3] See fragment *b*.4.

[4] Thus the confiscated houses of line 14 were perhaps the houses previously owned by cleruchs.

[5] See above p. 174.

earlier date the Spartans had not been averse to a peace treaty
leaving Athens in possession of them.[1]

In the present state of our knowledge it must be confessed that
there is no entirely satisfactory way of reconstructing the situation of these islands in detail at the time in question. It is perhaps advisable, therefore, for the present purposes to concentrate attention on the broader issues. Just as Thucydides thought
of Lemnos and Imbros as Athenian settlements abroad very
closely connected to Athens, so the fourth-century evidence
shows that in Greek eyes generally they were in a special position as possessions of Athens. The reason why this was so, in
contrast to many other areas which the Athenians had claimed
in the fifth century, is not to be sought in any special legal
position. Hampl regarded the islands as examples of his
'Poleis ohne Territorium',[2] which supported his principle that
the metropolis did not relinquish its legal possession of the land
of its colony. But Athens claimed many other territories in the
fifth century, on which she had not founded colonies,[3] and the
reason why her claim to these was not generally recognized was
that there was still a Greek population to oppose it.[4] There was
no opponent with a good claim to the islands of Lemnos,
Imbros and Scyros.

Her claim to the colonies is thus hardly to be based on
Hampl's principle about colonies, but it is true that her first
colonists on Lemnos were apparently not cleruchs yet Athens in
effect possessed the island. She could, for example, establish a
cleruchy on it. However, Athens' general behaviour as an
imperial state and examples from other Greek colonies provide
sufficient explanation for the position of Lemnos. It has been
seen that some other mother cities treated colonies effectively as
possessions, even though the colonies were not part of the
founding state,[5] and in founding a cleruchy on the land of her
colony, Athens was perhaps only exercising on a large scale, and
in an unusual way, the mother city's right, which we have
noticed elsewhere,[6] of sending in further settlers to a colony.

[1] See Aeschines, II.76.   [2] *Klio* xxxii 1939, 29–32.
[3] Even if she had founded cleruchies, but these are not separate cities in
Hampl's legal sense.
[4] Cf. Andocides' distinctions between the three islands and other past
possessions of Athens, III.9, 14 f.
[5] See especially Chapters V and VII.   [6] See Chapter IV.

When one remembers Athens' great power, and her high-handed treatment of cities unrelated to her, the control she exercised over her colonists on Lemnos is not surprising. The real weakness of Hampl's thesis, here as elsewhere, is his rigid concept of the polis 'im Rechtssinne'. A colony like Lemnos was in practice, owing to its mother city's power, very far from being a fully independent city, whatever the legal forms.[1]

From the point of view of our understanding of cleruchies, and their place in Greek colonization generally, perhaps the most significant conclusion from this long study of the doubtful cases is that, although a distinction of language was available, Greek authors of the classical period could describe cleruchies in the same terms as other colonies. In retaining the citizenship of the metropolis the cleruch appears strikingly different from normal Greek colonists, and yet this difference was not so important in the eyes of an observer like Thucydides that he felt the need to exclude the cleruchy from his concept of a colony. There could be no clearer warning to modern investigators that it is unhistorical to postulate rigid theoretical distinctions in Greek colonies.[2] Thucydides' concept of the colony was sufficiently wide to embrace both completely independent settlements and extensions of the founding state.

In view of this it is necessary to consider the cleruch's position and compare it with that of other Greek colonists. From this discussion we may exclude any cleruchs who stayed in Athens and did not reside on their lots, if such existed, since they were in practice not colonists. It is the cleruchies which formed a new community which concern us.

As an Athenian citizen the cleruch may be assumed to have been liable to the duties of Athenian citizen, in so far as his place of residence allowed. Thus the mutilated inscriptions about Hestiaea seem to imply that the cleruchs were liable to *eisphora* as we have seen,[3] and although absolutely indisputable evidence is lacking,[4] there should be no doubt that cleruchs

[1] Will is rightly critical of Hampl's thesis about Lemnos; see *La Nouvelle Clio* vi 1954, 457 f.
[2] This is a serious weakness in Will's paper, op. cit.; see especially 459. For all that he is right to compare the cleruchy with other colonies showing similar features to a lesser extent.   [3] See above pp. 171 f.
[4] There is definite evidence if, as I believe, Hestiaea and Aegina were cleruchies (see Thuc. VII.57.2), or if the Lemnians and Imbrians whom

were liable to general military service. Although they may have
served as garrisons in some difficult areas,[1] Jones is right to cast
a doubt on the theory that all cleruchies had this function.[2] It is
true that the one quite certain instance of military service by
cleruchs was in the vicinity of the cleruchy,[3] but presumably
Athens made use of them when and where they were needed.
Apart from financial obligations[4] and military service, however,
we are not informed about the cleruch's obligation as a citizen
living abroad, though we may note that, like other colonists,
they made offerings to the gods of the mother city.[5]

Among other colonies we have seen instances which seem
comparable with Athenian cleruchs, as Cythera for example,
and perhaps the colonies of Sybaris and Syracuse.[6] These may
have been extensions of the founding state, which could be regarded as colonies because of the practical effect of distance.
Some colonies of Corinth were very often associated with
Corinth in war, though the evidence falls short of showing that
Corinth could command their military support.[7] A true
parallel among Greek colonies for the cleruch's financial obligations to the mother city is not found. The colonies of Sinope
were bound to pay sums to the metropolis, but their payment is
called tribute ($\delta\acute{a}\sigma\mu o\nu$).[8] The only other clear evidence on the
subject is from the foundation decree about Naupactus, where
the colonists were expressly freed from taxes owed as citizens of
the mother community.[9]

Although instances comparable to the Athenian cleruchies
can be found among other Greek colonies, as large settlements

---

Thucydides mentions (III.5.1; IV.28.4; V.8.2; VII.57.2) as serving with
the Athenians, were the cleruchs. Similarly the lists of the fallen which
include Lemnians show that cleruchs served with the Athenians, if the
Lemnians there named were the cleruchs (see above, pp. 179f).

[1] As in the Thracian Chersonese; see Plut. *Per.* XIX.I.

[2] *Athenian Democracy* 174 f.

[3] When the Athenians ordered the cleruchs at Chalcis to help Eretria in
490, see Hdt. VI.100.1.

[4] Among these the cleruch was either wholly or partly exempt from the
trierarchy in the fourth century; see Busolt/Swoboda 1276 and n. 5.

[5] See *IG* I².274, 178 ($\varkappa\lambda\acute{\eta}\varrho o\upsilon\chi o\iota$ $\grave{a}\nu\acute{e}\theta\varepsilon\sigma[\alpha\nu]$), which may be compared with
the offerings of $\acute{e}\pi o\iota\varkappa o\iota$ at Potidaea (Tod 60) and an $\grave{a}\pi o\iota\varkappa\acute{\iota}a$ of uncertain
locality (*IG* I².396, see *ATL* III 283 ff). Cf. also the religious obligation of
the colonists to Brea, and of the Athenian allies; see above, Chapter IV.

[6] See Chapter V.   [7] See Chapter VII.
[8] Xen. *Anab.* V.v.10.   [9] See Chapter IV.

of citizens abroad they are different in degree from most Greek colonies. In discussing the question of mutual citizenship we saw that though colonies and mother cities found it easy to open their citizenship to each other, the normal rule was certainly for the colonists to lose their old citizenship.[1] It was for this reason that most Greek colonies did not form a means of political expansion for the mother city. In the cleruchy the Athenians had produced a colony to fulfil this purpose. It is therefore interesting that they did not invariably use it, and it is worth while to seek the reasons why one settlement was a cleruchy and another not.

It is easy to understand that a colony which became a new Greek state was out of the question when the settlement was on the land of an existing Greek city, as, for example, at Mytilene, and there is, in fact, no example of anything but a cleruchy being founded in these circumstances. When, on the other hand, the population of a captured Greek city had been entirely expelled, the Athenians apparently sometimes established a cleruchy, but not always. For though it seems most probable, if not certain, that Hestiaea, Aegina and Melos were cleruchies, Potidaea was not.[2] It is this instance which invalidates an old suggestion that cleruchies were established in Greek cities and *apoikiai* were planted on the territory of barbarians.[3]

The only obvious difference between the settlements at Aegina and Potidaea of almost exactly the same date is that Potidaea was much further from Athens. It is noticeable too that the earliest cleruchy definitely attested, that at Chalcis, was very close to Attica. It seems possible, therefore, that the cleruchy, as an extension of the founding state, was at first only felt to be possible on land close to Athens. The best analogies for the Athenian cleruchies in Greek colonization in general have been seen to be colonies at a short distance from their mother cities. It therefore appears that the unusual character of the cleruchy is to be explained by the practical effect of Athens' naval power and political ambition, which enabled her to overcome the difficulties which prevented most Greek mother cities from expanding their state by means of colonies. The dependent colonies of Corinth were probably the result of a similar ability

[1] See Chapter VI. [2] See above pp. 170 ff., 177 n. 3.
[3] See De Bougainville, op. cit., p. 21.

o

in the mother city to conquer the effects of distance, as has been seen, but in the cleruchy Athens had succeeded to an even greater degree.

Other imperial colonies

We may now turn to the Athenian colonies which were certainly not cleruchies. The foundations of several of these, which were discussed in Chapter III, show that they were established with imperial aspirations. It is necessary here to investigate how far their subsequent relations to Athens bore out the intentions of the founders. The Spartan colony at Heraclea in Trachis, Sinope's extensive control over her South Pontic colonies, and, to a far smaller extent, the Adriatic colonies of Dionysius I, represent valuable comparative material, which justifies their place in this chapter, but Athens inevitably demands most attention.

The position of Sigeum regarding Athens has been confused in modern literature, because Berve's extreme view that it was an independent possession of the tyrant house[1] provoked replies that went too far in their attempt to prove its connection with the state of Athens.[2] In general terms Sigeum's relationship with Athens was not exceptionally close except under the tyranny. When Hippias withdrew there[3] he came under the protection of the Persians,[4] and Sigeum's relations with Athens were presumably largely cut off until after the Persian Wars. As a regular ally in the Delian League and a vital position on the Hellespont Sigeum was then no doubt effectively under Athenian control, but the evidence does not suggest greater dependence than that of other subordinate allies.

It was argued above[5] that the establishment of Hegesistratus as ruler of Sigeum should be regarded as part of an Athenian policy to control the Hellespont, and this involves the assumption that Sigeum became a dependent colony. On the other hand, the evidence does not show that the colonists had any special legal status, as for example Athenian citizenship. The famous monument of Phanodicus[6] on which there is an Attic

---

[1] *Miltiades, Hermes* Einzelschriften 2, 1937, 26 ff.
[2] See especially Ehrenberg, *Aspects of the Ancient World*, 116–43; Bengtson, *Sitz. Bayr. Akad.* 1939, 7–67.
[3] Hdt. V.94.1.   [4] Cf. V.96.2.
[5] See Chapter III.   [6] Hicks and Hill 7; *Syll.*[3] 2.

and Ionic inscription, whatever its exact explanation,[1] can hardly be made to show the legal status of the colonists. The Attic dialect is used to address Sigeans, and this shows that the Athenian settlers had become in effect Sigeans. While it may be wrong to conclude from this that the settlers had lost their Athenian citizenship,[2] it is worse to use the fact that a non-Athenian employed the Attic dialect as evidence for Sigeum's political position.[3] Attic is simply used to address speakers of Attic. Political conclusions from the presence of a temple of Athena[4] are similarly out of place.

In a highly poetic passage Aeschylus gives mythical justification for Athenian possessions in the Troad (*Eum.* 397 ff), and Herodotus' account of the Athenian defence of their colonization of Sigeum (V.94.2) is a prose version of the same idea, but such evidence does not reveal the precise legal status of the settlers or their land. On the other hand Hippias' withdrawal to Sigeum[5] and a fifth-century Athenian decree praising the Sigeans[6] would both be hard to understand if the colonists had remained Athenian citizens. Furthermore, if the argument above about Lemnos is correct,[7] the fact that Sigeum was a tribute-paying member of the Athenian Empire[8] precludes the possibility that it was a cleruchy.[9]

The early Athenian settlement on the Thracian Chersonese was also a subject of dispute between Berve and his critics, and

---

[1] In spite of Van Compernolle's defence (*Antiquité Classique* xxii 1953, 61 n. 8) Brouwer's theory (*REG* xli 1928, 107 ff) that the inscription is not a grave relief but a votive monument, recording the offerings not of one man but two, the first of whom was the grandfather, the second the grandson, must be abandoned. See the criticisms, from different points of view, by Guarducci, *Ann. d. scuol. arch. d. Atene* iii–v 1941–3, 135–40, and Johansen, *Attic Grave Reliefs of the Classical Period*, 105. But even if we revert to the older opinion that both texts refer to one man, the document is still difficult to explain satisfactorily, though many suggestions have been made; see, e.g., Hicks and Hill notes to no. 7, *Syll.*[3] notes to no. 2, and Guarducci 136 f.
[2] As Berve, *Miltiades*, 30.
[3] As Bengton, *Sitz. Bayr. Akad.* 1939, 21, who follows Brouwers.
[4] As Bengtson, loc. cit.   [5] Hdt. V.94.1.
[6] *IG* I².32, republished by Meritt, *Hesperia* v 1936, 361 f.
[7] See p. 177.
[8] See *ATL* I Register, s.v. Σιγειῆς; III 206 n. 55.
[9] It should be remarked that Sigeum is generally recognized to have been no cleruchy; cf., for example, Ehrenberg, *Aspects of the Ancient World*, 119, even though he thinks that 'municipal cleruchies' could pay tribute (135 f).

we have seen reason to prefer Berve's opinion that Miltiades the Elder's colonization was a private enterprise.[1] If this is right, the colonists clearly did not retain their Athenian citizenship. The action of the Peisistratids in sending Miltiades the Younger to rule the Chersonese not long after Hegesistratus was set over Sigeum[2] made it in effect an Athenian possession, and all the evidence for its dependent position comes from after this time.

In detail the political and topographical problems of the Chersonese are very complicated.[3] However, the only important question for the present purpose is whether the cities of the area were independent of each other in the sixth century or formed a single state. Ehrenberg's conclusion that there was no single state of the Chersonesites at this period[4] seems well supported by the admittedly rather slight evidence, in which case it also seems probable that Miltiades the Elder's Athenian settlers were not established in one city. His enterprise was certainly not the foundation of a regular colony, for he became oikist of the Chersonesites,[5] who would include both the colonists and the original inhabitants. This special nature of the Chersonese must be remembered when it is discussed as an Athenian colony.

Conclusions about the status of the Chersonese, or of the Athenian settlers in it, have been drawn by modern scholars from Miltiades' trial for tyranny in the Chersonese. Herodotus' words (VI.104.2.) show that a definite trial was held and Miltiades was acquitted.[6] The acquittal was taken by Berve to show that the Athenian settlers of the Chersonese were not citizens of Athens. This line of argument was rejected by Ehrenberg (121) on the grounds that there must have been many possibilities of refuting such a charge. In this he is right, but it was common knowledge that Miltiades had been tyrant of the Chersonese,[7] so that some line of defence other than denial that he had been a tyrant must presumably have been found. Both writers however accept as definite that Miltiades must have been accused of tyranny over Athenian citizens, and Bengtson is of the same opinion,[8] though he avoids legal definitions and

[1] See Chapter III.   [2] See Chapter III.
[3] They are well treated by Ehrenberg, *Aspects of the Ancient World*, 121 ff.
[4] Ibid.   [5] Cf. Hdt. VI.38.1.
[6] As A. von Blumenthal showed, *Hermes* lxxii 1937, 476 f.
[7] Cf. Hdt. IV.137.1.   [8] *Sitz. Bayr. Akad.* 1939, 19.

merely affirms that the settlers must have been considered Athenians.

But it seems a mistake to take this trial as good evidence for the status of the Athenian settlers on the Chersonese. The main issue at stake was whether Miltiades should be admitted to Athens. His absence from Athens for at least twenty years may have meant that his opponents could find no other charge sufficiently serious for their purpose, and in the atmosphere of the post-Peisistratid democracy a charge of tyranny might be expected to be effective whatever the legal position.[1] Miltiades had been set up as a tyrant by tyrants, and the legal status of his subjects, some, if not most, of whom were not even of Athenian origin, was probably of small importance. To say, therefore, that there were Athenian citizens in the Chersonese[2] is only possible if one ignores the Athenian atmosphere of the time and the odium against tyrants as such.

Miltiades' return to Athens and tenure of the office of *strategos* has been used to show that the Athenian colonists of the Chersonese could return to full citizenship at Athens,[3] or, more generally, that all colonists of the later period had a similar right.[4] It seems very dangerous to draw general conclusions from the career of an outstanding nobleman like Miltiades, who may have been free from normal legal limitations. In any case he was not in the same position as the other Athenian colonists of the Chersonese. They were the descendants of settlers of the middle of the sixth century; he was specially sent out to rule between 524 and 513.[5] No one would suggest that Peisistratus had to justify his Athenian citizenship when he returned from ruling Rhaecelus, and it seems most probable that Miltiades was regarded as an Athenian citizen throughout, as is suggested by Herodotus' words describing his return: ἀπικόμενον ἐς τὴν ἑωυτοῦ[6] (VI.104.2).

A bronze helmet dedicated by Miltiades at Olympia has, however, been taken to show the opposite. The inscription on this runs Μιλτιάδες ἀνέ[κεν τ]ôι Δί,[7] and the absence of the

---

[1] Cf. the ostracisms of the 'friends of the tyrants'; Arist. *Ath. Pol.* 22.6.
[2] As Walker *CAH* IV. 171, and Ehrenberg, 121.
[3] As by Bengtson op. cit. 17 f.
[4] See Will, *La Nouvelle Clio* vi 1954, 453.   [5] See Chapter III.
[6] 'When he arrived in his own country'.
[7] ' Miltiades dedicated to Zeus.'

ethnic has been interpreted as perhaps showing that Miltiades was then tyrant of the Chersonese,[1] and so, it is implied, not entitled to be called Athenian. The notorious dedication of Pausanias at Delphi,[2] however, is sufficient to show that in such inscriptions great individuals did not need to state their city. Miltiades should therefore be regarded as a special case, and general conclusions about either the Athenian settlers on the Chersonese or Greek colonists in general are not to be drawn from his career.

The Athenian occupation of Lemnos was justified by a mythical story that the Pelasgians had promised to hand over their land to the Athenians when 'a ship sailing with the north wind comes from your land to ours in a day'.[3] When the Athenians controlled the Chersonese they demanded that the inhabitants of Lemnos should fulfil their old promise.[4] This has been taken to show that the Chersonese became Athenian territory. However such a formal explanation seems inappropriate. It is worth noting that the people of Myrina would not acknowledge εἶναι τὴν Χερσόνησον Ἀττικήν,[5] which suggests that the legal position was not clear. The Athenians presumably argued that the Chersonese was Athenian territory to obtain mythical, or traditional, justification for their occupation of Lemnos of a similar kind to that advanced about Sigeum.

Evidence about the Chersonese in later times seems also to suggest that the Athenian claim to it did not rest on any formal basis. Since Cimon had to re-acquire the Chersonese after the Persian Wars,[6] it may be assumed that it ceased to be under Athenian control with the departure of Miltiades. The later despatch of a cleruchy to the Chersonese[7] is therefore a result of the practical Athenian control established by Cimon, rather than any formal claims, and this is borne out by the information that the Cardians refused to receive Athenian cleruchs in the fourth century on the grounds that their land was their own and not Athenian.[8]

It seems right to conclude that the sixth-century Athenian

[1] See Kunze, *Gnomon* xxvi 1954, 142.   [2] Thuc. I.132.2.
[3] Hdt. VI.139.4.   [4] Hdt. VI.140.1.
[5] 'That the Chersonese is Attica'; Hdt. VI.140.2.
[6] Plut. *Cimon.* XIV.1.   [7] See above p. 178.
[8] See *Arg.* Dem. VIII.1–2.

colonization of the Chersonese did not create a cleruchy there[1] nor a formal claim that the Chersonese was Athenian land. Its dependence on Athens was a result of a Peisistratid policy of controlling the Hellespontine region, which was expressed in the rule of the Athenian Miltiades.[2] Both Sigeum and the Chersonese are therefore to be seen as examples of Athenian expansion in the later sixth century, but the dependence of the colonies was not expressed in special legal forms.[3] Athenian control over them was maintained by Athenian power, first under the tyrants and later under the imperial demos.

The foundations of the fifth-century Athenian settlements at Brea, Thurii and Amphipolis have already been discussed.[4] Brea has no history, so its subsequent relations with Athens are not known, but a clause in its foundation decree was used by Hampl to show that its land remained legally Athenian territority.[5] The clause in question provided that the cities should come to the help of Brea if its land was attacked, according to the agreement made about the cities of the Thraceward Region.[6] Hampl argues that the cities could not be bound by treaty to defend anything but Athenian state land, and adduces the silence of three alliance inscriptions to support his view. The oaths of the Chalcidians, Samians and the Bottiaean cities[7] should have mentioned not only the Athenians but also their colonies, if the allies were bound to help them. This argument is weak. The oaths mentioned are couched in general terms, the normal formula being that the cities will be faithful allies and help the Athenian demos. This does not suggest that there was

---

[1] Cf. Ehrenberg, *Aspects of the Ancient World*, 128.

[2] Cf. Ehrenberg, 127.

[3] An argument about the status of the colonists of Sigeum and the Chersonese was advanced by Will from the inscription *IG* I^2.928, of which he writes 'les morts sont classés sous leurs ethniques: Sigéens, Cardiens, Madytiens etc.' see *La Nouvelle Clio* vi 1954, 446. So he concludes that whatever the legal position of the companions of Miltiades the Elder and Hegesistratus, their descendants were simply Sigeans and Cardians. But this is based on error. In the inscription the only ethnics are Μαδ]ύτιοι (34) and Βυζά]ντιο[ι (98); the other names are place-names (Sigeum, Cardia, Thasos etc.) and show where the men fell. Only the Madytians can be used for Will's purpose and there may well have been no settlers of Athenian origin among them. This evidence is therefore irrelevant to the question of the colonists' status.

[4] See Chapter III.

[5] *Klio* xxxii, 1939, 34–6.

[6] Tod 44.13 ff. The clause is discussed above, Chapter III.

[7] Tod 42.22–31; *IG* I^2.50; Tod 68.16–22.

any strict distinction between the ways they might help the demos, and the Bottiaean undertaking to have the same friends and enemies as the Athenians (τ[οὺς αὐτοὺς φίλους καὶ ἐχθ]ροὺς νομιοῦμεν ὥσπερ ἂν ᾿Αθηναῖοι)[1] would surely cover a case such as that envisaged in the Brea decree. Moreover since we do not know the content of the agreement mentioned, it is impossible to draw conclusions from the duty imposed on the cities in question. All that is clear from the clause of the Brea decree is that the agreement contained the necessary arrangements for the case envisaged. No doubt if special formulae were required they were used. It is, therefore, impossible to show from the clause discussed that Brea was a 'Polis ohne Territorium'.

In the foundation of Thurii the Athenians took steps to establish a colony likely to help their interests in the West.[2] Quite soon, however, in 434/3, civil strife occurred among the colonists as to which city was their metropolis and who their oikist.[3] The dispute is described by Diodorus as between the Athenians and the Peloponnesians (XII.35.2.), though this may be an over-simplification, since there were settlers from many other parts of Greece.[4] The decision of the god at Delphi that he himself was the oikist of Thurii, and the implication that this decision was well received,[5] appear to be setbacks to Athenian intentions, but it also appears that the group of pro-Athenian settlers were trying to preserve the Athenian connection, and their acceptance of the god's decision may have been due not only to his authority in colonial matters[6] but also to his happy discovery of a middle road.

Thurii's behaviour in the Peloponnesian War shows that the pro-Athenian party were in the ascendant there until the Athenian defeat in Sicily. The Athenians were well received there in 415,[7] and Gylippus failed to win over the city in 414.[8] Demosthenes and Eurymedon found the pro-Athenian party in control and were not only able to hold a review, but even to persuade the Thurians to join enthusiastically in the Athenian

---

[1] Tod 68.18 f.   [2] See Chapter III.
[3] Diod. XII.35.1–3.
[4] As appears from the tribes Boiotia, Amphiktyonis, Ias, Euboeis and Nesiotis; see Diod. XII.11.3.
[5] Diod. XII.35.3.   [6] Cf. Chapter II.
[7] Diod. XIII.3.4.
[8] Thuc. VI.104.2.

campaign and have the same friends and enemies.[1] Even before the success of the pro-Athenian party recorded by Thucydides (VII.33.6) the Athenians were able to look for Alcibiades throughout the whole town.[2] The Athenian policy at the foundation of providing in the tribal arrangements for a pro-Athenian bloc had thus had some success. However, when the Sicilian Expedition failed, Thurii openly joined the Peloponnesian side[3] and expelled a large number of citizens for pro-Athenian sympathies.[4] The history of Thurii's subsequent relations with Athens shows that colonists of such mixed origins were not reliable friends of Athens, but this is hardly surprising in view of the special circumstances of the foundation and the contemporary divisions in the general Greek world.

Special circumstances were not present at Amphipolis; it was a new city and definitely an Athenian colony;[5] but the mixed origins of the settlers also told against the Athenian connection there. Although the Athenians intended that Amphipolis should be a strong point of their power in the Thraceward region, the size of population necessary for the city's safety[6] presumably prevented them from founding a colony entirely of their own citizens. The mixed origin of the settlers, if no other reason, makes it certain that Amphipolis was not a cleruchy, and there is no evidence to suggest that the settlers from Athens had a special status in the colony.[7] In view of its great importance to Athens, it is necessary to investigate whether the Athenians took any other special measures to control the colony.

In Amphipolis at the time of Brasidas' arrival there was an Athenian general, Eucles, whom Thucydides describes as guardian of the region (φύλαξ τοῦ χωρίου; IV.104.4). Eucles has

[1] Thuc. VII.33.6. The numbers given by Thucydides, 700 hoplites and 300 ἀκοντισταί are, as Pappritz noted (*Thurii*, Diss. Berlin 1891, 65), very small when compared with Diodorus' figures of Thurian forces against the Lucanians (XIV.101.2). But Pappritz gives other examples of great differences between Diodorus' figures and Thucydides', and so it cannot be argued that the Thurian support was niggardly.

[2] Thuc. VI.61.6 f.   [3] See, e.g., Thuc. VIII.84.2.

[4] [Plut]. *Vita dec. orat.* 835E.

[5] The foundation of Amphipolis is discussed in Chapter III.

[6] See Chapter III.

[7] Some passages in Thucydides (IV.105.2 and 106.1) might be held to suggest that the settlers from Athens had kept their Athenian citizenship. I therefore discuss them in detail in Appendix VI, where I try to show that it would be wrong to draw such a conclusion.

been called 'der athenische Gouverneur',[1] but the implication
that Athens set a regular governor over Amphipolis is not justified by Thucydides' narrative. It is clear from Thucydides' description (ibid.) of Eucles as the general (τοῦ στρατηγοῦ), and his
immediately subsequent description of himself as the other
general of the Thraceward region, that Eucles was one of the
two generals responsible for the defence of the Thraceward
Region, and his headquarters were at Amphipolis. He is not
therefore quite the same as the φύλακες and ἐπίσκοποι whom the
Athenians sent to supervise dependent cities,[2] though even
these may have not been permanent officials. Eucles is rather to
be compared with the Corinthian ἄρχων sent to Ambracia in
426,[3] than with the Corinthian ἐπιδημιουργοί regularly sent to
Potidaea.[4] It is nevertheless important to note that the headquarters of one of the two Athenian generals in the Thraceward
Region were at the colony of Amphipolis. The defence and
effective control of the town was intended to be in Athens'
hands.

One of the reasons for Amphipolis' value to Athens stated by
Thucydides (IV.108.2) was χρημάτων πρόσοδος. This phrase,
to judge by Thucydides' normal usage,[5] should mean revenues
to the state, rather than the profits of individual Athenians
through trade with Amphipolis. Thus Gomme talks of the 'important revenue' which Amphipolis provided as additional to
the tribute (φόρος).[6] It cannot be determined whether the
revenue came from a direct levy or an indirect tax like the 5 per
cent toll imposed at the Piraeus[7] and the duties levied by
Thasos,[8] but perhaps the latter is more probable. For Amphipolis remained famous for its revenues, as is shown by a passage
of Isocrates (V.5), where he affirms that Philip should value the
friendship of Athens more than the revenues (προσόδους) from

---

[1] See Papastavrou, Klio Beiheft 38, 1936, 16.

[2] These are the terms of the Suda (s.v. ἐπίσκοπος) where they are equated
with the Spartan harmosts; the remark goes back to Theophrastus, see
Harpocration s.v. Ἐπίσκοπος. But Highby argues convincingly that the
Athenian ἐπίσκοποι were, in contrast to the harmosts, not permanent and
regular officials. See The Erythrae Decree, Klio Beiheft 36, 1936, 18-20.

[3] See above p. 137 n. 1.   [4] See above pp. 136 f.

[5] See the examples of his uses of the word πρόσοδος listed by Bétant, Lexicon
Thucydideum s.v.   [6] Historia ii 1953, 2 f.

[7] See [Xen.] Ath. Pol. I.17, and Frisch, The Constitution of the Athenians,
227.   [8] See Chapter V.

Amphipolis. Such a reputation is perhaps most easily explained by the fact that Amphipolis was a great *entrepreneur* city, where tolls could be profitably and easily levied. But whatever the exact nature of the revenue, Athens may be said to have imposed financial obligations on her colony.

We do not know why Amphipolis and other colonies of Athens founded after the Persian Wars did not pay tribute, though we can conjecture that a payment made by formal allies was considered inappropriate for Athens' own colonies. Even so, payments by Amphipolis might be justified, if justification were felt necessary, by the fact that Amphipolis, like the allies, enjoyed Athenian protection. If, on the other hand, Hampl is right and Amphipolis was a city on Athenian territory, a payment to Athens could be regarded as a kind of rent. For when the ambassadors from Sinope justified their interest in the treatment of Cotyora, they said

Κοτυορῖται δὲ οὗτοι εἰσὶ μὲν ἡμέτεροι ἄποικοι, καὶ τὴν χώραν ἡμεῖς αὐτοῖς ταύτην παραδεδώκαμεν βαρβάρους ἀφελόμενοι· διὸ καὶ δασμὸν ἡμῖν φέρουσιν οὗτοι τεταγμένον καὶ Κερασούντιοι καὶ Τραπεζούντιοι.[1]

It was on the basis of this statement and his conclusions about Amphipolis that Hampl formulated his principle that mother cities remained legally in possession of the territory of their colonies, and his argument regarding Sinope and her colonies needs to be examined before the discussion of Amphipolis can be satisfactorily concluded.

Hampl interprets the passage just quoted as showing that the Sinopeans did not give up their right to the territory, but merely allowed their colonists to inhabit it as tenants, on consideration of their fixed payments of tribute.[2] He finds support in the reason given by Xenophon for the coming of the ambassadors from Sinope (V.v.7):

φοβούμενοι περὶ τῶν Κοτυοριτῶν τῆς τε πόλεως (ἦν γὰρ ἐκείνων καὶ φόρον ἐκείνοις ἔφερον) καὶ περὶ τῆς χώρας, ὅτι ἤκουον δῃουμένην.[3]

---

[1] Xen. *Anab.* V.v.10: 'These Cotyorites are our colonists and we gave over this territory to them, after we had taken it from barbarians. For this reason they pay a fixed tribute, as also the people of Cerasus and Trapezus.'

[2] His discussion of Sinope and her colonies is in *Klio* xxxii 1939, 5 ff.

[3] 'They were afraid both for the city of the Cotyorites (for it was theirs and paid tribute to them) and for their land, because they heard it was being laid waste.'

To make his argument complete Hampl asserts that the colonists were not citizens of Sinope abroad, and although his individual arguments are not very strong, he is almost certainly right in this conclusion. The distance of the colonies from Sinope, if nothing else, makes it improbable that they were part of the state of Sinope. So, if the territory of the colonies was legally Sinope's, then they were, as Hampl calls them, 'Poleis ohne Territorum'.

In the first passage quoted above, *Anab.* V.v. 10, the Sinopean ambassadors say that they gave over the land to their colonists and the colonists in return pay tribute. This is not, as it stands, evidence that Sinope maintained a legal claim to the land of her colonies. Nor are the words ἦν γὰρ ἐκείνων of the second passage, for it can be shown by detailed study of similar Thucydidean passages[1] that such expressions imply political control in general, but have no precise or regular legal significance. That Xenophon's words here lack such precise significance may be shown by comparing Xenophon's reply to the ambassadors with what the ambassadors are actually reported as saying. For Xenophon says (V.v.19) Κοτυωρίτας δέ, οὓς ὑμετέρους φατὲ εἶναι.[2] Whereas the ambassadors in fact said (V.v.10) simply that the Cotyorites were colonists from Sinope (ἡμετέροι ἄποικοι).

But while these passages from Xenophon do not seem to justify the separation of inhabitants and territory postulated by Hampl for the colonies of Sinope, the payment of tribute and the reason given for it are both interesting in themselves and for the sake of comparison. The justification for the payment of tribute by the colony—that the mother city had won the land from the barbarians and given it to the colonists—is strikingly similar to one of the Theban arguments for their right to control Plataea.[3] They do not mention tribute, but the general hegemony that they claim may be compared with Sinope's position regarding her colonies, for the tribute was only one aspect of her control. We also learn from Xenophon's account that the ambassadors from Sinope could give orders to the people of Cotyora (V.v.24.), and that there was a harmost

---

[1] See my article in *Historia* xi 1962, 246 ff.

[2] 'The Cotyorites whom you state to be yours.'

[3] Thuc. III.61.2. The relations of Thebes and Plataea are discussed above, pp. 126 f.

from Sinope at Cotyora (V.v.19). The justification for their tribute may therefore be compared with the Theban justification for a general hegemony. Perhaps it was an accepted argument for the right of mother cities to control their colonies.

In order to show that Amphipolis was a 'Polis ohne Territorium', Hampl argued first that it was a separate city in a legal sense, and secondly that Athens remained the legal possessor of its land.[1] As we have seen,[2] there is no need to doubt that Amphipolis was a normal Greek colony in the sense that it formed a new city-state. The evidence for the second of Hampl's arguments begins with the clause relating to Amphipolis in the Peace of Nicias: ἀποδόντων δὲ Ἀθηναίοις Λακεδαιμόνιοι καὶ ξύμμαχοι Ἀμφίπολιν.[3] This Hampl compares with the clause relating to Panactum, which is couched in exactly the same terms and which undoubtedly refers, he maintains, to Athenian territory. In fact Panactum was probably disputed territory between Thebes and Athens.[4] But it is more important, as we have also seen, that phrases like those about Amphipolis and Panactum could be applied to areas which were not legally part of the territory of those to whom they were to be returned.[5] The phrases imply political control in general, as is shown by a comparison with another phrase in the Peace of Nicias: 'concerning Scione and Torone and Sermyle and any other city which the Athenians possess (ἔχουσιν)'.[6] If the word ἔχουσιν could be used for the relationship of Athens to her subject allies, ἀποδόντων, referring to Amphipolis, cannot be pressed into yielding the conclusion that Athens claimed legal possession of the territory of Amphipolis. The same view should be taken of three fourth-century passages adduced by Hampl to show that Amphipolis' territory was legally Athenian. Aeschines remarks (II.32), with reference to the peace treaty of 375/4, that Amyntas voted to join with the other Greeks in helping to recover for the Athenians Amphipolis, which was theirs (Ἀμφίπολιν τὴν Ἀθηναίων). Demosthenes says (XIX.253) that

[1] Op. cit. 2–5. His conclusion is accepted by Westlake, *Hermes* xc 1962, 280.
[2] P. 199; cf. Appendix VI.
[3] 'The Spartans and their allies shall give back Amphipolis to the Athenians.' Thuc. V.18.5.
[4] See my discussion *Historia* xi 1962, 247.
[5] See Chapter VII.　　　　　　　　　　[6] Thuc. V.18.8.

the great king and all the Greeks recognized that Amphipolis belonged to the Athenians. Both these statements and the passage [Dem.] VII.29, where the words are similar, are to be understood as referring to Athens' claim that Amphipolis should be in general subject to her. None suggests that the people and territory should be legally distinguished from each other in the way that Hampl proposes.

On the other hand the whole passage Aeschines II.29–33 is more complicated. Here Aeschines tell of his representations as ambassador to Philip on the question of Amphipolis; he explains (31) how he went over the possession of the land from the beginning, recounting how Acamas, the son of Theseus, had received it as the dowry of his wife; and he says that at the time it had been in place to tell the story as accurately as possible, but that now he will be more concise. So he relates how he turned to the clause in the peace of 375/4 noted above, and claimed that Philip should not work against the actions of his father Amyntas, ending with the words:

εἰ δ᾽ ἀντιποιῇ κατὰ πόλεμον λαβὼν εἰκότως ἔχειν, εἰ μὲν πρὸς ἡμᾶς πολεμήσας δοριάλωτον τὴν πόλιν εἷλες, κυρίως ἔχεις τῷ τοῦ πολέμου νόμῳ κτησάμενος· εἰ δ᾽ Ἀμφιπολίτας ἀφείλου τὴν Ἀθηναίων πόλιν, οὐ τἀκείνων ἔχεις ἀλλὰ τὴν Ἀθηναίων χώραν.[1]

This quite clearly makes a distinction between land and people, city and inhabitants.

When Aeschines justified Athens' claims to Amphipolis in this way the city had not only been free from Athens in practice since 424, but its Athenian settlers had presumably left, and Athens had been repudiated as the mother city.[2] It may well be that these events appeared to Athenians to be the theft of their city, so that they regarded the inhabitants remaining as illegally occupying their possession. This may or may not be the explanation for Aeschines' expression,[3] but it is necessary to

[1] 'But if you claim that you took the city in war and thus rightfully possess it, if it was against us that you fought and took the city by force, you hold it justly according to the law of war. But if you took from the Amphipolitans the Athenians' city, you hold not their property but the Athenians' land.'

[2] This was the effect of their action in transferring the oikist's honours and destroying all memory of Hagnon's foundation; Thuc. V.11.1.

[3] Aeschines' arguments are part of a well-developed campaign of propaganda and counter-propaganda. The highly artificial justification from the mythical past on which Philip's claims to Amphipolis were also based

remember that Athenian claims to the city after its break from
Athens may well have been different from her attitude when it
was still an Athenian colony. This suggestion seems to be confirmed by the theoretical conclusions which follow if one accepts
Hampl's contention that the colony's land was Athens' land
from the beginning.

If Amphipolis' land was Athenian state land like Attica, the
foreign settlers must have been given the right of possession,
ἔγκτησις, in order to possess it. This right was not freely given at
Athens; by no means all metics possessed it, and it remained an
important privilege.[1] It is also relevant that the first preserved
instance of the grant of ἔγκτησις at Athens is not till 424/3.[2] Is it
to be assumed that this privilege was given to a large number of
foreign settlers at Amphipolis?

If, on the other hand, this somewhat absurd conclusion is
avoided by saying that the settlers did not have the right of
possession of their allotments but paid a rent for them to Athens,
in the way that Hampl interprets the tribute of Sinope's
colonies, we must accept that the settlers of Athenian origin
were willing to pay rent to the state for occupying allotments of
Athenian state land. Since the citizens of a Greek city did not
pay rent to the state for their land—for this would be paying
rent to themselves[3]—this possibility too may be confidently
dismissed. These formal arguments are necessary to disprove

---

may be seen in Speusippus' letter to Philip, 5 f; see Bickermann and Sykutris,
'Speusipps Brief an König Philipp', *Ber.sächs.Akad.Wiss.*, Phil. Hist. Klasse,
lxxix 1927, 9 and 26 f.

[1] See M. Clerc, *Les Métèques Athéniennes* (Paris 1893) 195 f.

[2] The word occurs or is plausibly restored in *IG* I².70 (see new text
SEG X. 84.11 ff) and 83 (see new text *SEG* X.91.22), the inscriptions being
dated to 424/3 and 421/0 respectively. The most striking early instance was
in 410/9, when ἔγκτησις was granted to Thrasybulus' accomplices in the
assassination of Phrynichus; see Tod 86.30.

[3] The whole question of ownership and property in Greece is discussed in
detail by Vinogradoff, *Outlines of Historical Jurisprudence* II ch. X. The fundamental basis for property ownership was the state who gave the κλῆρος. The
inalienability of the κλῆρος (Vinogradoff, 208) and the revolutionary cry
γῆς ἀναδασμός reflect this. However, it is clear from the phrase ἐγκτῆσθαι
κυρίως applied to property ownership (204) that, in practice, possession was
complete apart from, in some instances, right of disposal. There is never any
suggestion of the citizens paying rent to the state for the land that they
occupied, which would be most surprising in a society where no differentiation was made between the state and the citizens acting in a body (see
Vinogradoff, 102–5).

Hampl's over-formal idea that Amphipolis was a 'Polis ohne Territorium'. They show that such a special status is not to be attributed to Amphipolis.

How did the relations between Athens and Amphipolis work out in fact? The headquarters of one of the Athenian generals for the region were at Amphipolis and the Athenians probably imposed some financial obligations on the colony, but the only other factor relevant to the maintenance of the Athenian connection was the democratic constitution.[1] The Athenians could hope that this would make the city loyal to Athens,[2] but if any other attempt was made to secure Amphipolis' loyalty to Athens it failed. Thucydides relates (IV.103.2) that there were people ready to betray the city to Brasidas, that the Argilian settlers were in touch with their former fellow-countrymen, who were urging them to betray the city (103.4) and that the Amphipolitans were all suspicious of each other (104.1).

It seems clear that the normal difficulties in achieving unity in a mixed colony[3] were present to Athens' disadvantage. Because the settlers from other cities were not tied by kin to Athens, they were ready to give up the city to Brasidas,[4] and to fight against the Athenians in the Amphipolis campaign.[5] After that they were unwilling to return to their previous situation and instead repudiated the Athenian connection.[6] The Athenian dilemma was that they could not found so large a colony from their citizens alone and they could not rely on the loyalty of settlers of mixed origin.

The same fate befell the Spartan hopes of Heraclea in Trachis. It was founded to subserve Spartan war aims and the settlers were very numerous and of mixed origins.[7] The Spartans exercised a close control over the colony. It provided troops for Sparta's campaigns, as, for example, for an expedition to Naupactus immediately after the foundation,[8] and in 385 before Haliartus.[9] The evidence also shows that Sparta sent a regular official to govern it. When the Boeotians took control of the place in 420 a Spartan was expelled for misgovernment.[10] When Thucydides gives reasons (III.93.2) for the colony's

[1] See Chapter III.
[2] See Chapter III.
[3] See Arist. *Pol.* 1303 b 25.
[4] Thuc. IV. 106.2.
[5] Thuc. V.9.7.
[6] Thuc. V.11.1.
[7] See Chapter III.
[8] Thuc. III.100.2.
[9] Xen. *Hell.* III.v.6.
[10] Thuc. V.52.1.

failure he includes the behaviour of these officials (ἄρχοντες αὐτῶν τῶν Λακεδαιμονίων οἱ ἀφικνούμενοι). Finally, Xenophon mentions a harmost, Labotas, who fell there in battle (*Hell.* I.ii.18). This evidence is conclusive,[1] and Heraclea may be added to the very small list of colonies in which officials sent regularly by the mother city are attested.

In spite of this close control, however, Heraclea proved a broken reed for Sparta, and it seems likely that the reason was the mixed origin of the settlers. Although Thucydides does not mention strife between the racial groups among his reasons for the failure of the colony (III.93.2), it would be reasonable to assume that this mixed origin was the basis for the objection to the Spartan rule. The Spartan settlers themselves would hardly have been frightened off by the harsh rule of their own people, and this assumption may be supported by Diodorus' account (XIV.38.4) of the stasis at Heraclea in 399, which the Spartans settled by sending out Herippidas, who surrounded the people in assembly with his hoplites and killed five hundred of them.[2] This must mean that the stasis was considered to be against Spartan interests, and it would be a probable inference that some of the people of non-Spartan origin had formed an anti-Spartan party and became Herippidas' victims.

In 395, after Haliartus, the Boeotians and Argives took the city by treachery, (which also reveals disunity in a colony of mixed origins), killed the Spartans that they took there, and allowed the settlers of Peloponnesian origin to leave with their possessions. They then handed over the city to the Trachinians, the old inhabitants of the region.[3] This information not only shows that the settlers of different origins had remained distinct, but it also reinforces the conjecture that it was the settlers of other than Spartan and Peloponnesian origin who had earlier objected to Spartan rule and left; for it appears that by 395 the majority of the population was of Peloponnesian origin.

We may therefore conclude that Heraclea, which was like Amphipolis in its size and mixed nature, and in the intentions of the metropolis, was also like Amphipolis in failing to provide a

---

[1] Cf. Parke, *JHS* l 1930, 76, who suggests that the practice established in this colony was extended later to Sparta's subordinate allies.

[2] The unpleasant details are to be found in Polyaenus II.21.

[3] Diod. XIV.82.6 ff.

P

strong point of Spartan power abroad, because the mixed
origin of the settlers made the colony divided and unreliable.

Among late imperial colonies the settlements in the Adriatic
attributed to Dionysius I of Syracuse deserve a mention. The
sources for this colonization are exceptionally bad, and as a
result its extent and nature are disputed. But while Beaumont
seems to have been right in showing that the bases for a belief
that Dionysius had an empire all over the Adriatic are extremely feeble,[1] Gitti is also right in showing that Beaumont
went too far in his disbelief.[2]

The most important evidence is the passage Diod. XV.13.1,
where we are told that Dionysius decided to found cities in the
Adriatic,

διανοούμενος τὸν Ἰόνιον καλούμενον πόρον ἰδιοποιεῖσθαι, ἵνα τὸν ἐπὶ
τὴν Ἤπειρον πλοῦν ἀσφαλῆ κατασκευάσῃ καὶ πόλεις ἔχῃ ἰδίας εἰς τὸ
δύνασθαι ναυσὶ καθορμισθῆναι.[3]

The first necessity is to establish the meaning of πόρον. This is
discussed by Gitti in an appendix to his article, where he makes
a crucial mistake. For he discusses the meaning not of Ἰόνιος
πόρος but of Ἰόνιος κόλπος. No one would deny his contention
that Ἰόνιος κόλπος meant in the fourth century the whole
Adriatic, but Ἰόνιος πόρος should rather be the Ionian straits,
which, as it happens, suits much better Dionysius' aims described in the sentence quoted; for he wanted a safe crossing to
Epirus and harbours at which his ships would call.

In general, however, Gitti is to be followed in his attempted
reconstruction of the extent of Dionysius' empire in the Adriatic.
Uncertain though each individual case remains, Dionysius
seems to have founded a few settlements in the Adriatic and to
have had considerable interests in the area of the Dalmatian
Coast.[4] Unfortunately the paucity of the evidence conceals from
us the methods that Dionysius used to control his colonies.
Diodorus' general statement of his imperial ambitions is supported by one single detail: there was a governor of the colony

[1] JHS lvi 1936, 202 f.   [2] La Parola del Passato vii 1952, 161–91.
[3] 'Intending to possess the so-called Ionian straits, in order to make safe
the crossing to Epirus and to have his own cities in which ships could
anchor.'
[4] See Gitti, 178 ff, for Dionysius' settlements and interests on the East
coast of the Adriatic.

at Lissus appointed by Dionysius.[1] This is to be set beside the official from Sinope at Cotyora, the Spartan governors of Heraclea and the Corinthian officers at Potidaea, and understood as a sign of the mother city's control over the affairs of the colony. Otherwise we can say no more than that it seems probable that Dionysius used colonies for his imperial aims.

In this chapter we have seen examples of very close control imposed on colonies founded with imperial intentions. Although Hampl's theory that colonies became 'Poleis ohne Territorium' has been found without substance, some of the colonies discussed were clearly in general terms regarded as the possessions of the mother city. There was, therefore, clearly no theoretical objection to colonies closely dependent on the mother city, or to the use of colonies to build up power oversea.

The examples all come from a late period in Greek colonization. Only the notable control exercised by Sinope over her colonies[2] might have been established at an earlier period. Xenophon's story does not reveal when the practices began, and the colonies were probably all founded a very long time before the events described.[3] But without further knowledge it would be dangerous to assume that Sinope's control was very ancient. Its existence is perhaps to be explained by the fact that the cities were on the edge of the Greek world, and therefore felt the need to combine in face of the barbarians whom they constantly feared.[4] In such circumstances very close relations and tight control may have been acceptable for practical reasons. However, though exceptional circumstances may have produced exceptional arrangements, the justification of Sinope's position related by Xenophon shows that the mother city's claim to control her colonies was not thought abnormal.

Athens' relations to her colonies seem to represent the most extreme control by the metropolis. Some of her colonies, the cleruchies, were actual extensions of the Athenian state, and even those without this status were treated as her possessions. It was emphasized above that the cleruchies and the descriptions

---

[1] Diod. XV.14.2.   [2] See above pp. 201 ff.
[3] The foundation dates of Cotyora and Cerasus are not recorded, but the Eusebian date for Trapezus is 756. I discuss the dates of Greek colonies in the Black Sea in *Bull. Inst. Class. Studies* v 1958, 25 ff.
[4] Cf. Xen. *Anab* V.v.23.

of them by ancient writers show that a Greek colony could theoretically in the fifth century be a settlement of citizens abroad. The cleruchy appears to be the answer to the problem of normal Greek colonization, for the state and its population were not diminished. But lack of numbers and perhaps the feeling that Athenian citizens should only be settled fairly close to Athens meant that the cleruchy could not be used for large, distant, imperial foundations. The substitute, the mixed colony, proved unsatisfactory as a way of extending the mother city's power abroad.

Both the limitations of the cleruchy and the failure of the mixed colony to serve imperial ends suggest that colonization was, even in the late period, not an ideal way for Greek cities to expand. If the distance from the metropolis was great and the numbers of the colonists needed to be large, a satisfactory dependent colony was hard to establish. Thus the very close control exercised by Athens and some other mother cities in the later period shows that there was no theoretical objection to colonial empires, but in practice they remained difficult to create and maintain.

CHAPTER X

CONCLUSION

THE great difficulty of this investigation, as was stated in Chapter I, is that the sources which provide the evidence are mostly centuries later than the foundations of the colonies. There is no completely satisfactory escape from this difficulty, and a large proportion of the instances of the relations between colonies and their mother cities that we have discussed belong to the fifth and fourth centuries. However, there is enough evidence about earlier times to reinforce the arguments advanced in Chapter I to show that the relationship was important from the beginning. From the seventh century there are, for example, the substance of the foundation decree for Cyrene,[1] the foundation of Epidamnus and Selinus by oikists summoned by Corcyra from Corinth and by Megara Hyblaea from Megara in Greece,[2] the dedication of Geloans to Athena Lindia,[3] and the reception of Bacchiad exiles at Corcyra.[4] Also from early times we have Thasos' relations with Paros and several instances, some more, some less certain, of mother cities' control over colonies at a short distance.[5] This evidence seems to be sufficient to disprove any idea that the relations between colonies and mother cities increased in importance in the fifth century. We know more about these relations from the fifth century onwards simply because there is more evidence from those times for Greek history in general.

The idea that the Cypselid colonies of Corinth and those of Athens represented a new type and are entirely different from those founded earlier[6] is also wrong, at least in emphasis. It is quite true that Corinth and Athens, owing to a combination of imperial ambitions and ability to overcome the effects of distance, exercised an unusual degree of control over their colonies, control which was reflected at the foundation of the

[1] See Chapter II.   [2] See Chapter II.   [3] See Chapter VIII.
[4] See Chapter VI.   [5] See Chapter V.
[6] This is Will's thesis, *La Nouvelle Clio* vi 1954, 413–60.

colonies in the position of the oikist. But the evidence for similar control by other mother cities, some of it of early date,[1] shows that it is wrong to conceive of a sharp line dividing the colonies of Corinth and Athens from the rest. In fact this assumption too depends finally on an argument from silence, for it is about these colonies that we are best informed.

However, there still remains another, wider, application of the argument from silence. When the number of Greek colonies is considered and the length of time in question, the evidence for the relations between Greek colonies and mother cities that we have reviewed must seem small in quantity. Should one, therefore, conclude that it is all exceptional? That the great silence reveals the general rule, and any relationship attested between a Greek colony and its mother city is an exception from it?

It is very rare to be able to argue confidently from the absence of evidence that a colony and mother city maintained no relationship. Such an argument is perhaps admissible, however, in the case of Thera and Cyrene. When the colony was experiencing political difficulties under Battus III, it sent to Delphi for advice and the oracle suggested that Demonax of Mantinea be appointed mediator.[2] At an earlier date Battus Eudaimon acted through Delphi in inviting settlers from all Greece to strengthen the colony.[3] On both occasions Thera, the mother city, is conspicuously absent, and this is especially noticeable when new settlers were invited; for, as we have seen, it had been provided in the foundation decree that the mother city could send further settlers to the colony.[4]

To argue generally, however, that where evidence is lacking the colony maintained no relations with its mother city would be an unsound procedure, and is shown to be unjustified by the new evidence on the subject, largely from inscriptions, which has been added in comparatively recent times. If epigraphical discoveries of modern times have provided evidence for strikingly close relations between Thasos and her colonies, or between Miletus and hers, or between Argos, Cnossus and Tylissus, not to mention less notable examples, it is surely right to conclude that more evidence would show more instances of

[1] See Chapter V.   [2] See Hdt. IV.161.1; Plut. *De mul. virt.* 261B.
[3] See Hdt. IV.159. 1 ff.   [4] See Chapter IV.

relations between colonies and mother cities. In general too the
evidence that we possess seems to be sufficient in quantity and
sufficiently widely spread to be regarded as reasonably representative of the whole field of Greek colonial relationships.

The new evidence also helps to free Thucydides from the
charge that he overestimated the importance of these relationships. His information, for instance, about the religious obligations owed by colonies to their mother cities is confirmed as
generally valid by inscriptions about the offerings of colonies to
the gods of the metropolis.[1] But such information is perhaps less
striking than his emphasis on the relationship's effect in creating
wartime alliances. Apart from the instances mentioned above in
Chapter I, which included Melos' relationship to Sparta and
that of the Ionian cities to Athens,[2] his idea that the relationship justified an alliance is clearly revealed by his statements
regarding two occasions which concerned the relationship of
Sparta and Doris. Here too the relationship of colony and
metropolis,[3] if based on actual events at all, went back for its
origin to the times of the migrations.

When the Phocians attacked Doris in c. 457 and took one of
the townships there, the Spartans sent 1500 hoplites of their
own and 10,000 of the allies and compelled the Phocians to give
the city back.[4] The expedition has been thought far too large
simply for the coercion of the Phocians,[5] and it led to the
Battle of Tanagra, which suggests that the Spartans went prepared to fight it out with the Athenians. Thucydides, however,
considers it unnecessary to give any other motive than that
implied in his beginning: καὶ Φωκέων στρατευσάντων ἐς Δωριᾶς
τὴν Λακεδαιμονίων μητρόπολιν.[6] The second occasion was in 426.
The Trachinians were being attacked by the Oetaeans; they
sent to Sparta for help and with them went an embassy from
Doris, 'the metropolis of the Spartans' (ἡ μητρόπολις τῶν
Λακεδαιμονίων), for Doris too was suffering Oetaean attacks.[7]
The Spartans again sent help and Thucydides gives us their
motives; they wanted to help the Trachinians and Dorians, but

[1] See Chapter VIII.
[2] See Chapter I.
[3] Thuc. I.107.2, Hdt. VIII.31.
[4] Thuc. I.107.2.
[5] Cf. CAH. V.79 ff.
[6] 'And when the Phocians attacked Doris, the mother country of the
Spartans.'
[7] Thuc. III.92.1-4.

at the same time they thought that the enterprise would be to their advantage in the war against the Athenians. On neither of these occasions does Thucydides distinguish between pretext and true motive, though he is accustomed to make such distinctions. A modern observer would conclude that the Spartans used their relationship as a pretext on both occasions, and the reason why Thucydides did not, apparently, see it as such must be that he regarded the desire to help a related city as a normal motive for war.

An inscription which includes records of Melian contributions to the Peloponnesian war fund in the Archidamian War[1] is perhaps evidence for the support in war that Thucydides found normal between colony and mother city. But the effect of the relations between colonies and mother cities regarding war is more clearly illustrated by another inscription, which we have already discussed. In the latter stage of the Peloponnesian War the Neapolitans fought, and were later reconciled, with their mother city Thasos.[2] The stone concerning this is contemporary evidence to support that from Thucydides and other writers, and shows the shame attached to wars between colonies and mother cities; its converse implication is that they were natural allies. Of this too we have an example known solely from an inscription: the alliance in the latter part of the sixth century of Epizephyrian Locri and its two colonies Hipponium and Medma.[3]

Thucydides also implies that a mother city should have a position of undefined hegemony,[4] and here he is more fully supported by evidence from inscriptions. That relating to the Locrian colony at Naupactus contains a clause that the colony should not secede from its metropolis;[5] the Thasian inscription encouraging delation shows an even more marked control by a mother city over its colonies;[6] and the inscriptions about Argos, Cnossus and Tylissus reveal that the colonies accorded a general primacy to their mother city.[7] Beside these may be set the remarks of the ambassador from Sinope at Cotyora.[8] In

---

[1] Tod 62; cf. Adcock, *Mélanges Glotz*, 1–6. The Melian contributions are recorded in lines 24 ff, 36 ff.

[2] See Chapter V.   [3] See Chapter V.

[4] I.25.3 f; 38.2–5.   [5] Tod 24.11 f; see above, Chapter IV.

[6] See Chapter V.   [7] See Chapter VIII.

[8] See Chapter IX.

none of these cases did the mother city's control over its colonies need special explanation. Thucydides is representing the general view, which saw nothing surprising in mother cities that controlled their colonies.

On this matter it is clear that there were commonly-held and fairly consistent opinions in Greece. Another important question is whether there were similar fixed ideas about the relationship in all its aspects, or, more simply, whether it was homogeneous throughout the Greek world. In the realm of ideas it is clear from the evidence on the act of foundation discussed in Part I that there were fixed general principles about the way a colony should be established, and that it was generally believed that the new community was in many senses an extension of the old, so that their continuing relationship was a matter of importance to both. On the other hand each foundation probably differed from others in the detailed arrangements, if any, made for that relationship. Such differences were seen in the foundation decrees discussed above in Chapter IV.

Even more in the development of the subsequent relationship there was variety rather than uniformity. For here practical circumstances overrode theoretical principles, and the relationship was close or loose, good or bad, according to such factors as the distance separating colony and metropolis, or the ambitions of the metropolis, or the individual interests of the two communities, which might coincide or conflict.[1] In general the closest relations between colonies and mother cities have been found where the colonies were not far from the mother city, or where the mother city was sufficiently powerful and ambitious to overcome the obstacle of distance. So though there was no theoretical objection to Greek mother cities which controlled their colonies, practical factors, distance and the power of the metropolis, generally determined the degree to which a mother city exercised or tried to exercise such control.

But the aspects of the relationship which depended on the mother city's power and ambitions are only a part, and perhaps not the most important part, of the relations between Greek

[1] Corcyra is an example of a colony which had interests which conflicted with those of its metropolis; see Chapter VII. On the other hand there may have been coincidence of interests between Sinope and her South Pontic colonies; see Chapter IX.

colonies and mother cities in general. In Chapters VI and VIII we saw relations which did not depend on such influences: the opening of the citizenship of one community to the other, for instance, or the religious connections between them, or the reconciliation of colonies' quarrels by their mother cities. Such relations may be regarded as the fundamental or general basis of the connection between colonies and mother cities, on which closer relationships could be built if circumstances were favourable.

It is above all the religious relations which show the fundamental nature of the colony-metropolis relationship. There could be no more serious mistake than to think that this relationship is shown to be purely formal and of no real significance by the fact that the complaints of Corinth against Corcyra recorded by Thucydides only become specific in the field of religion.[1] It shows rather the depth and antiquity of this kind of relationship.

The earliest way in which Greek communities were joined with each other was by having the same sanctuary and the same cults. Thus the early Greek leagues were religious leagues in the sense that they were based on a common religious centre and worship.[2] The religious function of such leagues may have been primary, but the religious and political aspects were originally not separate.[3] The more purely political leagues of the classical period sometimes had their roots in the older type. So the Panionion was the centre of the political union of the Ionian cities at the time of the Ionian Revolt,[4] and the Delian League had as its centre the home of ancient Ionian religious gatherings.[5] The relationship between colony and mother city perhaps became more exclusively political at the same time, but the ancient forms of expressing their union remained important. So some of the Corinthian colonies seem to be similar to subord-

---

[1] Cf. Beaumont, *JHS* lvi 1936, 183, who writes: 'Is it really credible that the Corinthians disliked the Corcyreans to such an extent for the reasons he (i.e. Thucydides) gives?' and considers the Corinthian claims 'a trifling concession to sentiment'.

[2] As e.g. the Amphictyonies, the Panionion, the Calaurian League. For an account of these see Ehrenberg, *Der Staat der Griechen* I, 82–5.

[3] Cf. Ehrenberg p. 83: 'eine absolute Scheidung von religiöser und politischer sphäre den Dingen Gewalt antut'.

[4] Hdt. VI.7; cf. Ehrenberg 83, 93.

[5] See Thuc. III.104.3 ff.

inate allies,[1] but their loyalty was expressed by the fulfilment of their religious obligations.[2]

It should now be clear why Thucydides was shocked at the violation of the relations of kinship between colonies and mother cities in the Sicilian campaign.[3] The League of Delos, being based in his view on ancient Ionian kinship, did not generally flout such ties, but there were many individual instances where political alignments of the later fifth century cut across the old relationships, which he regarded as traditional and right. His basic ideas are the product of traditions from an older Greek world, which were no longer always effective in the times that he described.

The relationship of colony and mother city often provided from early times a way of bridging the gulf between independent city states. Nearly three centuries separated the beginning of the great colonizing movement and the first writing of history, and we know comparatively little of the relations between Greek states during this time. Our knowledge and understanding are enhanced, if we realize that a regular and effective link between them was the relationship of colony and mother city.

[1] See Chapter VII.   [2] See Thuc. I.25.4.
[3] VII.57; see above, Chapter I.

APPENDIX I

CORINTH'S WESTERN AIMS
IN THE 8TH CENTURY

THE colonization of Syracuse and Corcyra in the later eighth century has been regarded as the means by which Corinth consciously sought a predominant trading position in the West. Thus we should have a very early example of colonies established to fulfil a mother city's own commercial aims, which implies the intention that the colonies be closely related or actually dependent and, incidentally, a corresponding diminution in the independence of the oikists.

The hypothesis was originally put forward by Blakeway,[1] and appears with further arguments in Dunbabin's *The Western Greeks*.[2] The starting point was the belief that there was trade with the West before any of the western colonies was founded, in which no one state predominated, whereas from the time of the early colonies in Sicily and Italy till the end of the seventh century trade with the West was allegedly monopolized by Corinth. It was, therefore, suggested that Corinth's colonization was designed to win this commercial supremacy. This hypothesis was attacked by R. M. Cook,[3] who held that the archaeological evidence showed neither that Corinth had a complete monopoly nor that she had achieved commercial prominence suddenly.[4] But recent archaeological work has shown that there is no evidence for trade with the West before the first colonies were founded. Apart from Mycenean pottery,[5] the earliest

---

[1] *BSA* xxxiii 1933, 202 ff.   [2] Pp. 10–17.

[3] *JHS* lxvi 1946, 80 f; *CR* lxiii 1949, 113 ff.

[4] He also pointed out that the thesis of a western monopoly must be judged against the predominance of Corinthian pottery in mainland markets too in this period; *JHS* lxvi 1946, 84.

[5] Mycenean pottery has been found on various sites in the West. It is studied in full by Lord William Taylour, *Mycenean Pottery in Italy* (Cambridge 1958). Proof of continuity of contact between Greece and Italy from the Mycenean period to that of the first colonies is not found. Such continuity has been assumed by S. A. Immerwahr in her review of Lord William Taylour's book (*AJA* lxiii 1959, 295 ff), but a single sherd which may be

Greek material in the West has been found at the Greek colony of Pithecusae on Ischia.[1] Thus the hypothesis that there was a connection between colonization and a change in the character of the trade loses its archaeological support.

An attempt to save it has been made[2] by attributing the character of a trading post to the colony of Pithecusae. But there is nothing to indicate that it had this character rather than that of a normal colony,[3] and Strabo's information (V.247) that the inhabitants owed their early prosperity to fruitfulness (εὐτυχήσαντες δι᾽ εὐκαρπίαν) implies that its economy was agricultural. Its offshore position could as well have been chosen for safety as for trade. It was the security provided by the sea which led many Greek colonists to choose a site on an island close to the shore or a peninsula.[4] But though there no longer seems to be an archaeological basis for Blakeway's and Dunbabin's hypothesis, the other arguments that they advanced might appear to stand independently.[5]

Support for the hypothesis was found in Strabo's account (VI.269) that Corcyra and Syracuse were established at the same date. Eusebius, however, gives 709 as the date of Corcyra's foundation.[6] Strabo's account has a suspect appearance; it combines the foundation not only of Corcyra and Syracuse but also of Croton. Dunbabin (15 f) rejects the synchronization of Croton and Syracuse on the grounds that such synchronizations are automatically suspect, though both he and Blakeway

---

protogeometric found at Scoglio del Tonno, Taranto (*Mycenean Pottery in Italy*, no. 165, p. 118, pl. 14:19) is hardly a sufficient basis for this assumption. It suggests possible sporadic contacts between the Ionian Islands and the heel of Italy (cf. Lord William Taylour 119, 186 f).

[1] See Vallet, *Rhégion et Zancle* ch. I, especially 43 f.

[2] By S. A. Immerwahr, 295 n. 1.

[3] As R. M. Cook has convincingly shown; *Historia* xi 1962, 113 f. On the differences between a trading post and a normal colony see Chapter I above.

[4] Examples: Sinope, see Polyb. IV.56.5 ff; Iasos, see *AM* xv 1895, 139, and plan Pl. III; Syracuse, see Thuc. VI.3.2. For more examples and valuable discussion of this point see J. M. Cook, *Greek Settlement in the Eastern Aegean and Asia Minor*, *CAH*, I and II revised Edition, 24 f.

[5] Good points against the view that Corinth's early colonization was for trade were made by Gwynn, *JHS* xxxviii 1918, 92 f; more recently Will (*Korinthiaka* 321 ff) has briefly listed arguments against it.

[6] A date in the last decades of the eighth century is made certain by recent archaeological investigations at Corcyra (see Μ. Παρασκευαΐδης, Καθημερινή (Athens) 16.iii.1961), but they cannot settle the dispute between 733 and 709.

accept the synchronization of Syracuse and Corcyra. The existence of the Eusebian date, however, suggests strongly that this synchronization is equally suspect, and it may be added that if there was no pre-colonization trade the realization of Corcyra's importance as a port of call to the West[1] would only be likely after the foundations of the Sicilian colonies. It would thus be easy to understand that the Corinthian occupation of Corcyra came later. If Corcyra was founded in 709 and Syracuse in 733 their foundations were not part of a single Corinthian state policy.

The fact that both Archias and Chersicrates were probably Bacchiads[2] was taken to suggest the state organization which the theory requires. Late sources tell us of private reasons why these two wanted to leave Corinth,[3] but even if these are considered of doubtful value, a member of the ruling clan could clearly be required as oikist without the expedition necessarily being a planned act of state, as Theras and Dorieus show.[4] And if Syracuse was largely founded by Archias' initiative Thucydides' wording (VI.3.2), in which Archias is the prime mover and not οἱ Κορίνθιοι, is explained. The story of Aethiops, who bartered his allotment of land for a honey cake on the voyage out,[5] can hardly be used against this. Blakeway maintained (p. 206 and n. 1) that it showed that 'the expedition was carefully planned before the fleet set sail' and 'the division of land was made before the expedition started'. But every settler must have known he would receive an allotment; he could barter it before the actual division was made.

Arguments for the theory confined to the two Corinthian foundations are thus seen to be weak, but there remains the wider suggestion that Corinth and Chalcis can be seen to have

[1] See Thuc. I.36.2; 44.3.

[2] Archias is described as a Heraclid by Thucydides, VI.3.2., as is Chersicrates by Strabo, VI.269. The description has usually been taken to mean they were Bacchiads, e.g. by Bérard, 118 f. The point seems to be made certain by Arist. frg. 611, 19: Κόρινθος: ἐβασίλευσε δὲ καὶ Βακαῖος τρίτος κτλ. ... ᾧ θυγατέρες μὲν τρεῖς, υἱοὶ δὲ ἑπτά, οἱ τὸ γένος οὕτως ηὔξησαν ὥστε Βακχίδας καὶ Ἡρακλείδων καλεῖσθαι τοὺς ἀπ' αὐτῶν. Chersicrates is expressly stated to have been a Bacchiad by the scholiast to Ap. Rhod. IV. 1212, 1216; see Timaeus frg. 80, FGH IIIB 623 f.

[3] For Chersicrates see schol. Ap. Rhod. ibid.; for Archias, [Plut.] Am. Narr. 772E ff; Diod. VIII. 8. Cf. Bérard, 119.

[4] Hdt. IV.147 ff; V.42.

[5] Athenaeus 167d, the ultimate source being Archilochus.

been working in concert with regard to their western colonization.[1]

Dunbabin suggested that this can be seen in the siting of the
early Sicilian colonies.[2] The Chalcidians secured themselves the
rich Laestrygonian plain by the colonies of Naxos, Catane and
Leontini, while Syracuse was the best harbour in Eastern
Sicily. Evidence of Corinthian and Chalcidian co-operation is
also seen in the Corinthian expulsion of Eretrians from Corcyra[3]

[1] See Blakeway 205 ff., Dunbabin 10–17.

[2] Dunbabin's theories rest partly on the Thucydidean chronology for the
Sicilian colonies, a system which he ably defended in Appendix I. The dates
of these colonies have been the subject of much recent work, culminating in
the long book of R. Van Compernolle, *Étude de Chronologie et d' Historiographie
Siciliotes* (Brussels 1960). Thucydides' dates have been attacked from two
points of view. Vallet and Villard supported the earlier dates for Naxos and
Megara found in inferior sources (Naxos 757, Megara 757–50, Syracuse 733)
mainly on archaeological grounds; see *BCH* lxvii 1952, 289–346. For a
further statement of these views and references to opposition to them see
Vallet, *Rhégion et Zancle*, chs. I and II, and p. 47 n. 1. There is an admirably
balanced brief discussion of the subject by Bijvanck, *Bull. van d. Verein. tot.
Bevord. d. Kennis van d. Antieke Beschaving* (Leiden) xxxiv 1959, 68–71, expressing a cautious confidence in the traditional chronology. To my mind
the archaeological dating is not sufficiently certain to be preferable to the
detailed and self-consistent Thucydidean account. Much of the dating of
eighth- and seventh-century Greek history depends on Payne's absolute dates
for Protocorinthian and Corinthian, the only external supports for which
came from the foundation dates of Syracuse and Selinus given by Thucydides; cf. Hopper, *BSA* xliv 1949, 169 ff. It now seems, however, that the
Bocchoris scarab excavated by Buchner at Pithecusae (not yet published by
Buchner; see however, *La Parola del Passato* liv 1957, 225, and Trendall,
Archaeology in Sicily and Magna Graecia, with *JHS* lxxvii 1957, 41) provides
valid external confirmation for Payne's dating of the beginning of Proto-
corinthian. An attempt to lower drastically the traditional dating of
Geometric and Protocorinthian is shown to be without basis by Boardman,
Historia vii 1958, 250.

Van Compernolle attacks Thucydides' dates on the grounds that (1) they
were taken over from Antiochus and (2) they were worked out by reckoning
generations in a completely unhistorical and artificial way. That Thucydides used Antiochus seems most probable, as Dover has also shown (*Maia*
vi 1953, 1 ff) but even Van Compernolle's most subtle and complicated
arguments have not removed the strong objections to the theory that
Thucydides' dates are the result of adding artificial generations. These are
expressed by Westlake in a very judicious review of Van Compernolle (*C.R.*
n.s. xii 1962, 266 ff) including what is perhaps the strongest: 'Such methods
would have shocked Thucydides profoundly'.

[3] Plut. *QG* XI. The passage is described as 'unique' and 'of dubious
authority' by Halliday, who is also inclined to reject the synchronization of
Syracuse and Corcyra; see *Greek Questions of Plutarch*, 53 f. But it would be
wrong to reject it out of hand, and Blakeway argues well in support of it, 205
n. 4.

and the ejection of Megarian settlers from the Chalcidian colony Leontini.[1] In the first of these events the Corinthians are thought to be acting against Chalcis' enemies, in the second Chalcidians against Corinth's; for Corinth was at war with Megara in the last quarter of the eighth century.[2]

The expulsion of the Megarian colonists from Leontini must be considered in conjunction with Thucydides' information (VI.4.1) that they were received into Leontini in the first place. This hardly suggests Chalcidian enmity against the Megarians. Their later expulsion would be naturally attributable to the civil strife common in mixed colonies. The expulsion of the Eretrian settlers from Corcyra seems to be irrelevant through chronological difficulties. If we date it with Dunbabin and Blakeway to 733, we seem to be too early for the hostility between Chalcis and Eretria;[3] not long before, they co-operated in founding Cumae.[4] If we date it to 709, that is too late to be connected with the earliest Sicilian colonization. Of all these arguments, therefore, there only remains the hypothesis that the Corinthians took the best harbour, the Chalcidians the best land, and that this shows an agreement on spheres of influence. It seems possible that an amicable division was made among the settlers of the new island, but an agreement between two mother cities in the eighth century on spheres of influence has an anachronistic air. Nor does the siting of the colonies alone

[1] Thuc. VI.41; Polyaen. V.5.1–11.

[2] For this war see Hammond, *BSA* xlix 1954, 93 ff.

[3] The date of the Lelantine War is notoriously uncertain. But it is only by referring the event on Corcyra to it (and to 733) and by including the expulsion of the Megarian colonists from Leontini similarly, that it is put so close to the co-operation of the protagonists at Cumae; see, for example, Forrest's discussion, *Historia* vi 1957, 161 ff, where these indications are used to give the high date. If the Archilochus fragment (Diehl[3] 3) refers to the war it is easier to think of a date nearer 700; cf. Forrest, 163. Similarly if Ameinocles' shipbuilding at Samos (Thuc. I.13.3) is attached to the war, as Forrest, 161, this gives us the date *c.* 704. In some sensible and restrained observations on the war, which are to be preferred to the views followed by Forrest, Boardman suggests two phases of conflict, but this is partly to explain the Corcyrean episode which he too attributes to the war; see *BSA* lii 1957, 27 ff. For a useful collection of the literary sources for the war and an attempt to reconcile their divergent implications see Will, *Korinthiaka* 391–404. But the idea of a war lasting (with intervals) from *c.* 700 to *c.* 550 seems a desperate expedient, and general considerations about Ionian conditions suggest that the war was before 670, see Roebuck, *Ionian Trade and Colonization* 73 n. 8.

[4] See Dunbabin 3, 5 ff.

prove any long term planning and co-operation. Thus this far-going hypothesis regarding the nature of the colonization of Syracuse and Corcyra seems not to be well founded; so that there is no need to attribute here a special character to the oikists or act of foundation in general.

APPENDIX II

TRANSLATIONS
OF FOUNDATION DECREES[1]

1. *Cyrene*[2]

   Ὅρκιον τῶν οἰκιστήρων.

   [Ἔ]δοξε τᾶι ἐκκλησίαι · ἐπεὶ Ἀπόλλων αὐτομάτιξεν Β[άτ]
25 τωι καὶ Θηραίοις ἀποι[κίξαι] Κυράναν, ὁριστὸν δοκεῖ Θη[ραί
   ο]ις ἀποπέμπεν ἐς τὰν [Λιβ]ύαν Βάττομ μὲν ἀρχαγέτα[ν
   τ]ε καὶ βασιλῆα · ἑταίρους δὲ τοὺς Θηραίους πλέν· ἐπὶ τᾶι ἴσα[ι
   κ]αὶ τᾶι ὁμοίαι πλὲν κατὰ τὸν οἶκον· υἰὸν δὲ ἕνα καταλ[έ
   γεσθαί τ[ῶ οἴκω ἑκάστω, πλὲν δὲ] τοὺς ἡβῶντας, καὶ τῶν [ἄλ
30 λ]ων Θηραίων ἐλεύθερος, [ὅ κα λῆι], πλέν. Αἰ μὲν δέ κα
                                                            κατέχ[ων]
   τι τὰν οἰκισίαν οἱ ἄποικοι, τῶν οἰκείων τὸγ καταπλέον[τα]
   ὕστερον εἰς Λιβύαν καὶ πολιτήιας καὶ τιμᾶμ πεδέχ[εν]
   καὶ γᾶς τᾶς ἀδεσπότω ἀπολαγχάνεν. Αἰ δέ κα μὴ κατ[έχ]
   ωντι τὰν οἰκισίαν μηδὲ οἱ Θηραῖοί μιν δύνανται ἐπικουρέ
35 ν, ἀλλὰ ἀνάγκαι ἀχθῶντι ἔτη ἐπὶ πέντε, ἐκ τᾶς γᾶς ἀπίμ[εν]
   ἀδιέως Θήρανδε ἐπὶ τὰ αὐτῶγ χρήματα καὶ ἦμεμ πολιάτ
   ας. Ὁ δέ κα μὴ λῆι πλὲν ἀποστελλοίσας τᾶς πόλιος, θανά[σι]
   μος τένται καὶ τὰ χρήματα ἔστω αὐτοῦ δαμόσια. Ὁ δὲ ἀπ
   οδεκόμενος ἢ ἀδήιζων ἢ πατὴρ υἰὸν ἢ ἀδελφεὸς ἀδελ
40 φεὸν παισεῖται ἅπερ ὁ μὴ λέων πλέν. Ἐπὶ τούτοις ὅρκια ἐπ
   οιήσαντο οἵ τε αὐτεῖ μένον[τ]ες καὶ οἱ πλέοντες οἰκίξοντε
   ς καὶ ἀρὰς ἐποιήσαντο τὸς ταῦτα παρβεῶντας καὶ μὴ ἐμ

---

[1] These translations are intended to provide no more than close render-
ings of the three main texts discussed above in Chapter IV. References to
publications of the documents will be found there. Italics are used to indicate words which are uncertain owing to gaps in the originals or for any
other reason.

[2] As this text is less easily consulted than those referring to Naupactus and
Brea, I print the Greek, i.e. the relevant portion of *SEG* IX.3 except in lines
28 f, where I give Wilhelm's text. On this see my discussion in *JHS* lxxx 1960,
98. Translations of the text which I have consulted with profit in preparing
my own are those of Oliverio, *Riv. di Fil.* vi 1928, 222 ff.; Chamoux, *Cyrène
sous la monarchie des Battiades*, 106 f.; and one prepared for teaching purposes
by my colleague Mr. C. A. Rodewald.

μένοντας ἢ τῶν ἐλλιβύαι οἰκεόντων ἢ τῶν αὐτεῖ μεν
ὄντων. Κηρίνος πλάσσαντες κολοσὸς κατέκαιον ἐπα
45 ρεώμενοι πάντες συνενθόντες καὶ ἄνδρες καὶ γυναῖκ
ες καὶ παῖδες καὶ παιδίσκαι · τὸμ μὴ ἐμμένοντα τούτοις
τοῖς ὁρκίοις ἀλλὰ παρβεῶντα καταλείβεσθαί νιν καὶ κα
ταρρὲν ὥσπερ τὸς κολοσός, καὶ αὐτὸν καὶ γόνον καὶ χρή
ματα. Τοῖσι δὲ ἐμμένοισιν τούτοις τοῖς ὁρκίοις καὶ τοῖς
50 πλέοισι ἐλλιβύαν κ[αὶ] τ[οῖς μέ]νοισι ἐν Θήραι ἦμεν πολλ
ὰ καὶ ἀγαθὰ καὶ αὐ[τοῖς καὶ γό]νοις.

AGREEMENT[1] OF THE FOUNDERS

Decided by the assembly. Since Apollo has given a spon-
taneous prophesy[2] to Battus and the Theraeans ordering them
to colonize Cyrene, the Theraeans resolve that Battus be sent to
Libya as leader and king: that the Theraeans sail as his companions: that they sail on fair and equal terms, *according to
family*;[3] that one son be conscripted *from each family*; *that those
who sail* be in the prime of life;[4] and that, of the rest of the
Theraeans, any free man *who wishes* may sail. If the colonists
establish the settlement, any of their fellow-citizens[5] who later
sails to Libya shall have a share in citizenship and honours and
shall be allotted a portion of the unoccupied land. But if they
do not establish the settlement and the Theraeans are unable to
help them and they suffer inescapable troubles *up to* five years,[6]
let them return from that land without fear to Thera, to their
possessions and to be citizens. But he who is unwilling to sail
when the city sends him shall be liable to punishment by death
and his goods shall be confiscated. And he who receives or protects another, even if it be a father his son or brother his brother,
shall suffer the same penalty as the man unwilling to sail. On

[1] For this rendering of ὅρκιον see my remarks in *JHS* lxxx 1960, 103 f.
[2] I gladly take this opportunity of acknowledging the correctness of
Parke's interpretation here (*JHS* lxxxii 1962, 145 f), which I follow in
preference to my earlier mistaken opinion of the force of αὐτομάτιξεν.
[3] On this uncertain part of the document see my discussion in *JHS* lxxx
1960, 98.
[4] This translation of τοὺς ἡβῶντας is preferred to simply 'the adults' (as,
e.g., Wilhelm, *Griechische Inschriften rechtlichen Inhalts*, 6), since it takes
account of the other meaning of ἡβάω (to be in the flower of youth) and the
needs of a colonial expedition.
[5] On this translation of οἰκείων see above p. 64 n. 1.
[6] For another possible interpretation of this phrase see above p. 53 n. 1.

these conditions they made an agreement, those who stayed
here and those who sailed on the colonial expedition, and they
put curses on those who should transgress these conditions and
not abide by them, whether those living in Libya or those staying in Thera. They moulded wax images and burnt them while
they uttered the following imprecation, all of them, having
come together, men and women, boys and girls. May he who
does not abide by this agreement but transgresses it melt away
and dissolve like the images, himself and his seed and his
property. But for those who abide by the agreement, both those
who sail to Libya and those who remain in Thera, may there be
abundance and prosperity both for themselves and their descendants.

2. Naupactus[1]

The colony at Naupactus is to be established on the following
terms. The Hypocnemidian Locrian, when he becomes a
Naupactian, shall, being a Naupactian, have the right, when
present, to sacrifice and obtain a share of the sacrifice, in the
places where a stranger is permitted by sacred law, if he so
wish.[2] If he so wish he shall make offerings and receive a share
both in the sacrifices of the people and those of the societies, he
and his family for ever. The colonists of the Hypocnemidian
Locrians shall not pay tax among the Hypocnemidian Locrians
until one of them becomes again a Hypocnemidian Locrian. If
the colonist wishes to return, it shall be allowed without payment of fees[3] so long as he leaves for the household[4] a grown son
or brother. If the Hypocnemidian Locrians are driven out of
Naupactus by force, they shall be permitted to return, each to
his previous home, without entry fees. They shall pay no tax
except in common with the West Locrians.

---

[1] Translations of this text and commentaries which I have consulted with
profit in preparing my version are those of Meister, *Ber. d. sächs. Gesell. d. Wiss.
zu Leipzig*, Phil. Hist. Klasse, 1895, 272 ff, Tod 24, and Buck, *The Greek
Dialects*, (Chicago 1955) 250 ff.

[2] On the difficulties of punctuation and interpretation in this sentence see
above pp. 49 ff.

[3] The word ἐνετήρια only occurs here; on its possible meanings see above
p. 52 n. 1.

[4] I translate τὰ ἐν τᾶι ἱστίαι according to Meister's interpretation, who
sees the τὰ as an accusative of respect meaning 'with regard to' or the like.
Cf. also Tod p. 34.

1. The colonists to Naupactus are to take an oath not to secede voluntarily from the Opuntians by any means or device whatever. If they wish it shall be permitted, thirty years after the swearing of the oath, for one hundred men from the Naupactians to administer the oath to the Opuntians, and the Opuntians to the Naupactians.

2. Whoever of the colonists defaults in his tax payments in Naupactus shall be excluded from the Locrians until he pay his lawful dues to the Naupactians.

3. If the colonist have no successors in his house, nor heir among the colonists in Naupactus, the next of kin among the Hypocnemidian Locrians shall inherit, wherever he may come from among the Locrians,[1] so long as he comes in person, whether man or boy, within three months. But otherwise the laws of the Naupactians shall be applied.

4. If the colonist return from Naupactus to the Hypocnemidian Locrians he shall have it proclaimed in the market-place at Naupactus, and among the Hypocnemidian Locrians he shall have it announced in the market-place of his city of origin.

5. Whenever a member of the Percothariae and Mysacheis himself becomes a Naupactian, his property in Naupactus shall also be subject to the laws of Naupactus. But his property among the Hypocnemidian Locrians shall be subject to the laws of the Hypocnemidian Locrians, as the laws of the Hypocnemidian Locrian city of each individual stand. But if one of the Percothariae and Mysacheis return under the laws relating to the colonists, he shall be subject to his own laws, each in his city.

6. If the settler in Naupactus shall have brothers, as the law stands in each city of the Hypocnemidian Locrians, if the brother die, the colonist shall take possession of the property, that is shall possess his due share.

7. The colonists to Naupactus shall have precedence in bringing suits before the judges; the Hypocnemidian Locrian shall bring suits and answer suits *against himself*[2] in Opus on the

---

[1] I translate according to Meister's punctuation here in preference to Tod's, as it seems to me more in tune with the order of words, but certainty is not attainable. See above p. 54 n. 3.

[2] Here I prefer Buck's interpretation of κατὰ ϝέος to Tod's ('so far as he is concerned').

same day. *Those who are the magistrates of the year*[1] shall appoint a
prostates[2] for the colonist from the Locrians, and from the
colonists for the Locrian.

8. Whoever of the colonists to Naupactus leaves behind a
father and leaves his property with his father, shall be allowed,
when the father dies, to recover his share.

9. Whoever shall violate these decisions by any means or
device whatever, except after a decree both of the assembly of
the Thousand at Opus and the assembly of the colonists at
Naupactus, shall be outlawed and his property shall be confiscated. The magistrate shall grant a trial to the accuser within
thirty days, if thirty days of his magistracy are left. If he does
not grant a trial to the accuser, he shall be outlawed and his
property confiscated, his land together with his servants. They
are to swear the oath prescribed by law. The votes are to be
cast into an urn. And the statute for the Hypocnemidian
Locrians is to be valid in the same way for the settlers from
Chaleum with Antiphatas.

3. Brea[3]

The adjutants for the oikist shall make *provision for the
sacrifice*[4] in order to obtain favourable omens *for*[5] the colony, as
they shall decide. Ten distributors of land shall be chosen, one
from each tribe. These shall allot the land. Democlides shall
establish the colony with full powers to the best of his ability.
The sacred precincts that have been set apart are to be left as
they are, but no further precincts are to be consecrated. The
colony is to make an offering of a cow and panoply to the Great
Panathenaea and a phallus to the Dionysia. If anyone attacks

[1] This phrase is a crux which cannot be certainly solved. I follow Tod and
Buck, and give what seems to be the most probable meaning.

[2] On the exact meaning of this word see above p. 59 n. 4.

[3] Because the beginning of the text has been lost the meaning of the
mutilated opening phrases is not clear enough for an informative translation.
I therefore begin with the first complete sentence, line 3. Tod's remarks on
the opening phrases (p. 89) are still valid in spite of later attempts to restore
and interpret them. See above p. 60 n. 1.

[4] This is a translation of Meritt's text (*Hesperia* X 1941, 319; also printed
in Hill, *Sources*,[2] B.55), but he offered it in full knowledge of its uncertainty,
for the sake of example only.

[5] The force of ὑπέρ here is not quite clear, since 'on behalf of' or 'in the
name of' are equally possible, as Daux pointed out; see *REG* xlviii 1935, 63
n. 3.

the territory of the colonists, the cities are to bring help as quickly as possible according to the treaty which was made, when . . . was first secretary of the council, concerning the cities of the Thraceward Region.

This decree is to be written on a stele and placed on the acropolis; the colonists are to provide the stele at their own cost. If anyone puts a motion to the vote contrary to the stele, or speaks against it as a public orator, or attempts to persuade others to rescind or annul in any way any of the provisions decreed, he shall be deprived of civil rights together with his sons and his property shall be confiscated, and one tenth shall go to the goddess, unless the colonists themselves make some request *on their own behalf*.[1]

Those in the army who are enrolled as additional colonists shall settle at Brea within thirty days of their arrival in Athens. The colonial expedition is to set off within thirty days, and Aeschines shall accompany it and pay the expenses.

Phantocles proposed: Concerning the colony to Brea, let it be as Democlides proposed, but the prytaneis of the Erechtheid tribe shall introduce Phantocles to the council in its first sitting. The colonists to Brea shall be from the Thetes and Zeugitae.

---

[1] The restored words περὶ σφῶν are uncertain.

APPENDIX III

THE FORM OF THE
NAUPACTUS FOUNDATION DECREE

IT was noted in Chapter IV[1] that in the Naupactus foundation decree the first paragraph (1–11) is without a number
and contains several provisions. All the subsequent paragraphs
are numbered and each contains strictly one provision only.
Why does the numbering not begin at the beginning, and does
the distinction reflect significant differences between the numbered and unnumbered provisions?

To dismiss the distinction as a matter of chance seems unjustified. It is hardly likely that the idea of numbering occurred
to the inscriber after four provisions were already cut, or that
such an illogical formal arrangement would have persisted in a
copy, which is what we have.[2] Nor can the arrangement be explained, as by Meyer,[3] by the analogy of the Corpus Iuris,
where the second paragraph receives the number 1, the first,
the *principium*, remaining unnumbered. For, as Meister remarked (301), this explanation would only be valid if the pre-
liminary section consisted of a single provision.

But Meister's own subtle and complicated explanation (301 f)
is also open to objection. He suggested that the inscription
contains not one but two decrees. The first contained general
conditions which had to be passed before the colony could be
decreed by the Hypocnemidian Locrians, or the colonists enrol
themselves. The second began with the act by which the
colonists completely committed themselves, the oath not to
secede, after which the Thousand of Opus[4] could conclude a
treaty with the colonists, of which the numbered part of the inscription is the record. So he saw a chronological order in the
decree: first an announcement of general provisions, then the

[1] See Chapter IV also for publications of the inscription and commentaries.
[2] This is inferred from lines 46 f and the inscription's provenance; see Tod
I p. 33.
[3] *Forschungen zur alten Geschichte* I 296.   [4] Cf. line 39.

enrolment of the colonists and their oath, then further provisions based on a treaty between the colonists and the Thousand of Opus. His main argument for this lay in his opinion that the first numbered paragraph (11), *Ἔνορρον τοῖς ἐπιϝοίροις ἐν Ναύπακτον μὴ 'ποστᾶμεν*, must describe an act already accomplished. Taking the view that it is impossible to understand the imperative *εἶμεν*, he supplied *ἐστι*, and translated 'the colonists are bound by oath', which he took to show that the oath had already been sworn.

However, this concept of an oath and enrolment which changed the status of the colonists regarding the mother city is not justified by the decree. There is no difference in the character of the provisions of the first paragraph and the subsequent ones in this respect: both are equally binding on the colonists. If the first could be passed without an oath of the colonists, why not the subsequent ones? Furthermore, the whole tone of the decree makes the concept of a treaty untenable. It shows throughout conditions imposed on the colonists. The analogy of the Brea decree[1] seems admissible here; the provision (26–9) for recruits there shows that detailed conditions could be laid down before some of the colonists had enrolled themselves. They do not form a body with which a treaty could be made.

Formal support for Meister's assumption of a break in the decree is also lacking, since all the provisions follow naturally on the first words: *Ἐν Ναύπακτον κὰ τῶνδε ϝαπιϝοικία*. Only, therefore, if his contention is inescapable that *ἐστι* must be supplied in line 11, is there any reason for assuming that the first numbered paragraph begins a new decree. His view did not convince the compilers of Liddell & Scott (s.v. *ἔνορκος*), who supply *εἶμεν*. And if *ἐστι* is understood, the sentence differs not only from all the preceding sentences, but also from all those that follow. If this phrase describes a past act and what follows is a new decree, how is one to construe the infinitives of the remaining clauses? *ἐξεῖμεν* (12), to mention only the first, becomes grammatically inexplicable. If, however, all the infinitives depend, as seems natural, on the first words of the decree, then the intrusive statement of fact becomes impossible. Thus Meister's explanation of the paragraphing problem by postulating two decrees is to be rejected.

[1] Tod 44.

If there is significance in the irregular form it must lie in a difference between the provisions of the first part and those of the numbered sections. And a difference has been generally recognized. The first paragraph has been thought to contain 'dispositions générales', the rest 'dispositions particulières'.[1] Meister (301) accepted this distinction: 'dieser Unterschied ist ganz unverkennbar'. To establish it we need only consider the two kinds of arrangements which occur in both the unnumbered and numbered parts.

Taxes or tribute are dealt with in lines 4–6, 10 f, and (B) 14–16. In the first two places the colonist's tax liability regarding his old community and his new is established,[2] the third is concerned with possible tax-defaulting in Naupactus. Clearly this last has a less general and fundamental significance than the two sections in the unnumbered part. Arrangements for the return of colonists are made in lines 6–10 and (Δ) 19–22. In the first the principles about return are established entire, the second lays down the procedure to be followed by the returning colonist. A similar inference may be drawn from the fact that the religious provision occurs in the first, unnumbered, part. For this would clearly be a matter of general importance. We may, therefore, conclude that the distinction in form was intentionally made in order to express a real difference in the character of the provisions: those of a general character and greatest importance were placed in the first section.

[1] The words are those of the editors of the *Recueil des inscriptions iuridiques grecques* 187. Their further suggestion (ibid.) that the unnumbered part is a kind of synopsis, which the numbered provisions fill out, gives, however, a false picture. Where, to take one obvious example, is there any reference to religion after lines 1–4?

[2] For full discussion see Chapter IV.

APPENDIX IV

CORINTH AND MEGARA

THE earliest recorded instance of Corinth's colonial relationships, if the sources[1] may be trusted, concerns Megara. The account given is that the Megarians were Corinthian colonists and in such a dependent position that when a Bacchiad died men and women from Megara had to go to Corinth to mourn him. They decided to revolt, stoned envoys from Corinth who came to warn them to desist, and finally won a battle against the Corinthians.

The sources are inferior and their indication of date is limited to the implication that the events took place during the Bacchiad rule at Corinth, but Hammond[2] has made a good case, even if his arguments are of varying worth, for dating the events to the last quarter of the eighth century and connecting them with the war in which Orsippus of Megara distinguished himself.[3] As a result of the war Megara lost territory to Corinth but won independence. Can it, however, be established that Megara counted as a colony of Corinth? The ancient sources[4] give as founders either the Dorians generally, or the Corinthians and Messenians, or the Corinthians alone, as in the accounts under discussion. This evidence makes it at least possible that the Megarians could be regarded as colonists of Corinth, and the events described may therefore be a very early instance of a mother city's attempt to control a colony and the colony's war of independence. Even so, certain reservations must remain. It may be that Aristotle's *Megarian Constitution*[5] and even the Corinthian poet Eumelus[6] were the authorities on

[1] These are: Schol. Pind. *Nem.* VII.155; schol. Plato *Euthydem.* 292E; schol. Aristophanes *Frogs* 443; Zenob. V.8 (for edition see above p.32 n.5).
[2] *BSA* xlix 1954, 93 ff.
[3] See Hicks and Hill 1 with notes; cf. Paus. I.xliv.1 and Hammond 97 f.
[4] Listed in *RE* s.v. Megara 180 f.
[5] See Halliday, *Greek Questions of Plutarch*, 92.
[6] As suggested by Hammond, 95. However, little certain is known of Eumelus and his eighth-century date is not beyond dispute; see Will, *Korinthiaka* 124 ff, though some of his arguments against the traditional date are to be rejected; see my article *Bull. Inst. Class. Studies* v 1958, 35.

which the extant accounts were based, but these accounts are very late and may be unreliable at least in their emphasis on Megara's position as a colony of Corinth. It is certain that Megara, lying next to Corinth and surrounded by Greek states, was no normal colony, so that Corinth's domination and the war should perhaps hardly be included in colonial relationships.

APPENDIX V

THE ARGIVE DECREE ABOUT CNOSSUS AND TYLISSUS

I REPRODUCE here Vollgraff's text of the two large fragments of the Argive decree about Cnossus and Tylissus.[1]

V

```
     .... [ἱαρὰ παρ]εχόντο τοὶ πα-
     [ρὰ τõν Ἀργεί]ον, δέρματα δὲ φ-
     [ερόσθο Ϝοι Κν]όϜιοι. πρὸ Ταυ-
     [ροφονίον? θύε]ν ἐν Τυλισõι Ϝ-
 5   [άρνα ϜΕρμᾶι?, ἀμ]νὰν δὲ καὶ δι-
     [δόμεν Δαίραι?.] σπονδὰς νεοτ-
     [έρας] μέ τίθεσθαι μεδατέρο-
     [νς, αἴ] μὲ συνδοκοῖ τõι πλέθε-
     [ι, συνβ]άλλεσθαι δὲ τὰν τρίτ-
10   [αν αἶσ]αν τὸς Ἀργείος τᾶν ψά-
     [φον · καῖ] τινας τõν εὐμενέον
     δυσμενέας τιθείμεθα καὶ τ-
     õν δυσμενέον εὐμενέας, μὲ θ-
     έσθαι, αἰ μὲ συνδοκοῖ τõι πλ-
15   έθει, συνβάλλεσθαι δὲ τὸνς
     ἐκ Τυλισõ τᾶν ψάφον τὰν τρί-
     ταν αἶσαν. αἰ δὲ μάχα γένοιτ-
     ο μὲ παρέντον τõν ἀτέρον, σπ-
     ονδὰνς θέσθο 'ν τõι δεομένο-
20   ι πέντε ἀμέρανς. αἱ στρατήα
     ἐνσ[ιείε]ϝνς τὰν γᾶν τὰν Κνο-
     Ϝίαν, [Τυλισίονς] ὀφελῆν παντ-
     ὶ σθένει [κὰτ τὸ δυνατόν. σῖτον]
     παρεχόν[το Ϝοι ΚνόϜιοι τοῖ]-
25   ς Ἀργείο[ις ΚνοϜοῖ, τοὶ δ' Ἀργ]-
     εῖοι τοῖ[ς ἐν Τυλισõι. σιταρ]-
```

[1] For references and explanations of abbreviations used see Chapter VIII.

(κ)ἐν στρα[τήαν τριάκοντα ἀμ]-
ερᾶν· αἰ δ[έ κ᾽ ἀποστήλοντι, ἀπ]-
ίμεν τὰν [στρατήαν ἐπ᾽ οἶκον]-
30 ς. κἐν Τυλ[ισοῖ κατ ταὐτά. ἠ δ]-
έ κα ϝαρθ[αίαι ὄϝιν θύομεν, ἀ]-
πάγεσθα[ι καὶ τἀπόλλονι ϝάρ]-
να. αἴ κ᾽ ἔνθ[ει τις Κνοσίον ἐν]-
[ς Ἄργος],

VI

A   νες
            τὸν χõ[ρον τõ]ν Ἀ[χ]α-
[ρναίον τõι Τυλισίοι ἐξἔμ]εν ξύλλεσθαι πλὰ[ν] τ-
[ὰ μέρε τὰ Κνοσίον συντ]έλλοντα ἐνς πόλιν. ἠότ[ι]
5 [δέ κα ἐκ δυσμενέ]ον ℎέλομες συνανϝότεροι, δα[σ]-
[μõι τõν κὰτ γ]ᾶν τὸ τρίτον μέρος ἔχεν πάντον, τ[õ]-
[ν δὲ κὰτ] θάλασαν τὰ ℎέμισα ἔχεν πάντον · τὰν δὲ [δ]-
[εκ]άταν τὸνς Κνοσίονς ἔχεν, ℎότι χ᾽ἔλομες κοι[ν]-
[ᾶ]ι · τõν δὲ φαλύρον τὰ μέν καλλ(ι)στεῖα Πυθόδε ἀπ[ά]-
10 γεν κοινᾶι ἀμφοτέρονς, τὰ δ᾽ ἄλλα τõι[Ἄρει Κνοσ]-
οῖ ἀντιθέμεν κοινᾶι ἀμφοτέρονς. ἐξ[αγογὰν δ᾽ ἔ̄]-
μεν Κνοσόθεν ἐνς Τυλισὸν κἐκ Τυλι[σõ Κνοσόνδ]-
ε· α[ἰ] δὲ πέρανδε ἐξάγοι, τελίτο ℎόσσα[περ ℎοι Κν]-
όσιοι· τὰ δ᾽ ἐκ Τυλισõ ἐξαγέσθο ℎόπυ[ί κα χρẽι. τõ]-
15 ι Ποσειδᾶνι τõι ἐν Ἰυτõι τὸν Κνοσίο[ν ἰαρέα θύ]-
εν. τᾶι ℎέραι ἐν Ἐραίοι θύεν βõν θέλει[αν ἀμφοτ]-
έρον[ς κ]οινᾶι, θύεν δὲ πρὸ ϝακινθ[ίον]........
.κο....κ.................................
....
20 ....
B ....ανοντο...........πρ[α]-
τομενίαν ἄγεν κατὰ ταὐτ[ὰ κατὰ τὸ δόγμα] τὸ ἀμ[φ]-
οτέρον. χρέματα δὲ μὲ ᾽νπιπασκέσθο ℎο Κνόσιο[ς]
ἐν Τυλισõι, ℎο δὲ Τυλίσιος ἐν Κνοσοῖ ℎο χρέιζ[ο]-
25 ν. μὲ δὲ χόρας ἀποτάμνεσθαι μεδατέρονς μεδ᾽ ἄ[π]-
ανσαν ἀφαιρίσθαι. ὅροι τᾶς γᾶς · ℎυõν ὄρος καὶ Α-
ἰετοι κάρταμίτιον καὶ τὸ τõ Ἀρχõ τέμενος κα[ὶ]
ℎο ποταμὸς κὲλ Λευκόπορον κἀγάθοια, ℎᾶι ℎύδο-

ρ ῥεῖ τόμβριον, καὶ Λᾶος. Ͱῖ κα τõι Μαχανεῖ θύομ-
30 ες τὸνς Ϝεξέκοντα τελέονς ὄϝινς, καὶ τᾶι Ͱ(έ)ραι
τὸ σκέλος Ϝεκάστο διδόμεν τõ θύματος. αἱ δὲ συ-
μπλέονες πόλιες ἐκ πολεμίον ἕλοιεν χρέματα,
Ͱόπαι συγγνοῖεν Ͱοι Κνόσιοι καὶ τοὶ Ἀργεῖοι,
Ͱούτο ἔμεν. τõι Ἄρει καὶ τἀφροδίται τὸν Κνοσί-
35 ον ἰαρέα θύεν, φέρεν δὲ τὸ σκέλος Ϝεκάστο. τὸν Ἀ-
ρχὸν τὸ τέμενος ἔχεν τὸν Ἀχάρναι · τοῖς θύονσι
ξένια παρέχεν τὸνς Κνοσίονς, τὸνς δ᾽ Ἀργείονς
τõι χορõι. ἐν Τυλισõι αἴ κα καλῆι Ͱο Κνόσιος πρεσγέαν, Ͱέπεσθαι Ͱόπυί κα δέεται, καἴ χὂ Τυλίσ-
40 ιος, τὸν Κνόσιον κατὰ ταὐτά · αἰ δὲ μὲ δοῖεν ξένι-
α, βολὰ ἐπαγέτο ῥύτιον δέκα στατέρον αὐτίκα ἐ-
πὶ κόσμος, κὲν Τυλισõι κατὰ ταὐτὰ Ͱο Κνόσιος.
Ͱα στάλα ἔσστα ἐπὶ Μελάντα βασιλέος. ἀϜρέτευ-
ε Λυκοτάδας Ͱυλλεύς. ἀλιαίαι ἔδοξε τᾶι τõν
45 ἰαρõν · ἃ (Ϝρέτευε) βολᾶς Ἀρχίστρατος Λυκοφρονίδας ·
τοὶ Τυλίσιοι ποὶ τὰν στάλαν ποιγραψάνσθο τάδε ·
αἴ τις ἀφικνοῖτο Τυλισίον ἐνς Ἄργος, κατὰ ταὐτά
σφιν ἔστο Ͱᾱιπερ Κνοσίοις.

V

Those from the *Argives* shall provide the *victims* and the
Cnossians shall take the hides. Before the Taurophonion (?)
shall be sacrificed in Tylissus a *ram* to ? and a ? . . .

Neither shall make new treaties unless the assembly[2] so
decides; and the Argives shall have the third share[3] of the
votes. And if we make enemies of any of our friends, or friends
of our enemies, we shall not do so unless it is agreed by the
assembly; those from Tylissus shall have the third share of the
votes.

If a battle occurs with one of the allies absent, a truce may be

[1] Versions and commentaries which I have consulted with profit in
preparing this translation are those of Vollgraff (see above p. 154), Tod (33)
and Buck (*The Greek Dialects* no. 85). Italics indicate words supplied.

[2] For this translation of πλῆθος see below pp. 240 f, where the possibilities
are discussed.

[3] For the meaning of αἶσα see below p. 240.

made in case of need for five days. If an army invades the territory of Cnossus, the *Tylissians* shall bring help with all their
strength *as far as they can*. *The Cnossians* shall provide *food* for
the Argives *at Cnossus*, but the Argives for those *at Tylissus*.
The army shall receive pay for *thirty* days; but if *they send it
away*, the *soldiers* shall return *to their homes*. And *the same conditions shall apply* in Tylissus. When *we sacrifice a ewe* to Arthaia,
we shall offer also a ram to *Apollo*. And if *any Cnossian* comes *to
Argos* . . .

VI

The *Tylissians* may plunder the land of ? . . . except the *parts*
belonging to the city *of the Cnossians*. And as to the booty
which we win both together from *the enemy*, in the division
they (i.e. the Tylissians) shall have a third part of everything
taken on land, but a half of everything taken on sea. And the
Cnossians shall have a tithe of what we take in common. Of the
spoils we shall, both together, offer the most fine to Delphi, but
the rest we shall, both together, dedicate to Ares at Cnossus.
There shall be freedom of export from Cnossus to Tylissus and
from Tylissus to Cnossus. But if any Tylissian export beyond let
him pay the same as the Cnossians. But goods from Tylissus may
be exported wherever it is *necessary*.[1] Let the *priest* of the
Cnossians sacrifice to Poseidon in Iutos. We are to sacrifice
both in common a heifer to Hera in the Heraeum; the sacrifice
is to be before the Hyacinthia. . . .

They shall keep the first day of the month alike *according to
the decree* (?) of both. The Cnossian may not possess property
in Tylissus, but the Tylissian who wishes may do so in Cnossus.
Let neither cut off a part of (the other's) land, nor take away
the whole.

The frontiers of the land: the Mountain of Swine, and the
Eagles, and the Artemisium, and the precinct of Archos, and
the river, and towards Leucoporus and Agathoea where the
rainwater flows, and Laos. When we sacrifice to Machaneus the
sixty full-grown rams, we shall give to Hera too the leg of each
victim. If several cities win booty from the enemy, as the

---

[1] Here Tod and Buck supply words meaning wish rather than need: κα
λει (Buck), κα λωιη (Tod). I translate Vollgraff's supplement.

Cnossians and Argives jointly decide, so let it be. Let the priest of the Cnossians sacrifice to Ares and Aphrodite, and let him keep a leg of each victim. Archos shall keep the precinct in Acharne. The Cnossians shall provide hospitality for those who sacrifice, but the Argives for the choir.[1] If the Cnossians demand at Tylissus the despatch of an embassy, let it be sent for whatever purpose[2] it is required, and if the Tylissian make a similar request, let the Cnossian grant it in the same way. But if they do not provide hospitality, the council shall immediately impose a fine of ten staters on the *kosmoi*, and the same rule shall apply to the Cnossian in Tylissus. This stele was erected when Melantas was king and Lykotadas of the tribe Hylleis was president.

Decree of the assembly for sacred matters: Archistratos of the Lykophron phratry was president of the council. Let the Tylissians add to the stele the following: if any of the Tylissians arrive in Argos, let him receive the same treatment as the Cnossians.

Kahrstedt has argued[3] that the Argive decree about Cnossus and Tylissus establishes a treaty between Argos and Cnossus only, Tylissus being merely a foreign possession of Argos. The key to this argument is the status of Tylissus. For since most of the provisions of the decree are expressly agreements between Cnossus and Tylissus, it can only be confined to Argos and Cnossus if Tylissus is not an independent state but, as Kahrstedt proposes, a piece of Argive territory. Any evidence which shows Tylissus to be an independent state is, therefore, fatal to Kahrstedt's hypothesis.

The amendment (VI.44 ff), by which Tylissians visiting Argos had the same rights as Cnossians, shows clearly that the two communities had the same status. Kahrstedt recognizes this (84), but as the amendment was passed a little later than the rest of the decree, he suggests that Tylissus had regained her independence in the intervening period. It seems somewhat improbable, if the decree was based on Tylissus' status as a

---

[1] Vollgraff offered a new punctuation here (*Verhand.* 76) which seems superior to the earlier version to be seen in Buck and Tod.

[2] To take ϝόπυί in a local sense is unsatisfactory, as Vollgraff has shown, *Verhand.* 81.

[3] See above p. 157.

R

dependent possession of Argos, that its only recognition of a
momentous change in that status should be a short amendment
regulating the position of Tylissians visiting Argos. But there is
no need to press the argument from the amendment. Within the
document as it originally stood there are provisions which put
Tylissus' independent status beyond doubt.

Even if we ignore for the moment the provisions which are
expressed without names, and which Kahrstedt (79) assumes to
have referred to Cnossus and Argos, there are among the provisions where the Tylissians are expressly named several which
suggest Tylissus' independence, and two which seem to prove it.
The agreements about trade (VI.11 ff), about help in war
(V.20 ff), and about the provision of ξένια (VI.40 ff), would all
be normally understood to show that Tylissus stood, in principle, on the same footing as Cnossus; however, even if these
could be regarded as conditions imposed by Argos on her subject, such an explanation is impossible for the passages V.15 ff
and VI.38 ff.

In the first of these the Tylissians are accorded one third of
the votes in the πλῆθος when any questions about friends or
enemies are to be decided. Vollgraff has shown[1] that the word
πλῆθος must here mean the assembly of the allies to which dele-
gates are sent, and this is strongly suggested by the actual words
of the decree: συνβάλλεσθαι δὲ τὸνς ἐκ Τυλίσο τᾶν ψᾶφον τὰν
τρίταν αἶσαν.[2] Thus, whatever exact procedure lay behind this
provision,[3] Tylissus clearly participated in the alliance as an
independent state. This conclusion is avoided by Kahrstedt,
who proposed to understand the words quite differently.[4]
πλῆθος is taken to mean the assembly in the several cities, αἶσα is
understood as turn,[5] and the whole thought to provide that the
Tylissian assembly should vote third in time. It is hard to see
what meaning such a procedure could have, and the unusual
translation of αἶσα is difficult to defend,[6] but it is unnecessary to

---

[1] *Verhand.* 21.   [2] As Vollgraff noted, *Verhand.* 25.

[3] The chief difficulty is that we do not know the constituents of the πλῆθος.
Without this essential knowledge only guesses can be made about the exact
force of the provision; see Vollgraff, *Verhand.* 22.

[4] For his discussion of the whole passage, see 87 ff.

[5] See Kahrstedt 90. The translation of αἶσα as share or part is justified by
Vollgraff in an exhaustive note, *Verhand.* 23.

[6] Cf. Vollgraff, *Verhand.* 25, who dismisses Kahrstedt's suggestions with
the words 'cette solution fantaisiste'.

argue the matter further, since assemblies of the people with the power that this provision postulates did not exist in Crete at the time of the decree.[1]

The second passage (VI.38 ff) provides for the summoning of embassies between Cnossus and Tylissus on terms of equality: ἐν Τυλίσοι αἴ κα καλῆι Ͱο Κνόσιος πρεσγέαν, Ͱέπεσθαι Ͱόπυί κα δέεται· καἴ χὀ Τυλίσιος, τὸν Κνόσιον κατὰ ταὐτά. Kahrstedt avoids the necessary assumption that Tylissus is an independent state by a totally different interpretation of the passage (75 ff). He argues that the passage means 'if the Cnossians demand the rights of a stranger etc.' He maintains first that the normal interpretation is impossible because the singular of the ethnic cannot be used to designate the whole state. This is false, as Vollgraff shows.[2] Secondly, he defends his unusual translation of πρεσγέαν as if it were equivalent to ξένια by two supposed analogies from Cretan inscriptions. The word πρειγήϊα (neuter plural) occurs in a Cretan agreement of the second century,[3] and has been understood to mean gifts of honour,[4] but it seems very questionable to regard it as analogous to πρεσγέαν, which must be a feminine noun of the first declension, and for which the true Cretan analogy would seem to be πρειγηΐα, meaning embassy and attested in an agreement between Lato and Olus.[5] The second analogy proposed are the Cretan officials called πρείγιστοι. These appear in Cretan inscriptions[6] and seem simply to be the elders;[7] they act, on one occasion, if the κόσμοι fail.[8] Kahrstedt notes this meaning. However, because they are dealing with foreigners in some of the instances where they occur,[9] he regards them as πρόξενοι. Kahrstedt thus attributes an unsupported meaning to the word πρείγιστοι, in order to find an analogy for an unexampled meaning of the word πρεσγέαν. It may be added that καλέω is not the natural word to express the meaning that he requires, and on his interpretation the phrase Ͱέπεσθαι Ͱόπυί κα δέεται becomes very difficult to understand.

If the document contains an agreement between Argos and Cnossus only, the provisions in which an unnamed 'we' or

---

[1] See Vollgraff *Verhand.* 20 ff.   [2] *Verhand.* 80; cf. Tod p. 62.
[3] *IC* III.iii.4.30.   [4] See Liddell and Scott s.v. πρειγήϊα, πρεσβεῖον.
[5] See *IC* I.xvi.22; cf. Liddell & Scott s.v. πρειγηΐα.
[6] E.g. *IC* IV.80.11; 184.13.   [7] Cf. Guarducci, *IC* IV p. 267.
[8] *IC* IV.80.11.   [9] As *IC* IV.80.11; 184.13.

'both' form the subject should refer to Argos and Cnossus. This is Kahrstedt's contention and necessarily an important part of his case. The provisions in question immediately follow or precede others in which the partners in the agreements are expressly Cnossus and Tylissus. It is, therefore, natural in a consecutive reading of the document to understand the names Cnossus and Tylissus in the provisions where no name is given, and this has been the interpretation of the epigraphists who have published the document.[1] In view of this Kahrstedt's thesis can only be maintained if the individual provisions under discussion seem to suit Argos and Cnossus much better than Cnossus and Tylissus.

The first of these provisions (VI.4 ff) makes arrangements about the division of booty which 'we take both together'. The expression is somewhat loose in detail, but the lines have been generally understood[2] to mean that Cnossus' partner took a third of the booty in land operations, and half in successes on sea. The general character of the provision would suggest that Tylissus was this partner, for such agreements about divisions of booty were regularly made between Cretan cities.[3] Furthermore, the earlier provision (V.20 ff) for Tylissians[4] to help Cnossus strongly suggests that the war partners throughout were Cnossus and Tylissus. Finally, it would be surprising to find Argos the equal of Cnossus in sea power, but her inferior on land.[5] For in the Peloponnesian War Argive hoplites are important,[6] her navy conspicuously absent.[7] Although the suggestion has been made that there were small contingents of Argive soldiers on Crete,[8] the above arguments seem to make it

[1] In addition to Vollgraff, see Hiller *Syll.*[3] notes to 56; Tod I pp. 61-3; Guarducci *IC* I p. 58.

[2] See Tod's translation, p. 61, and Vollgraff's translation and commentary, *Verhand.* 10, 43 ff.

[3] Vollgraff gives examples; see *Verhand.* 44.

[4] The name is restored, but the supplement seems certain.

[5] In such arrangements the booty was divided according to the military contribution; for examples which make this point expressly see Vollgraff, *Verhand.* 44.

[6] See Thuc. VII.20.1; 26.1; 44.6, for her contributions as an ally in an overseas campaign.

[7] Cf. Thuc. V.56.2, where the Argives blame the Athenians for allowing the Spartans to send help to Epidaurus by sea.

[8] By Vollgraff, *Verhand.* 32, in connection with his restorations in V.23-6. But neither the restorations nor their meaning are sufficiently certain to be called evidence.

much more probable that the provision concerns Cnossus and Tylissus than Cnossus and Argos.

The next provision (VI.9 ff) arranges for the offering to the gods by 'both in common' of the first fruits from the spoil. Kahrstedt argues (79) that, if one of the gods is Ares at Cnossus,[1] the Pythian, the other god to benefit, must be the god of a state with closer relations to Delphi than Cnossus. Tylissus, he adds, had no treasury at Delphi. But the fact that the Pythian receives the best of the spoil shows that he is honoured not as a god of one of the contracting states, but as a great international deity. For, since Cnossus received more than its partner in the division of the spoil, and since the tithe went to Cnossus, the Cnossian deity would be expected to be the better treated, if it were a question of giving the gods of the two contracting states their share. It may be added that Tylissus was presumably too small and unimportant to have a treasury at Delphi. There is, therefore, no reason to assume that Argos was one of the un-named 'both' in this provision.

The sacrifices of 'both in common' (VI.16 f) to Hera in the Heraeum (τᾶι Ϝέραι ἐν ᾿Εραίοι) raise the question whether this is Argive Hera. Vollgraff originally suggested[2] that a Cretan Hera was meant, and that ᾿Εραίοι is the name of a month and specifies the time of the sacrifice. Although there are serious objections to this view,[3] and although Vollgraff himself has long since recognized[4] that the goddess named must be Hera of the famous Argive Heraeum, the effect of his earlier suggestion is still to be seen in more recent works of reference.[5] It should therefore be emphasized that 'Hera in (the) Heraeum' in an Argive decree cannot be other than the great Argive deity.[6]

---

[1] The restoration is justified by Vollgraff, *Verhand*. 45.   [2] *BCH* 1913, 196 f.

[3] While it is true that a month of this name is attested at Olus (see *IC* I.xvi.5.88) the name cannot refer to a month here for two reasons. Firstly, as Vollgraff noted (*Mnemosyne* xlii 1914, 90) the time indication is given by the next phrase, θύεν δὲ πρὸ Ϝακινθ[ίον (17), and secondly, ἐν with the name of a month seems not to occur (I rely on the examples of the chronological uses of ἐν in Liddell and Scott s.v.). The normal expression is to give the name of the month in the genitive together with the word μῆνος; e.g. Tod 66.6 f, *IC* l.xvi.3.2–4; 5.88.

[4] See *Mnemosyne* xlii 1914, 90; cf. *Verhand*. 51 f and n. 237.

[5] See especially Guarducci *IC* I p. 58, but Tod also writes (I.p.61) 'whether the famous Argive Heraeum or a Cretan temple is not clear'.

[6] For the antiquity and prestige of Hera at Argos see Waldstein, *The Argive Heraeum*, I 3 ff.

It seems unlikely that Argos would arrange to make sacrifices with Cnossus to her own great goddess. When the Athenians imposed sacrifices to Athenian gods on Brea and on Erythrae and other allies,[1] they did not arrange to join in the sacrifices themselves. It therefore seems unlikely in this provision too that Argos was Cnossus' partner.

It is arranged that both states should have the same first day of the month (VI.21 f). Kahrstedt suggested (81) that this was to facilitate mutual celebrations in Cnossus and Argos, but it is not known that the many Greek calendars made attendance at Panhellenic festivals difficult to synchronize. It is neighbours with commercial relations who need to have the same first day of the month, which was the normal day for the settlement of debts.[2]

The final provision in which the names are not expressed (VI.29 ff) arranges that 'when we sacrifice to Machaneus the sixty full-grown rams, we shall give to Hera too the leg of each victim'.[3] The sacrifice to Machaneus, apparently a Cnossian deity, seems to be a practice already established, and the offerings of the legs to Hera an innovation.[4] It would be slightly surprising if the Argives had been participating in such a large offering to a Cnossian god, and more surprising that they should arrange for the first time for part of the offering to go to Hera. There is, on the other hand, nothing surprising in the provision if it refers to Cnossus and Tylissus.

In none of these provisions is it more probable that the two partners were Argos and Cnossus. On the contrary, all are more intelligible if they refer to Cnossus and Tylissus, as a natural reading of the Greek suggests. It may therefore be assumed that when they were concerned in a provision the Argives were expressly named.

If the phrases governed by an unspecified 'we' or 'both' are to be referred to Cnossus and Tylissus, and if Tylissus was an independent state at the time of the decree, Kahrstedt's thesis fails. The document cannot be regarded as an agreement between Argos and Cnossus alone.

---

[1] See above Chapter IV.
[2] Cf. Aristophanes *Clouds* 113 ff; Vollgraff *Verhand.* 53.
[3] Cf. Vollgraff's commentary, *Verhand.* 59.
[4] See Vollgraff's long discussion, *Verhand.* 59 ff, especially 70.

APPENDIX VI

THE CITIZENS OF AMPHIPOLIS

IN his account of Brasidas' capture of Amphipolis Thucydides makes certain statements about the citizens of Amphipolis from which it might be deduced that the Athenian settlers had kept Athenian citizenship. The three crucial phrases all occur in the space of a dozen lines. First (IV.105.2) Brasidas proclaimed that anyone Ἀμφιπολιτῶν καὶ Ἀθηναίων τῶν ἐνόντων could stay with possession of his belongings, or leave, taking his belongings, within five days. Secondly, the majority changed their mind when they heard this proclamation (106.1)

ἄλλως τε καὶ βραχὺ μὲν Ἀθηναίων ἐμπολιτεῦον, τὸ δὲ πλέον ξύμμεικτον.

Finally (ibid.), the proclamation was considered fair when compared with their fears

οἱ μὲν Ἀθηναῖοι διὰ τὸ ἄσμενοι ἂν ἐξελθεῖν, ἡγούμενοι οὐκ ἐν ὁμοίῳ
σφίσι τὰ δεινὰ εἶναι καὶ ἅμα οὐ προσδεχόμενοι βοήθειαν ἐν τάχει, ὁ δὲ
ἄλλος ὅμιλος πόλεώς τε ἐν τῷ ἴσῳ οὐ στερισκόμενοι καὶ κινδύνου
παρὰ δόξαν ἀφιέμενοι.

It would be very surprising if these Athenians, referred to three times in so short a space, were not the same people each time. Hampl's discussion[1] is unsatisfactory, because he takes the Athenians of the first passage as temporary residents (5), while referring the second passage to permanent citizens of Amphipolis (4). His reason is a mistaken interpretation of the words τῶν ἐνόντων in the first passage. He finds these words more suitable to temporary residents than permanent citizens. This would be a valid interpretation if the words applied to the Athenians only, but an examination of the context reveals that they qualify both the Athenians and the Amphipolitans. The

---

[1] *Klio* xxxii 1939, 2–5. It is surprising to find Hampl's treatment tacitly approved and his conclusion accepted by Westlake, *Hermes* xc 1962, 280.

contrast is between those who were inside the city and still free from Brasidas, and those over whom he had control outside. [1]

In discussing the questions who these Athenians were and what status they had in the colony, it is important to remember the circumstances of Amphipolis. It was only some thirteen years since the foundation, and there would probably be quite a number of temporary inhabitants from Athens, traders and the like, in the city. [2] It was also wartime, and civil strife in Greek cities was a familiar evil. Few Athenians would feel confident in a city under the protection of Sparta, even if they had been citizens of Amphipolis for thirteen years.

The people in Amphipolis whom Thucydides could call Athenians must have been either the permanent settlers of Athenian origin, or the temporary residents from Athens, or both these groups. It seems unlikely that he could be referring to the permanent settlers only, for the temporary residents would be in the lead among those who were glad to leave of the third passage. The choice therefore lies between the temporary residents only and both groups together.

The first passage, which distinguishes between the Athenians and the Amphipolitans, could clearly be interpreted as referring to temporary residents only, and so could the third passage which describes the Athenians as glad to leave. But the second passage seems to exclude the possibility that Thucydides only had temporary residents in mind. For the words ἄλλως τε καὶ βραχὺ μὲν ᾿Αθηναίων ἐμπολιτεῦον, τὸ δὲ πλέον ξύμμεικτον lose their significance in the context if the Athenians referred to are merely the temporary residents. Thucydides is explaining why the majority decided to accept Brasidas' offer; it is because, compared with the majority of mixed origins, the Athenians were too few to be politically dominant. These Athenians can hardly have been temporary residents, since even if Athenians temporarily in Amphipolis had political rights, [3] Thucydides could scarcely contrast Athenians with τὸ πλέον ξύμμεικτον if this description embraced Athenian settlers who had left

[1] See Thuc. IV.103.5 and 106.1, where the matter is emphasized.

[2] We may assume that Athenian trade with Amphipolis was not confined to the shiptimber that Thucydides expressly mentions (IV.108.1), but even if this were all, its importance suggests there would always be Athenian citizens in Amphipolis for commercial reasons.

[3] As, for example, Milesians in Olbia; see Chapter VI.

Athens at most thirteen years earlier. Finally, though the word
ἐμπολιτεύω should not necessarily be given so legal a meaning as
'to hold civil rights in',[1] it is not likely that Thucydides would
have chosen it had he been referring solely to temporary residents.

By a process of elimination, therefore, it follows that Thucydides is referring to both temporary residents and permanent
settlers of Athenian origin in the passages under discussion. At
first sight this seems the most natural conclusion; Thucydides
was an Athenian himself and would think of all those of
Athenian origin as Athenians; but such a conclusion raises
other questions. If these Athenians included permanent settlers
of Athenian origin, then those settlers were distinguished from
the Ἀμφιπολίτων of the first passage, from τὸ πλέον ξύμμεικτον
the second and from ὁ ἄλλος ὅμιλος of the third. The first of
these is the most striking, so that the others, being mere reflec-
tions of it, need not be considered separately. Do these distinctions imply that the Athenian settlers of Amphipolis had kept
their Athenian citizenship?

Examples have been adduced above which show that Greek
writers used ethnics inconsistently;[2] for on any one occasion
their choice of name could be influenced either by considerations of origin, or of locality, or of citizenship. On grounds of
analogy, therefore, it does not necessarily follow from Thucydides' words that these Athenians were not legally Amphipolitans. And on the argument from plausibility such a conclusion seems highly improbable. For it is virtually impossible to
believe that a colony could be established of which one section
remained citizens of another city. Such discrimination would
hardly have been endured by the settlers of non-Athenian
origin, and could not be reconciled with the principle of
equality, which was regularly found in Greek colonial enterprises.[3]

---

[1] This is the translation in Liddell and Scott s.v. Bétant is probably
nearer with his plain *inhabitare*; see *Lexicon Thucydideum* s.v. There is only one
other place where Thucydides uses the word, at IV.103.4, where it describes
the settlers in Amphipolis of Argilian origin, and there it need not imply
citizen rights. The only other approximately contemporary occurrence of
the word is in Isocrates (V.5) where it should probably be translated
'inhabitants' (ἀποικίαι αἵτινες . . . ἀπολωλέκασι τοὺς ἐμπολιτευθέντας). But
though the word may not carry implications about civil rights, it must be
at least allowed the sense 'to live in'.

[2] See Chapter VI.   [3] See Chapter IV.

s

If this argument is sound, we must accept that Thucydides could call Athenians and distinguish from Amphipolitans people who were citizens of Amphipolis. This seems a hard conclusion, but the circumstances of the time, which we have already emphasized, make it intelligible. In Thucydides' mind the important distinction was between those who were by origin connected to Athens, and so on the Athenian side in the crisis caused by Brasidas, and the greater number whose origin and loyalty were elsewhere.[1] Distinctions of legal citizenship were by comparison insignificant, and it would have blurred the important division of the moment if he had tried to express them. Here we have had to use periphrases like 'the settlers of Athenian origin', but it is not surprising that the historian chose to call them plainly Athenians.

It could still be argued that the last passage, especially the phrase διὰ τὸ ἄσμενοι ἂν ἐξελθεῖν must show that these 'Athenians' knew that they would return to citizen rights at Athens. For glad though they may have been to avoid the possible attacks of the pro-Spartan party, Brasidas' proclamation had ostensibly assured them of security in their rights at Amphipolis. It does not necessarily follow, however, that they were at that time citizens of Athens. We have already seen that some right of return to the metropolis was regularly conceded to colonists,[2] and fugitives were also often accorded a friendly reception.[3] In wartime refugees from a colony captured by the enemy, especially a colony not long established, could expect to be received into the metropolis.

We may conclude that Thucydides' account of the events in Amphipolis on the arrival of Brasidas does not show that the settlers of Athenian origin legally possessed a special status in the city.

---

[1] Westlake has shown (*Hermes* xc 1962, 276 ff) that Thucydides' account is apologetic and exaggerates the inconstancy of the Amphipolitans. This may also account for the distinction that he chooses to emphasize.

[2] See Chapters IV and VI.

[3] See Chapter VI.

INDEX

of Athenian colonies, 177 f, 201
at Naupactus, 47 f, 51, 232
of Sinope's colonies, 190, 200 f, 205
tribute lists, 81, 125, 177 f, 180
trierarchy, 190 n.
Troad, 193
Tylissus, Argive decree about Tylissus and Cnossus, 78, 214, Appendix V, 235–44
and Argos, Ch. VIII, 154–65, 212
and Cnossus, Ch. VIII, 154–65, 212, 239–44
status of, 239–44
tyrants, 30 f, 141, 195, 197
colonization of, 30 f, 33 f, 118, 141–3, 147 f, 151, 192, 211
Tyrsenians (see also Pelasgians), 176 n.

war, 95, 107 f, 139 n., 206, 233 f, 240, 242
aid in, 73 f, 97, 132, 135 f, 140 f,
144 f, 190, 213 f
between colonies and mother cities, 10, 86 f, 93, 147, 158, 183, 214
West Locris, Locrians, 45, 47–9, 58 n., 226
West Locrian settlement, 56 f, 59, 65, 111 n.

Xenagoras, 20 n.
Xenares, 39
Xenocritus, 36
Xenophon, 9, 11, 201–3
Xerxes, 109 n.

Zancle, Zancleans, 17 f, 21 n., 93 n., 94, 104, 113
Zeugitae, 61, 229
Zeus, 195
Homarios, 159
Meilichios, 15 n.
Zopyrion, 99